T0320933

VIRTUAL ETHNICITY

To my son Harvey Yuen,
the ultimate example of convergence

Virtual Ethnicity

Race, Resistance and the World Wide Web

LINDA LEUNG
University of Technology, Australia

ASHGATE

Published by
Ashgate Publishing Limited
Gower House
Croft Road
Aldershot
Hants GU11 3HR
England

Ashgate Publishing Company
Suite 420
101 Cherry Street
Burlington, VT 05401-4405
USA

Ashgate website: http://www.ashgate.com

British Library Cataloguing in Publication Data
Leung, Linda
Virtual ethnicity : race, resistance and the World Wide Web
1. Ethnicity - Computer network resources 2. World Wide Web - Social aspects 3. Internet - Social aspects 4. Racism
5. Minorities - Computer network resources
I. Title
305.8'002854678

Library of Congress Control Number: 2005921530

ISBN 978-0-7546-4303-6

Reprinted 2007

Printed and bound in Great Britain by MPG Books Ltd, Bodmin, Cornwall

Contents

Chapter 1

Introduction

The purpose of this book is to examine modes of ethnic minority production, representation and consumption on the World Wide Web. It is a latitudinal study which provides an empirical 'snapshot' of cyberspace in the late 1990s, a time when it was contended that the Internet was almost monolithically white and male. It attempts to do this by isolating the Web from the Internet as a whole, and studying its use in grounded contexts, such as in domestic and educational environments, so that the virtual realm is considered against the backdrop of relationships of power in everyday life. These aims of the research are investigated both theoretically and empirically.

Theoretically, the book effectively takes a media studies approach to the subject of representation. That is, the wealth of literature on the representation of race and ethnicity in film, television and popular culture is reviewed and used as a framework for examining the articulation of ethnic difference on the Web, as well as conceptualising the Web as a form of broadcast media and technology of representation. Specifically, it focuses on representations in or within cyberspace, as opposed to representations of cyberspace.

However, it is also envisaged that the process of looking at a newer technology like the Web challenges the way we think about old ones such as the broadcast media. To this end, the book takes a broader interdisciplinary approach: given the book is about how racial difference is portrayed, it also draws from cultural studies research (in chapter 2) to demonstrate that notions of ethnicity must be interrogated, are forever problematic and unfixed. Apart from studies of media, the book also borrows from a broader array of technology studies literature (in chapter 4) to show how minority groups adopt technology as part of their identity, or use technology for the purposes of representation. In addition, there is some discussion of literature pertaining to gender and technology (in chapter 6): as all the research subjects are women, it examines their engagement with computers, a technology in which they have been historically under-represented, both as producers and now to a lesser extent, consumers.

Empirically, the study aims to capitalise on my experiences in a larger research project which involved 14 ethnic minority women on a foundation course in new technology. These students, along with myself, became the research subjects in this study by looking at how ethnicity was articulated on the Web compared with other cultural forms. The research explores the findings of the 15 research subjects' (including myself) searches for Web sites and pages which depict their ethnicities. In doing so, it endeavours to highlight the strategic differences between self-constructed and objectified representations of ethnicity; and the genres of Web texts where such depictions can be found. In addition, the objective is also to identify who within these ethnic minority communities, is undertaking the task of online representation and on behalf of whom.

It is through its empirical dimension that this study strives to innovate methodologies for studying the Web whilst remaining interdisciplinary. In the process, it will investigate issues in researching and using this medium in both private and educational settings.

This chapter is where it all begins. It seeks, firstly, to describe the background to the research. Secondly, it attempts to define the technology with which the book is concerned, the World Wide Web, distinguishing it from the Internet as a whole. Thirdly, it outlines the subsequent chapters, sketching out the narrative of the book. The chapter summaries also define the terms and discuss the theoretical and methodological traditions employed in the research. Finally, the chapter concludes with a rationale for the research.

Background to Research

This book was born out of a wider research project on which I worked for two years and within which I was able to carve a space to further pursue and integrate my personal interests in information technology and questions of ethnicity. As Miller (1993: p.46) says, the personal legitimacy of a piece of research to the researcher is as important as the formal sanction it is given by an academic establishment. But personal interest also had to be balanced with pragmatism: as Ackers (1993: p.214) argues, access to the field is crucial in research. Therefore, this book could be considered the product of 'opportunistic research' (Hammersley and Atkinson 1995: p.36) in that it was conducted in parallel with my work as a Tutor/Researcher on a project funded by a British Telecom University Development Award.

When I joined the Department of Innovation Studies at the University of East London in September of 1996, my main involvement was in Project @THENE, a pilot initiative examining the use of information and communication technologies in distance education. One of the project's aims was to develop a foundation course in new technology, known as @THENE Year Zero. The course was to be for women from ethnic minority backgrounds and delivered by computer-supported distance learning. The existence of this course was justified through the university's acknowledgement that women, particularly those from ethnic minorities, are disadvantaged in terms of their access to information technology. Given my own background and identity as a woman from an ethnic minority, this was the aspect of @THENE which had the most personal resonance for me and was one of the motivations for working on the project. Therefore, it seemed more than appropriate to distil my research from the project by examining aspects of the relationship between ethnicity and technology.

The students on the @THENE Year Zero presented a ready-made group of 14 research subjects who, like myself, were women from ethnic backgrounds and had experienced marginalisation because of their respective ethnicities. It provided a common basis for comparison although the experiences, as expected, were incredibly diverse. My gender and ethnicity led me, at least, to have a close professional proximity to the group of women on the @THENE Year Zero: like many feminist strategies for technology (Faulkner 1996), the course sought to provide a learning environment where ethnic minority women's technical competence was increased through being taught by other women from ethnic minorities, such as myself.

Issues of ethnicity and representation are of particular personal importance to me because of my identity as an Australian-born woman of Chinese heritage. The lack of images in television, film and popular culture which reflect my subjectivity has resonated throughout my life and thus led me to incorporate my experiences as a woman from an ethnic background into the research. So this book is also the product of a kind of racial narcissicism, as Gilroy (1995: p.37) calls it, a desire to catch a glimpse of my own ethnicity on the Web, to compensate for its absence in other cultural forms.

In addition to my interest in issues of ethnicity, the research was informed by my educational background in media studies. Having completed undergraduate and postgraduate studies in this area, I wanted to utilise this body of knowledge, particularly that which related to representations of ethnicity in television and film. But rather than extend upon previous media research, I was interested in the degree to which this knowledge could be translated and adapted for a different kind of media. The Internet, being the medium of the moment, seemed comparatively undiscovered, particularly as a site of struggle between racism and anti-racism (Silk and Silk 1990 ix). While so much is known about how racism operates and is contested in the print and broadcast media, this had only been explored in a limited way in relation to new media. Thus, I integrated new media into my research, resulting in a study of representations of ethnicity on the World Wide Web.

Given the array of terms which are associated with the Internet (such as new media, cyberspace, the Information Superhighway), it seems appropriate to establish its parameters, and provide a definition which is adequate for the purposes of this research, particularly as this book concentrates on only one aspect of it.

Definition of Terms: The Internet and the World Wide Web

Despite the Internet's pervasion in public discourse, its identity and definition are still not entirely secure. Part of the difficulty in establishing its parameters of meaning is due to its multiple functions. The Internet is the overall structure which supports:

- electronic mail, a form of primarily one-to-one communication, although it also can be used to broadcast messages to many recipients
- computer conferencing, enabling multiple users to engage in joint activity or discussion
- access to other remote databases

- the transfer of files
- the World Wide Web, effectively a large decentralised database using hypertext to navigate through complex pathways to retrieve data (Hammersley and Atkinson 1995: p.201).

Therefore, there is no singular entity that is the Internet, but rather various overlapping and distinct aspects (Kendall 1999: p.70; Crane 2000: p.88): 'The Internet is more a networked schizophrenic, with multiple personalities that often have no idea that the others exist' (Costigan 1999: p.xx).

The Internet, in its physical form, is the amalgamation of a series of computer networks (Hall 1996c: p.376). Wide Area Networks (WANs) connect host computers and terminal servers, which in turn, function as gateways to Local Area Networks (LANs). The WANs are derived from the private and public sectors and include the networks of corporations, universities as well as telecommunications companies. Therefore, the Internet is a collection of *inter*connected *net*works. While the telephone, similarly, is constituted by intricate networks, the Internet, by contrast, can be considered a public medium in that the majority of information it handles is globally available and accessible. Because it is a product of the interdependence of industries and networks, the Internet is designed to handle diversity. Internetworking relies on the use of a uniform protocol rather than the use of a standard network system (Abbate 1994: p.199). That is, different network systems can communicate with each other through the use of a common computer language.

The Internet is accessed via computers but using telephone technology: the computer is connected to a telephone line, hence the term 'online'. Therefore, technically, it is not a broadcast medium (in the same sense as radio and television), although it is readily accessible to the public. Nevertheless, it also combines print and audio-visual technology. Overall, the Internet represents a merging of the publishing, broadcasting and computer industries (Barker and Tucker 1990: p.22; Crane 2000: p.88).

However, the Internet lacks a visible manifestation, unlike television and radio stations which can be physically identified through the location of their transmitters. As its physical locations – the servers which contain the texts that are published on the Internet – are widely dispersed, the Internet is highly unregulated. Moreover, it is difficult to pinpoint the geographical location of a server, thereby providing an opportunity to publicise a range of texts which may otherwise be censored or unshown within the print or broadcast media: 'Where a piece of information is when it is on the Internet is a little hard to describe. It is on a computer somewhere (maybe even on one's own), but it is available anywhere the Internet is' (Costigan 1999: xxii).

Therefore, the Internet enables the exchange of information across electronic 'free-space' or cyberspace (Shields 1996: p.1) transcending national borders and subsequently, bypassing legal and political constraints within any given country. Its main evolution has taken place in public institutions such as hospitals, universities and government departments undertaking co-operative research, which has meant a merging of disciplines and discourses. But with the increasing and now dominant involvement of the private sector, governments are increasingly unable to exercise control over information which is sent and received across its state boundaries. Its global access and participation make Internet regulation more difficult than that of telephone networks, which tend to be highly regulated within any given country. Its decentralised structure and constant expansion makes it difficult to 'map' or represent accurately interconnected sites (Shields 1996: p.1). As Jones (1999: p.6) contends, the Internet is not fixed, so can only be 'snapshot'.

Indeed, by the new millenium, commentators had given up attempts at quantifying Web content, concentrating instead on numbers of users. However, it was apparent that the Web is the most popular aspect of the Internet (Pastore 2000a; Nakamura 2002: p.109). In 1996, there were an estimated 500,000 Web sites (Hall 1996c: p.376) and 150 million Web pages (Kelly and Wolf 1997: p.71) produced and/or consumed by 40 million users in 150 countries (Meridian 1996). Kahle (1997) gave a more conservative estimate of 50 million Web pages in 1997 with the number doubling each year. This was expected to increase to 1 billion Web pages (Kelly and Wolf 1997: p.71) and 200 million users by the year 2000 (Meridian 1996).

But even given this level of usage and an apparent growth rate of 10% per month, Barry (1996: p.147) described the Internet as still being a 'digital dirt track' as opposed to an 'information superhighway'. Panos (1998) argued that it would remain a minority communications medium compared to the telephone. Indeed, the 50-100 million Internet users as at 1998 equated to less than 2% of the world's population (Hamman 1998). However, the worldwide Internet population as at 2002 was esimated between 580-655 million, with 90% of users concentrated in 20 countries. ClickZ (2004) forecasts a global total of 709-945 million Internet users in 2004.

Within these countries, the UK (where the empirical research was conducted) has approximately 21-34 million Internet users; compared to the US' 126-182 million Internet users (ibid). The UK lead the way in Europe in household Internet penetration in 2000 (Pastore 2000a), but is now second to Germany (ClickZ 2004).

The Internet, in the context of this research, refers only to the World Wide Web, and mainly to those static HTML pages which constituted it in the last years of the twentieth century (rather than to other functions such as electronic mail or MOOs/MUDs that can now be accessed via the Web). References to Web 'texts' and textual analysis of World Wide Web sites includes written text as well as images (still and moving), although in the latter half of the 1990s, there was much less capacity for sustaining moving images: the Internet was dominated mostly by written text and still graphics, as can be seen in the sites analysed as part of the empirical research in chapters 7 and 8. It regards both as contributing to overall representation in the same way that sound and moving images do so in film and television: that is, Web pages are regarded as cultural and sociological representations (Wakeford 2000: p.34), and as indicators of modes of production too (Nakamura 2002: p.108). The notion of Web production refers to the authors and process of creating Web texts; whereas Web consumption relates to interaction with the Web as a user, consumer or audience of its texts. The following chapter outline summarises the theories and methodologies used in this particular study of the Web.

Chapter Outline

It should be acknowledged that the theories and methodologies that have been referred to in the research, in actuality are my interpretation of those. That is, the body of knowledge which I have is at least 'secondhand'. My understanding of a particular theory may differ from that of the theorist, just as his/her knowledge has been based upon their reading of other theorists' work. Miller (1993: p.72) calls this the 'Chinese whispers' effect in the production of knowledge, quite apt in the context of this research study.

The review of literature is undertaken primarily in the first part of the book (Chapters 2, 3 and 4), discussing the implications of their findings for a medium such as the Web, and the possibilities of applying their methodologies to studying representation on the Web.

As this book is fundamentally concerned with issues of ethnicity, Chapter 2 will outline debates surrounding definitions of race, ethnicity and difference, providing some theoretical foundations which can then be explored empirically in the research. It looks particularly at Anglo-American differences in racial categories, attempting to differentiate the concept of ethnicity from notions of race, culture and nationality, and justify the focus on ethnicity in the research. Drawing on cultural studies writings on the politics of identity, it discusses the problematic notions of 'race' and 'blackness', and acknowledges the book's bias towards British terminologies of difference given that the research subjects and context are British. However, there is never an acceptance of static definitions of ethnicity: rather, the chapter introduces these terms, acknowledges that their appropriation differs according to cultural context, and returns to them later in the book (in Chapters 7 and 8) when examining how the research subjects adapt them for their own use.

Chapter 2 argues that on the one hand, ethnicity is a more particularistic form of identification than race: it allows for a spectrum of colour, not just black and white. Nor does it purport to have a scientific or biological basis, as race does. It embodies a wide range of experience, including those of people of colour, of imperialism, of religion, of migration. Yet it is also a term of marginalisation: everyone has an ethnicity yet it only seems to be applied to minorities. Anyone who is 'ethnic' either does not quite belong, or belongs elsewhere or on the peripheries. Thus, as Hall (1992: p.297) says, the meaning of ethnicity is a site of struggle and therefore, in seeking representations of ethnicity, the research examines Web sites or Web pages which articulate the struggle between hybridity, pluralism, diversity – and essentialism.

The theme that is carried through the book and applied to the Web is the analysis of how ethnic minorities have historically been represented in older media (in Chapter 3), and how such representations result from the structures and modes of production and consumption of those respective technologies. This chapter also looks at relevant theoretical and empirical research about how ethnic minorities are represented on the Internet. The ideas emerging from such a review are subsequently compared with the findings from the empirical work which is discussed in Chapters 7 and 8: How the research subjects distinguish between old and new media; whether they perceive differences in the way they consume television, film and the Internet; how the Web extends and diverges from historical representations of race.

Chapter 3 examines how the concepts of difference that were discussed in Chapter 2 have been articulated in the broadcast media and on the Internet. It explores the parallels between the ways in which race and ethnicity have been represented in the traditional mass media, as compared with cyberspace, interrogating the interconnectedness between the Internet and its antecedents (Jones 1999: p.22). It highlights the qualitiative differences between portrayals that have been constructed from the perspective of the 'white gaze', and images that have been created from within ethnic communities. That is, instances of ethnicity as the object of representation will be juxtaposed with examples of it as the subject of representation.

This chapter will also outline the methods by which race and representation in film and television have been studied. It discusses the potentialities and limitations of applying these approaches to the Web.

While the book investigates the extent to which the Web can be regarded as a form of broadcast media comparable to television, it also acknowledges the problems inherent in doing so. Therefore, Chapter 4 discusses how the Web has been conceptualised by other researchers, and looks at their perspectives on how the medium operates. In doing so, it provides some indication of its structure as well as modes of production and consumption, especially in relation to the participation of ethnic minorities.

A secondary aspect of the book explores the role of technology in the politics of identity. A selection of literature is reviewed in Chapter 4 in relation to technologies, (such as the VCR, video camcorder and turntables) which have been appropriated by minority groups. This historical comparison and contextualisation highlights the pervasive techno-utopian and dystopian discourses which have surrounded the Web and its technological precedents.

Chapter 4 argues that the Web should be constructed as a site of struggle, not escape. It is a place where the real and the virtual are not mutually exclusive, but where the former is played out in the latter. Therefore, cyberspace is a point of negotiation between resistance and power. It contends that relationships of power exist on the Web as they do in daily life, that the forces which exclude ethnic minorities in the everyday world also operate in cyberspace. But these marginalising forces do not function in a way which is so monolithic or totalitarian to rule out instances of resistance. So there is a tension between the capacity for the World Wide Web to offer alternative images of ethnicity to that of the broadcast media, and the influences of the real world which have constrained representations of ethnicity within popular culture.

This theoretical interrogration of ethnicity, representation and the Web is tested and contested empirically in the from Chapters 5 to 8. While Chapter 5 discusses the methodology of the empirical research, Chapters 6 to 8 discuss the findings (actual Web sites and television shows selected by the research subjects, and the interpretations of the ways in which race and ethnicity are articulated in the media texts by the research subjects) and return to the themes and ideas raised in the literature review (Chapters 2 to 4).

Chapter 5 introduces the empirical research, describing the wider context in which it took place, that is, as part of the larger research framework of Project @THENE. It highlights the methodological complexity of the research, the need to work within the feminist approaches utilised by Project @THENE while having to adopt and adapt other methods for this study. It illustrates the process of methodological improvisation and innovation necessary for this particular research situation and especially for studying the Web, for which there are no research traditions as yet.

Chapter 5 also explains how the research subjects, who were from the 1997/8 intake of students on the @THENE Year Zero course, came to be involved in the study. It examines my own position (as tutor, fellow research subject and woman from ethnic minority) in relation to the other research subjects and its inherent inequalities. The multi-dimensional role I have in the research characterises it as 'not (just) a job, but a way of life...one's life becomes woven into the research' (Ackers 1993: p.223), a marriage of the personal and the professional, of inside and outside. The difficulty in juggling these various personae and its implications for my relationship to the research subjects are discussed.

The chapter also details the tasks the research subjects and I completed for this study. The two research tasks, which were incorporated into the curriculum of the @THENE Year Zero, are discussed fully. The first research task ascertained the ethnic backgrounds of the students and their perceptions of the representations of their ethnic communities within the broadcast media. In addition, it gained an insight into how their relationship with technology might be informed by their ethnicities.

As part of the second research task, the research subjects were asked to 'surf' the World Wide Web for images which most adequately expressed their ethnic subjectivity. Subsequently, they were asked to provide responses on:

- the available range of texts on the World Wide Web which reflected their ethnicities
- aspects which were crucially absent or inappropriately present
- cross-media comparison with representations of their ethnicity in filmic or televisual texts
- alternative representations they would propose if they were to create their own Web site.

Furthermore, Chapter 5 provides an autobiographical examination of my approach to the research tasks. It emphasises the significant role of autobiography in the research tasks, as it transfers as much as possible the responsibility of representation away from myself as the researcher to the research subjects. In short, Chapter 5 explains the relationship between the online and offline in terms of the conditions of participation and the localised situations in which they were played out (Kendall 1999: pp.57-58).

Still working on the premise that online experiences are inextricable from offline ones (Jones 1999: p.xii), Chapter 6 ventures into the realm of cyberethnography, the offline collection of data about users (Wakeford 2000: p.38). To gain a more detailed insight into the research subjects' perspectives of the Web, the representation of ethnicity, the research tasks and the educational and domestic contexts in which they were conducted; I draw on interview material produced for Project @THENE. This interview material is used in Chapter 6 and provides an indication of the problems which arose during the execution of the research tasks, the conditions under which the research subjects interacted with the Web, especially in the domestic environment, as well as the methodological issues posed by doing research on the Web.

The chapter also returns to the theme of the role of technology in the politics of identity when looking at the ways in which the research subjects have integrated computers and the Internet into their everyday lives and their private spheres. Because the research subjects are all women who find themselves guardians of a 'borrowed' technology in their homes, this chapter draws upon literature in the area of gender and technology to analyse the impact of the computers and the Internet on their domestic relationships.

Chapters 7 and 8 analyse the Web sites and pages which the research subjects found in our journeys into cyberspace. As part of a qualitative study, these textual analyses are not so much concerned with generalisability (Denzin 1999: p.111), as with the insights they offer into their production and consumption (Mitra and Cohen 1999: p.181). The problematic nature of representation is discussed through the difficulties and resistance of the research subjects in defining and articulating their own ethnicities. Their perceptions of racial and ethnic representation in the media, particularly television, are explored and compared with the depictions of race and ethnicity they sought and/or found on the Web. The extent to which the Web continues traditional representational practices where ethnic minorities are concerned is examined alongside the opportunities for representation that are exemplified in their selection of texts. The findings demonstrate how historically dominant white author–white reader relations can be displaced by the participation of ethnic minorities on the Web. The possibilities for alternative forms of representation are shown in Web texts which assert ethnic author–white reader, or ethnic author–ethnic reader relationships. The various ways in which these dynamics operate through specific Web texts are debated through the perspectives of the research subjects. After all, it is in the act of consumption that texts become meaningful (Mitra and Cohen 1999: p.182).

Chapter 7 compares the experiential differences and similarities between consuming representations of ethnicity on the Web and the broadcast media. It looks particularly at sites which offered objectified representations of ethnicity, constructing ethnicity in terms of binary oppositions and notions of cultural purity. It offers readings based on the research subjects' conceptualisations of ethnicity and expectations of the Web both prior to and following their exploration of it.

Chapter 8 examines sites which contain self-produced representations of ethnicity, according to their producer/consumer or author/reader relations. It looks firstly at a mode of ethnic minority Web production which seeks to substitute dominant, white perspectives of ethnicity while still addressing a white audience. Secondly, it focuses on Web sites produced by ethnic minorities for ethnic communities, with particular attention paid to who is undertaking the task of representation and on behalf of whom. It avoids the simple conclusion that these are somehow better than Web texts which are not created by ethnic minorities. Rather, it uses the examples discussed to return to the question of representation initially raised by media studies. It asks how representation might be reframed in light of a medium like the Web where there are comparatively many more possible opportunities for self-representation.

What Does The Research Do That Is New?

The research draws from and extends upon a wide range of disciplines. In the wider context of Project @THENE, it contributes to feminist research on gender and technology. However, it brings to this, the consideration of an additional dimension, that of ethnicity, by studying the particular experience of women from ethnic minorities and their engagement with the World Wide Web. In examining the relationship between ethnicity and technology in a grounded local situation, as recommended by Brah (1992: p.139), it offers an alternative perspective to the pervasive notion that ethnic minorities are eternally 'victims of the digital divide', making race and technology incongruous (Nelson and Tu 2001: p.2). The research adds to the growing pool of empirical work on the representation of ethnic communities on the Internet, although and Sudan (2000: p.70) and Nakamura (2002: p.32) still lament the lack of research on issues of race and ethnicity in cyberspace. But while most of these empirical studies emerge from the US, this one is uniquely British. It also explores the ethnicity/technology relation in a new way, by adapting previous work on race and representation in media studies. In doing so, it attempts to rethink the relationship between media and new media. In this way, online experiences are studied in the context of other experiences of media (Sterne 1999: p.270).

Gender and Technology: Where Does Ethnicity Fit In?

There is a significant body of literature as summarised by Faulkner (1996), which discusses the relationship between gender and technology. It examines, for example, the sexual division of labour surrounding technologies, women's engagement with technologies as users rather than as designers, and women's under-representation in the information technology industry. However, the primacy of gender is often emphasised over its intersection with class, sexuality and ethnicity. Even within cybercultural studies literature, gender has been the focus over other aspects of identity (Kolko et al 2000: 8; Silver 2000: 135).

Both Project @THENE and my study acknowledge the particular inequalities women from ethnic minorities encounter, which are different to that of other women. The Project @THENE research contributes to this gender and technology literature by looking at the role of computers and the Internet in providing distant and flexible learning for mature women students from ethnic minorities. My study recognises that the examination of ethnicity on the Web cannot be adequately defined without reference to other aspects of identity (Hernton 1988: p.xi).

The research subjects provide insight into a culture of media and Internet consumption, but one that is from the margins. As women, they have been traditionally under-represented as consumers of information technology: in the UK particularly, Internet use has been consistently dominated by men (Pastore 2001; Greenspan 2003). As ethnic minority women, they are often not the targeted readers of the media texts they prefer to consume. The research is unique in its interpretation of media texts through the viewpoints of a group who find themselves both the subjects and objects of representations of race and ethnicity. As it involves a group of women using technology in a very specific and arguably unlikely context, the book aims to make a small contribution (in chapter 6) to the area of gender and technology studies which deals with women's engagement with technologies that were never intended for them.

Challenging the Anglo-American Divide Through Empirical Specificity

The Internet is worthy of examination because of its relative contemporaneity compared to other forms of broadcast media. However, given the initial US dominance of online production and consumption, studies of the Internet have tended to focus on the US. All the key texts relating to race and ethnicity on the Internet – such as Kolko et al's (2000) *Race in Cyberspace*; Nelson and Tu's (2001) *Technicolor*; and Nakamura's (2002) *Cybertypes* – emerge from the US, with little in the way of equivalent comprehensive studies of Web production and consumption in Britain. Acknowledging this ethnocentrism, Nakamura (2002: p.xix) calls for more research on issues of race and ethnicity in non-American cyberspaces.

The empirical research was conducted within a British university with London-based research subjects. Within this national, cultural and simultaneously localised socio-economic environment, notions of race, ethnicity and blackness are articulated very differently to those in the US. Yet in addition to British media and Web texts, those from the US also had a meaningful role in the construction of ethnic identity for the research subjects. In this study of Web consumption, the use of research subjects as cultural informants follows the tradition of British cultural studies.

The few grounded empirical studies which have been done about race and ethnicity in cyberspace tend to focus on one element of the Internet. Certainly, it has only been through empirical research that ethnicity and the Internet has been investigated in any detail, albeit mostly about US audiences and texts. For example, Gajjala (1999) and Mitra (1997) examine the construction of ethnic communities in newsgroups. Carstarphen and Lambiase (1998) analyse racist discourse in students' electronic discussions. Hoffman and Novak's (1998) study of discrepancies in Internet use between white and black people in the United States focuses on the World Wide Web. Hoffman and Novak's research is complemented by Lockard's (1999) content analysis of Web sites produced by ethnic minority groups. Kolko et al's (2000) edited collection looks at the representation of race and ethnicity in a broad range of texts across the digital realm including cyberpunk movies, video games, MOOs and Web sites. Likewise, Berry and Martin, Mallapragada, and Arnold and Plymire study various online ethnic communities on the Internet in Gauntlett's (2000) anthology. Ross and Greaves, and Nguyen's (2001) articles concentrate on Web sites created by ethnic producers for minority audiences. Finally, Nakamura (2002) focuses on the depiction of ethnicities in and about cyberspace, from graphic and text-based MOOs and MUDs to advertisements for Internet services.

It is obvious that between these studies of various elements of the Internet emerge different conclusions. For example, while Nakamura's research illustrates the absence of ethnic participation in LambdaMOO; Lockard, Hoffman and Novak's studies show evidence of significant black activity on the World Wide Web. In recognition of the need for research which regards the Internet as a technology constituted by a variety of unique protocols, with each needing to be examined differently, my research is concerned only with the World Wide Web. It also responds to Lockard's call for more qualitative studies of Web content, especially in-depth analyses of representations of ethnicity. Even at 2002, Nakamura says there remains a notable lack of research on race, racism and ethnicity particularly in non-American cyberspaces: 'It is crucial that scholarly inquiry examine the ways that racism is perpetuated by both globalism and communications technologies like the Internet across a range of discursive fields and cultural matrices' (Nakamura 2002: p.xviii, xix, 32).

Rethinking the Ethnicity/Technology, Media/New Media Relation

Given the dearth of empirical research on ethnicity and the Web, it is necessary to turn to other studies of ethnicity and technology. This relationship has been explored extensively in media studies, whereby the wealth of research on race and representation in the print and broadcast media provides a series of theoretical frameworks with which to consider depictions of ethnicity on the World Wide Web. By using old theories to study new media, a readymade structure for systematic scholarship is provided (Jones 1999: p.x) which assists in examining the tensions between the Web as a site of resistance, of self-constructed representations of ethnicity, and it being a site of ethnic objectification, where the 'white gaze' prevails. Traditional media studies offer a point of departure for looking at resistance on the Internet, and answering Jain's (1997) question: is the Internet a positive reinforcement of one's subjectivity or a cheap form of tourism, of looking at others? This juxtaposition of old and new also enable the former to be revisited and revised in light of emerging technologies.

In this sense, the book interrogates the content of the Internet from within the existing disciplinary and historical framework of media studies. That is, it considers representations of race on the Web to be media texts that can be compared and contrasted with those seen in television programmes and films. It regards the Internet as part of a wider media landscape, as a technology which borrows, hybridises and diversifies from its predecessors. In adopting this media studies lense, it examines ways in which the Web continues traditions in representation established in previous media, as well as offers new possibilities for representational practices. Thus, the empirical research looks at a range of media artefacts chosen by the research subjects, from TV shows to Web sites which portray ethnic minorities. The Anglo-American bias evident in availability and choice of media texts is explored, as is the absence and transience of ethnic minorities: British television programmes such as *EastEnders* and *The Real McCoy*, as well as Web sites such as BlackNet and The Chronicle are discussed in terms of their rendering of issues of race. These are critically juxtaposed with selected equivalent and abundant US media texts. Such an analysis contributes to media studies literature in that it extends other latitudinal studies which have focused on particular media texts specific to an historical period. Therefore, while media texts, whether TV shows or Web sites, may no longer be available, they are significant and indicative of social and representational trends at a particular period in time.

Nevertheless, in a study of ethnicity on the World Wide Web, the substantial literature on race and representation in the media is not entirely sufficient. Clearly, ideas which apply to film and television cannot be applied wholesale to the Web. But by using them comparatively, the limits of those media theories can be tested and subsequently, we can discover some things about how the Web operates. Not only can the debates about media as a tool of representation be challenged in this way, but also those which are concerned with the media as a technology. For example, the hopes and promises which were invested in broadcast media technologies such as television, video and community cable paralleled the rhetoric that surrounded the Internet in the mid to late 1990s.

In any case, there is more than a theoretical justification for juxtposing media and new media. Silverstone (1997) agrees that new ways of seeing media are needed given technological convergence. Certainly, the World Wide Web seems the most appropriate part of the Internet to be regarded as a form of broadcast media because it incorporates written text, moving and still images for public consumption, facilitating its comparison with television and film.

To perceive the Web in binary opposition to or superceding broadcast media technologies is problematic because technological convergence is ensuring that the previously unique characteristics of each are becoming increasingly integrated so that, for example, consumers can now buy computer monitors that also function as televisions. But this convergence extends beyond the technological artefacts themselves to the ways they are being used and the content that they carry. The selectivity afforded to the user when s/he 'surfs' the World Wide Web is being mimicked by the plethora of 'choice' realised through the proliferation of satellite, cable and digital interactive television. According to Nguyen and Alexander (1996: p.110), this heralds an era of 'demassification', in which audiences are fragmented and there is a movement away from mass production and marketing: 'It is about narrowcasting to defined, niche audiences, not broadcasting to all and sundry. And the market for these new services is, in a fundamental sense, global, not regional or national' (Horsman 1996: p.20).

Conversely, influenced by the growth of commercial interest in the Web and the need to locate smaller, self-organising, niche groups which the media historically never provided for; software developers are instigating strategies for making the Web more akin to a broadcast medium by directing content at the user. This movement is intensified by the carriage of content, through the use of bigger, thicker, faster transmission technologies for Internet access, such as cable and satellite instead of telephony (British Broadcasting Corporation 1997). Capable of carrying larger volumes of data at greater speeds, these will ensure that information is given to the Web user rather than sought.

Therefore, the similarity of the hardware utilised by the Web and broadcast media suggests that there are strong technical grounds for conceptualising it as a broadcast medium. This close connection is not only evident in their means of carriage (of data, messages, texts), but also in their content. The Web is being used as an arena for audiences to discuss and respond to programmes on television. In the United States, this has been particularly popular where issues of race are concerned. The *New York Times* reported a *Star Trek* Web-based debate on race issues after an episode of its spin-off series, *Deep Space 9*, dealt with race in mid-20th century America. Similarly, Oprah Online was flooded with messages in response to the topic of interracial marriages which was discussed on one of the Oprah Winfrey shows (Marriott 1998: p.1). In this sense, the Web complements television provision.

But in spite of the present and potential similarities between television and Web technologies and content, there are still significant differences in their modes of production, consumption and representation which should be acknowledged. In terms of production, the technical differences between the broadcast media and the Internet influence accessibility to each. Television uses mainly analogue and, to a lesser extent, digital technologies which are difficult to make compatible. By and large, cinema, television, photography and video produce analogue representations through photomechanical means. The broadcast media require separate hardware for production, distribution and consumption. In contrast, the Internet is purely digital: multimedia, virtual reality and computer networking produce digital images through strings of code constituted by binary digits (Dovey 1996: p.xii). Its 'interactivity' as defined by Dovey, that is 'the ability of the user to interact with information and image to change, reformulate or tailor the data to his or her own ends', gives it an added technical dimension that broadcast (analogue) media does not possess. The same technology is able to be used for production, distribution and consumption.

As a multimedia technology, the Internet is relatively cheap to access compared to broadcast media technologies (Barker and Tucker 1990: p.24). The technology associated with print and broadcast media is expensive as it is based on professional market pricing, compared with multimedia technology which is based on consumer market pricing.

In terms of consumption, Kelly and Wolf (1997: p.76) describe the fundamental difference between the broadcast media and the Web as one of 'push' and 'pull'.

Television, radio and film are classified as 'push' media because they are consumed within a shared context, in communal spaces, require minimal interaction and are highly regulated. A limited number of texts are presented to viewers via a few television channels and the degree of choice is very finite. In contrast, the Web is a 'pull' media because it necessitates the isolation and intervention of the user to extract information. The user sits alone before a monitor to view texts that have been subjected to no official scrutiny prior to being published. It is precisely these different modes of engagement which inform the unique representational practices of television and the Web.

The extent to which television and the Web can be compared will become evident in the course of this research. While it is apparent that the two media are, increasingly, utilising the same carriage technologies, the research will focus primarily on content and its relationship to production and consumption.

Summary

This chapter has sought to spell out the premise, aims and objectives of this book. In short, the research developed from a need to extend studies of gender and technology by considering other aspects of identity, such as ethnicity. In addition, it aims to be an empirical contribution to the expanding amount of material about the Internet which neither pays much attention to ethnicity or disciplines that have analysed the ethnicity/technology relation.

As part of examining ethnic minority Web consumption, representation and production empirically, the book strives to be specific about the technology being scrutinised: the World Wide Web has been defined as part of but distinct from the Internet as a whole. It also seeks to detail the context in which the study took place, that is, within a larger research project, in an educational institution with ethnic minority women students who participated as research subjects and gave an insight into their findings of ethnicity on the Web as well as the private spheres of their Web consumption.

Both the empirical and theoretical dimensions of the research aim to be interdisciplinary. That is, they seek to draw on disciplines relevant to different aspects of the research. While there is much written about the Web, media and cultural studies literature on identity politics, race and representation provides some balance in the examination of this technology/ethnicity equation. Therefore, in the following chapter, there is a further explanation of terms: given that the Web has already been defined, this other facet of the research, ethnicity, is explored and distinguished from notions such as race, culture and nationality.

Chapter 2

'Not Everything in Black and White Makes Sense': Differing Definitions of Difference

This chapter aims to examine the slippery discourses of race and ethnicity, and the particularities of defining difference on both sides of the Anglo-American Atlantic. Hence the reference to the 1997 advertising campaign for Guinness beer, 'not everything in black and white makes sense', seemed apt given the array of terminologies which have been used to describe non-whiteness, and the difficulties that each has had in articulating it throughout history into the 21st century.

Given this concern with definitions of difference, or what might be called 'identity politics', the brief review of literature in this chapter draws mainly from writings in cultural studies. It summarises contemporary conceptual and theoretical issues of ethnicity and identity, foregrounding the following chapter's review of media studies literature, which looks at the relationship between the representation of those concepts of difference and the technology that undetakes it, that is, how a medium informs the content it carries. The separation of the cultural studies and media studies literature reviews is necessary because they are disciplines which have previously been entangled but have subsequently established themselves in their own right through diverging theoretical interests, although they remain closely aligned (Turner 1990). Cultural studies has tended to be preoccupied with human subjects, whether they are working class communities, readers of texts or media audiences. Media studies has focused on media content and industries, and the process of mass communication. It has been influenced by North American academic traditions of studying the psychological effects of the mass media. In this sense, it overlaps with the more distinctly British discipline of cultural studies in its preoccupation with audiences and consumers. But where cultural studies examines popular and broader cultural phenomena, media studies concentrates on print and broadcast media cultures. It is firmly between these two areas that I locate myself as a researcher and this research: the study is as much an exploration of the Web as a form of new media and tool of production, consumption and representation by ethnic minorities; as it is about the intricacies and complexities of ethnicity itself.

This chapter seeks to explain the choice of ethnicity as the focus of the research by discussing the historical and cultural specificity of definitions of difference. It distinguishes between terms which define difference essentially, such as 'race' and 'nation', and those which encompass diverse experiences and subjectivities. It delineates between the concepts of race and ethnicity. It argues that there exists a struggle over the meaning of ethnicity, but proposes that it is precisely this tension in its definition that makes ethnicity appropriate for the purposes of this research. Moreover, it suggests that fundamentally, ethnicity cannot be defined without reference to class, gender, sexuality, age and other aspects of subjectivity.

The introduction to this book described how this study emerged from my participation in a larger research project, Project @THENE. One of its aims, as stated in its original bid for funding from British Telecom, was 'to increase access to higher education in IT-related subjects for students from non-traditional backgrounds – particularly women from **ethnic minority communities'** (*my emphasis*). Therefore, my study of ethnicity was framed by Project @THENE's specific concern with it.

But the vocabulary used in Project @THENE's funding bid also indicates an institutional acceptance of ethnicity to describe a certain kind of difference. It seems to be the term of this historical moment, at least in the British context. It is the consequence of constantly changing discourses of difference, of struggles for meaning that have taken place not only over time, but across other social and cultural locations.

Ethnicity can refer to identities in a dynamic state of diversity and hybridity, which are characterised by new and non-traditional differences and configurations. This conceptualisation of ethnicity acknowledges the past, but suggests that it is transformed and reinvented in the present (Ross 1996: p.xi). It includes migratory and diasporic experiences, and the inevitable processes of transcultural mixing which take place as a result: 'In the experience of migration, difference is confronted: boundaries are crossed; cultures are mingled; identities become blurred' (Robins 1991: p.42).

The parameters of ethnicity can be quite elastic so that it encompasses the wide range of difference which migration has produced. Indeed, the notion of diaspora fits well with this perspective of ethnicity, as it refers to the geographical dispersal of particular communities of people by force or choice, thus integrating the local with the global, and combining shared culture with different experiences (Gillespie 1995: p.6). According to Ang (1994: p.5), these communities are bound by real and/or symbolic ties to and collective memories of an original 'homeland'. By this definition, they can also be characterised as 'virtual' (Fernback 1999: pp.204-211): that is, these imagined connections parallel 'virtual communities' as they do diasporic ones. For example, the black diaspora is constituted by all those ethnicities that have emerged from the forced migration of Africans; there also exists, for instance, a Chinese diaspora which has developed from different historical circumstances. The notion of diaspora attempts to negotiate the constant tension between 'where you are from' and 'where you are at' (Gilroy 1990/1: pp.3-16). The breadth of diversity that is accommodated in this definition of ethnicity extends even further, beyond different social, political, cultural and historical experiences.

Brah (1992: p.131) argues that ethnicity also has to account for the experiential differences informed by gender, class and sexuality. That is, one's ethnicity cannot be understood in isolation from other dimensions of subjectivity, so that, for example, my experience of Chineseness is inextricably linked to my experience as a woman (of

Chinese heritage). The range of positions that this definition of ethnicity allows in terms of 'where you are at' or where you locate yourself other than geographically, means that ethnicity is no longer necessarily tied to one's origins or homeland. This dissociation of ethnicity from a particular space or period of time, according to Giddens (1991: p.2), is exascerbated by the role of technology in mediating social relations:

> ...modern social life is characterised by profound processes of the reorganisation of time and space...coupled to the expansion of disembedding mechanisms – mechanisms which prise social relations free from the hold of specific locales, recombining them across wide time-space distances.

It may be precisely these dislocating tendencies of contemporary existence that inspire a reaction to a flexible and fluid conceptualisation of ethnicity. Hall et al (1992) recognise that ethnicity is a term which is vulnerable to many forms of reappropriation, particularly essentialist ones which define it in terms of cultural purity. For those who seek to use it as a terminology of exclusion, ethnicity connotes distinct cultural features, traditions, customs and religions. It is a regressive construction of ethnicity founded upon an idealised and imagined past (Ross 1996: p.xi). The term 'ethnos' implies a sense of place and belonging and therefore links closely with a concept of a 'nation' and its 'natives' (Hall 1992). Modern nations utilise it as a vehicle for claiming that they are constituted by a singular 'ethnos' or family, a homogenous community which is threatened by other ethnicities. Simultaneously, ethnic communities themselves express their desire to return to origins through a form of 'ethnic absolutism' (Hall et al 1992: p.308): here, 'authenticity' is used as a form of political mobilization through which resources, economic or otherwise, can be claimed from the State (Yuval-Davis 1998: pp.138-139). Thus, the struggle over the meaning of ethnicity is also a struggle over who has the power to define where the boundaries of ethnic collectivities lie: as Werbner (1997: p.18) argues, ethnicity is defined as much internally as externally.

Ethnicity which is constructed on principles of exclusivity is exemplified in, for example, religious fundmentalism and attempts to forge a singular narrative of national culture. It is also manifest linguistically in terms such as 'ethnic minorities', which Lippard (1992: p.168) regards as a marginalising tactic: '...people of colour are the minority only in the United States and Canada. Globally, Caucasians are distinctly in the minority.'

Although everyone has an ethnicity, it has been applied only to particular ethnicities, mainly minority ones and those which are deemed to contradict or threaten the dominant culture or wider society (Solomos and Back 1996: p.131; Leicester 1993: p.16). The notion that non-whiteness can be classified according to ethnic minorities, while restrictive, does allow for more particularistic forms of identification than race. Ethnicity can refer to indigenous communities because of their association with their native land, but can also apply to immigrants because of their 'minority' status in a host society. In contrast, race operates on the basic binary opposition of black and white: 'It bears repetition that "race" (and) ethnicity...are not interchangeable terms.' (Gilroy 1987: pp.154-156)

Gilroy argues that there should be a clear conceptual distance between race and ethnicity. Race is written with quotation marks to highlight it as a problematic term. It is used with difficulty because of its focus on the physical body: skin colour, facial features, hair, physique, posterior, genitalia (Hernton 1988: p.xii; Leicester 1993: p.16). It utilises these symbolic markers of the body to make a socially constructed difference into a supposedly natural one: 'If this (racial) originality exists – and there is no doubt about it – it is due to geographical, historical and sociological circumstances, and not distinct aptitudes related to the anatomical or physiological constitution of black, yellow and white races.' (Lévi-Strauss 1977: p.324)

Indeed, as Lévi-Strauss points out, the concept of race emerged in a particular social and historical context. It was at the height of imperialism that the use of race as a category for describing difference gained prevalence, in conjunction with ideas of biological determinism. Race was characterised by:

- physically distinguishable traits which gave rise to the popular use of craniology, the study of skull size, up until 1940
- the assumption of blood or genetic difference based on distinctions between skin colour (Bottomley and de Lepervanche 1988: p.33).

These physiological characteristics were used to support 'survival of the fittest' theories, justifying competition between races and the superiority/inferiority of a particular race (Hoch 1979: p.47). While racial dualisms have been widely criticised for being scientifically invalid, they nevertheless persist in discourses of difference. Indeed, these beliefs about genetic hierarchies – whether individual, institutional or systemic – constitute racism (Leicester 1993: p.16).

Such dichotomies have been key to the formation of national identities. According to Said (1995: pp.1-3), European identity was forged in diametric opposition to the Orient. Invented by Europe, the Orient was instrumental in defining the West as everything that the East was not. This Orientalism, the construction of the Orient as the 'cultural contestant' of Europe, parallels the dichotomies of racism.

Chapter 7 of the book shows evidence of Orientalism on the Web found in my searches for representations of Chineseness. It also examines racism on the Web and in doing so, has to engage with terminologies of race. This book acknowledges that any notion of race premised on biological, anatomical or physiological characteristics is fundamentally flawed, but uses the term to refer to strategies for representing difference. For example, when referring to media studies literature on race and representation, I am alluding to research which shows difference to be depicted in terms of binary oppositions of race. The book also recognises that race remains in widespread use to delineate difference, perhaps more so in national contexts other than Britain. As Ifekwunigwe (1998: p.91) says, race is discursively privileged.

In the United States, terminologies of race still seem to be predominantly used: 'Race is the hottest topic in America. This country is obsessed with it.' (Greaves in Marriott 1998: p.1)

But in spite of its inadequacies, race has, in the US context, come to be associated with discourses of blackness. It has been appropriated in what Spivak (1993: pp.3-5) calls a 'strategic essentialism', a way of mobilising people for the sake of achieving a political objective. So that while blackness implies racial difference, it actually refers to those who have been subject to slavery, segregation, discrimination and economic exploitation (Silk and Silk 1990: p.viii). Thus, the concept of race becomes politicised when discussed in relation to blackness.

References to blackness are used to indicate political unity rather than to describe race. 'Black' is a symbol of oppression as well as resistance (Ross 1996: p.viii). It is intended as a sign of solidarity for those who have been discriminated against for their non-whiteness and to unite everyone who has experienced racism under the category of blackness in the fight against racism.

> What these communities have in common, which they represent through taking on the 'black' identity, is not that they are culturally, ethnically, linguistically or even physically the same, but that they are seen and treated as "the same" (ie non-white, "other") by the dominant culture' (Hall et al 1992: p.308).

But again, the variation in the meaning of 'black' according to history and geography should be considered. Hoch (1979: p.50) claims that in the 16th century, it referred to North African Moors, southern Italians – especially Sicilians, and Spaniards. In the United States, more contemporary notions of blackness mean people of African or Caribbean descent. The use of the term in Britain in the 1970s and 1980s was heavily inspired by the Black Power movement in the US, but was adapted to include people of South Asian descent, who as post-war immigrants, occupied a similar structural position as African-Caribbeans in British society (Brah 1992: pp.127-128). The differential use of terminologies of blackness across the Atlantic has not been without controversy.

As Brah points out, it was seen as problematic in Britain because of its original appropriation by black Americans to establish their own positive political and cultural identity. The American use of the term does not recognise as black other kinds of non-whiteness except people of African or Caribbean descent: with an African-American population of 40 million strong, perhaps it does not need to (Mashengele 1997: pp.311-315; Morrissey 2003). Therefore, it does not articulate the range and types of difference which characterise black Britishness. As such, many British Asians do not define themselves as black. As a person of Chinese heritage, I could be considered as black in Britain, but perhaps not in the United States. Indeed, Modood (1997: p.157) argues that British anti-racist movements which accepted the black/white opposition were complicated by the Asian presence, which triangulated this dualism. This fluidity in the definition of blackness represents the ongoing struggle for meaning in discourses of difference, and the inadequacies which still exist in language for articulating non-whiteness.

In order for blackness to retain a political resonance, it has to utilise the tactics of racism by premising itself upon a black/white binary opposition. But the question of who is included or excluded from blackness remains unresolved. In contrast, ethnicity has more semiotic mobility: although there are essentialist notions of ethnicity, there are also heterogenous conceptualisations of it. However, these have been criticised for being apolitical: as ethnicities become increasingly individualised, they also become depoliticised, removed from their relations of power. Ross (1996: p.vxi) argues that generality is necessary in defining ethnicity as attempts to describe it concretely easily degenerate into stereotype. Thus, there seem to be advantages and disadvantages to defining difference broadly as well as more specifically.

'It is all well and good to theorise the diaspora, the post-colony and the hybrid, but where this is never interrupted by the necessity of political work, it remains a vote for the status quo' (Hutnyk 1997: p.134). This chapter has merely been an extended definition of terms. The 'political work' which the book undertakes is an exploration of the ways in which difference is constructed from within, from without, across technologies and subjectivities, and the negotiations and struggles that take place in between. Firstly, it examines historical definitions of race and ethnicity across time and technologies. Secondly, it looks at how ethnicity is embodied in the ways in which the research subjects define themselves. That is, there is no attempt on my part to impose a set definition of ethnicity on the research tasks or findings: indeed, like the Internet, ethnicity is not fixed and so can only be 'snapshot' (Jones 1999: p.6). Instead, the book subscribes to Lippard's (1992: pp.167-168) proposal that 'a vital, sensible, and imaginative vocabulary can only be self-generated during the process of self-naming'. Thirdly, it uses the research subjects' conceptualisations of their own ethnicities as the basis for exploring the Web pages and sites they selected. In doing so, the research will gauge the capacity for the Web to accommodate a diverse range of representations of ethnicity.

The next chapter considers how the discourses of difference discussed above have been manifest in media images. Studies of representations of race and ethnicity in film and television are used as possible points of departure for analysing the construction of race and ethnicity on the Web.

Chapter 3

'It's All There in Black and White': Media Studies and the Theorising of Race and Ethnicity on the World Wide Web

The discourses of difference which were examined somewhat abstractly in the previous chapter will now be discussed more concretely. This chapter investigates how such discourses have been manifest in media images, particularly in the representations of race and ethnicity in film and television. This area of research forms a basis for critically analysing depictions of difference on the Web.

The chapter begins by reiterating the reasons for using media studies as a foundation for theorising the construction of race and ethnicity on the Web. This is followed by some thoughts on why the issue of representation is such an important one. The remainder of the chapter examines research on race and representation in the media, exploring the methods by which it has been studied in relation to the structures of the media industries as well as in the images produced. Where the latter is concerned, the findings of such media research provide a framework for analysing Web representations of race and ethnicity, especially in the context of who has power over the production of images and their interpretation.

Media Studies as a Departure Point: A Rationale

As mentioned in the introductory chapter, the case for conceptualising the Web as a form of broadcast media for the purpose of scrutinising depictions of ethnicity is not merely a personal one. While my research background is in media studies and I have felt that my identity as member of an ethnic minority has been subject to a poverty of representation in popular culture and media, other academics have also argued for a the study of new media through the theoretical frameworks by which we understand old media. After all, Internet research comes from, amongst other disciplines, media studies (Jones 1999: pp.x-xi).

Given that the convergence of previously distinct media technologies is taking place, it seems appropriate to cross-fertilise the theories and ideas that have circulated around each. The Internet is seen as the embodiment of this convergence, combining the technologies of telephony, broadcasting, computing and publishing (Barker and Tucker 1990: p.22) for the carriage of content. The World Wide Web, in particular, has been embraced as an extension of television, providing a forum for audiences to discuss and respond to programmes on television (Marriott 1998: p.1). But while the comparison of the World Wide Web with television may be appropriate, their commonalities should not be overemphasised. The technological convergence evident in the Web should not be mistaken as its substitution for television. The convergence of technologies associated with television and the Web is neither wholesale or even. That is, the different modes of production, consumption and representation of each medium need to be considered. As such, theories and ideas which have been applied to television can only have limited pertinence to the Web.

Thus research into representations of race and ethnicity in media and popular culture merely offers points of departure for scrutinising the equivalent on the Web. It provides a wealth of theoretical frameworks and case studies against which findings from the Web can be tested. It is also a way of gauging the extent to which the boundaries between television and the Web overlap in their renderings of race and ethnicity. Where they do not coincide, there is the opportunity for further enquiry, for discovering the idiosyncratic qualities of the Web's modes of operation in relation to issues of race and ethnicity.

Why is Representation Important?

The plethora of research devoted to depictions of race and ethnicity in popular culture indicates the significance granted to issues of representation, which seemingly arises from a belief in the power of the media. The potency of images has been studied in relation to their impact on attitudes and values. For example, television programmes have been examined in terms of the extent to which they can contest or affirm the racist beliefs of audiences (Hartmann and Husband 1973: pp.271-273). Thus representation is the point at which discourses of difference become visible. It is the manifestation of those abstract notions of race, or 'strategic essentialism' (Spivak 1993: pp.2-5), or hybridity, discussed in the previous chapter.

> ...how things are represented and the "machineries" and regimes of representation in a culture do play a constitutive, and not merely a reflexive, after-the-event, role...[they have] a formative, not merely an expressive, place in the constitution of social and political life...it is only within the discursive, and subject to its specific conditions, limits and modalities, do they have or can they be constructed within meaning... (Hall 1996b: p.443).

The abundance of research which exists on race and representation in media and popular culture is disproportionate to the few equivalent empirical studies that have been done on different aspects of the Internet. Because of this imbalance, it is important that the Web's particular representational practices are investigated, especially the process by which the concepts of race and ethnicity become apparent and tangible.The Internet is, after all, part of a wider media landscape and social phenomenon (Sterne 1999: p.271). Mitra (1997: pp.56, 60) argues that both the Internet and the traditional mass media need to be compared in terms of their contributions to the construction of national image, as national media depict the primary cultural practices of a nation.

Therefore the Internet, as an international medium, could be said to resonate with the icons and symbols of a global culture.

Researchers of the Internet have called for more study of issues of race and ethnicity in cyberspace, an area which has a notable lack of research (Sudan 2000: p.70; Nakamura 2002: p.32), even within the discipline of cyberculture studies (ibid: p.108). In his content analysis of Web sites produced by ethnic minority groups, Lockard (1999) recognises the need for further enquiry, particularly more qualitative analyses of Web representations: '...racial/ethnic nose counts in cyberspace are problematic in that they are rough estimates based on narrative surface facts, not an engagement with either representational contents or the agency of electronic representation'. This is a response to the growth of 'ratings studies' and statistical analyses of Web use by market research companies such as WebTrends and Nielsen//NetRatings (Mitra and Cohen 1999: p.180; Wakeford 2000: p.31).

Even where depictions of ethnicity have been examined in depth, such as in Nakamura's (2002: p.49) study of LambdaMOO, it is necessary to look critically at the possibilities offered by them: are they viable alternatives, 'critical rearticulations and recombinations of race, gender and class, and which also call the fixedness of these categories into question'? Or are they more of the same, 'tired reiteration(s) and reinstatement(s) of old hierarchies'? The study of representation in the media and the Web is a means of contesting regressive constructions of race, and a beginning point for formulating ways of transcending these in the production of new images.

What is Representation?

Representation is sometimes defined as merely the unproblematic reflection of reality. But as Hall (1996b: p.443) contends, while there may be an external reality to which symbols and images refer, it is only within the realm of representation that we can engage with it. However, the process of representation is political, biased in its particular modes of conveying meaning. This is more apparent in cyberspace than in the media.

While the Web affords a variety of representational strategies (Mitra and Cohen 1999: p.182), as Rubio (1996) argues, representations on the Web are nothing but hollow: 'For when you visit my home page, you don't get to meet me, but only a presentation of myself...'. He likens it to looking at the facade of a house yet never meeting the owner because s/he or it is never home. That is, the knowledge you garner from a Web page is inevitably superficial, only a skeletal imitation at best of what it is supposed to represent. This cynicism about the Web's capacity for representation mistakenly equates it with empowerment: 'If representational visibility equals power, then almost naked young white should be running Western culture' (Phelan in Nguyen 2001: p.182).

Studies of race and representation in the media should not be regarded as 'true' depictions of how ethnic minorities were at a particular period in history, but rather how they were thought of at that point in time. It is more an indication of the relationship between producer and consumer, who was constructing images of ethnicity in the media and for whom. Representations of ethnicity on the Web need to be similarly considered as 'snapshots' which can be pieced together in order to theorise the structure of the Internet, its modes of production and consumption (Jones 1999: p.6; Mitra and Cohen 1999: p.181; Sterne 1999: p.270).

Research on issues of race and ethnicity in cyberspace has already, to some extent, borrowed from the traditions of media studies. Just as representation in the *structures* of the media industries has been scrutinised, so too has issues of access and participation on the Internet. Representation in media *images* has also been studied extensively, in terms of both the absence and presence of ethnic minorities, as well as whether those presences are positive or negative. Because of the comparably short history of the Internet, its studies have been preoccupied with the absence of ethnic minority representation; and only a minimal amount of attention has been paid to how race and ethnicity are being constructed in cyberspace and by whom. These issues of inclusion and exclusion are as important to questions of racism as they are to representation (ibid 277; Leicester 1993: p.2).

Representation in Structures

As mentioned above, the structural relationship between ethnicity and technology has been investigated in detail by researchers of the media. For example, at the level of production, the print and broadcast media industries have been analysed and found to be hierarchical and inaccessible to ethnic minorities.

In his historical analysis of television production, Tunstall (1993: p.4) contends that the role of the television producer was modelled on the notion of a 'governor of a small colony'. This suggests that the practices of imperialism are inscribed in the structures of the television industry, and that this is evident in its race relations: '...undoubtedly people of British and north European Protestant origin have been the single, most powerful ethnic force (in the media)' (Tunstall 1977: pp.74-75).

The whiteness of the British media is not only characteristic of its television but also its film industry. As Isaac Julien, a black British filmmaker, said: 'British film culture is white, middle class, mostly male and heterosexual' (in Givanni 1995: p.9).

Furthermore, this lack of ethnic diversity could also be found in the print media industries. Of the 8000 journalists working in the provincial press in the mid 1990s, only 20 were black (Campaign for Press and Broadcasting Freedom 1996: p.10).

These patterns are not entirely dissimilar to the media industries in the United States, taking into consideration the different historical trajectories. Tunstall (1977: p.89) claimed that the majority of US newspapers, news agencies, magazines and television stations were white-controlled. Even considering that black people and European immigrants were involved in US film production at the beginning of the 20th century, their participation has fluctuated according to the economic health of the industry: as films were increasingly commercially financed through Wall Street, the industry also became more white (ibid); and when the industry underwent periods of depression, ethnic minorities were the first to be excluded from it (Silk and Silk

1990: pp.121-152). Leicester (1993: pp.18, 20) defines such exclusions of minority groups through white-powered systems, practices and procedures as institutional racism, although it is part of a wider structural racism which involves a history of social inequality.

It is through these detailed historical analyses that it becomes apparent that past exclusion from participation in the media has discouraged young black people from seeking careers in the industry, thereby perpetuating it as a white domain (Tulloch 1990: p.146). This sort of historical examination of the Internet, likewise, shows that access informs how race is articulated online (Nakamura 2002: p.7). It is the offline environment which determines the conditions for online participation, and as such, the dominant group to set norms in the online world are male and white (Kendall 1999: pp.57, 66). However, the study of these offline-online relationships has concentrated on Western countries, primarily the US.

Past research into the Internet's modes of production and participation suggested a similar pattern emerging to the broadcast media, that is, the apparent colonisation by the white Western middle classes (see Apple 1992: p.118; Johnson 1996: p.98; Spender 1996: p.118; Hoffman and Novak 1998: p.3; Interrogate the Internet 1996: pp.125-127; Kendall 1999: p.63; Pastore 2001; Greenspan 2003b). The profile of cyberspace was not only white, but also very masculine: back in 1993, Panos (1998) said that computer networks were as much as 95% male; in 1996, Interrogate the Internet (1996: pp.125-127) claimed that 73% of Internet users were male. In 1998, the gender ratio was estimated to be 63% men to 37% women, and Panos suggested that this had remained static for some years. In 2000-2001, Internet use in countries other than the US and Canada was still 52-63% male (Pastore 2000a, 2001). However, with women actually leading Internet use in the US and Canada, cyberspace appears to be getting less masculine.

With approximately 90% of users concentrated in 20 countries (ClickZ 2004), the Internet also seems to be less North American. Of the projected total of 709-945 million worldwide Internet users in 2004, the estimated 126-182 million Internet users in the US comprise a significant proportion but certainly not a majority. But does this actually mean that cyberspace is any less Western or even any less white? In 1998, it was speculated that Internet growth in developing countries was faster in developing countries than anywhere else (Panos 1998). By 2002, Internet use in the US still tripled that of China, its nearest rival; but the number of users across the Asia Pacific region approximated the US (Greenspan 2002). Meanwhile, within the US, Asian Americans were found to have a greater level of household Internet penetration, and be more experienced and active Internet users than their white counterparts (ClickZ 2001; Greenspan 2003a).

Nonetheless, African Americans and Hispanics have traditionally trailed Asians and Caucasians in online participation (ClickZ 2001; Morrissey 2003; Greenspan 2004a). But there have also been instances where the narrative of the homogenous and monolithic 'white middle class bohemia' (Johnson 1996: p.98) has been disrupted. The 1993 US census showed that 13% of black youth, 21.1% of Latino youth and 35.5% of white youth had access to a computer (Zipp 1997). The growth rate of the

Internet shows that these percentages have increased significantly. Hoffman and Novak's (1998) study of computer access and Internet use in the US shows evidence of significant black activity on the World Wide Web. Indeed, African Americans and Hispanics are more likely to use th Web for research purposes and chatrooms than their white counterparts (Greenspan 2004a). However, this sort of minority activity has not been explored to any extent that could be compared with the study of black participation in the media. But even with limited access, Mitra (1997: p.60) argues that any minority group is empowered to produce Web texts that can shape cyberspace as they would want and contribute to making it their own. Therefore, the Internet is seen as both an instrument for potential empowerment as well as entrenching privilege. Can minority resistance and activity flourish in an environment which Hall (1998a) regards as the antithesis of multiculturalism, where the audience is largely white and monolinguistic?

Lockard (1999) suggests that US dominance of cyberspace in the late 1990s in terms of users and content inevitably means that the Web contains 'heavily racialized – and implicitly racist – geographies', that it is a microcosm of the social contexts in which it is used:

> '...cyberspace is unmistakably signed with Euro-American whiteness. Such internalized online monoculturalism reiterates external racisms prevalent in American social structures...Simply, the local geography of cyberspace follows the lines and contours of American racism, sexism and classism.'

Therefore, the Web represents the existing inequalities between black and white people in post-colonial societies. These disparities stretch beyond online environments to the industries that create them: in the top fifty Silicon Valley companies in 2001, there were only five black directors and one Latino director (Hill 2001: p.25). According to Hossfeld (2001: p.36), the technology industries of Silicon Valley are dichotomised between white management and ethnic minority workers (Kumar 2001: p.79). In terms of consuming these technologies, black and Hispanic minority groups have consistently had the lowest levels of computer ownership (Hill 2001: p.17) and less access to computers in a school environment than their white counterparts (Robinson 1998: pp.139-140).

Research on the extent to which ethnic minority representation in the structures of the media reflects the broader community has provided a basis for further inquiry into ethnic minority participation on the Internet, and subsequently their representation in Web texts. As Givanni (1995: p.1) says, access and representation are twin subjects. That is, the images that are seen on film, television or the Web reflect and indicate something about the producers of those images: they are meaningful not only semiotically, but culturally, sociologically and politically (Wakeford 2000: p.34). So just as black people's representation on the screen is related to the structure, ideology and culture of media institutions (Young 1995: p.50), it should follow that equivalent depictions on the Web are informed by the structure, ideology and culture of the Internet. It is in imagery that one of the key elements of oppression, that is stereotyping, occurs (Leicester 1999: p.25).

Representation in Images

Studies of the lack of ethnic minority representation in the structures of the media has concluded that this is reflected in the lack of media representations of blackness (see Pascall 1982; Freeth 1982; Young 1995). That is, the absence of diverse people in the media is fundamental to the absence of diversity in content (Johnson 1996: p.96).

Historical studies of images of blackness have, as can be expected, emerged from Britain and the US. They have argued that racist representations on television are symptomatic of racism in popular culture generally (Berelson and Salter 1973: p.110). Or as Bobo (1993: p.273) proposes, racist representations have been continually reconstructed from previous media: that is, racism on television has been borrowed from film, which inherited it from radio, which in turn, appropriated it from print. The premise of these assertions is that ultimately, depictions of ethnic minorities are informed by the wider social and historical context in which they are produced (Hall 1981: pp.3-39). Thus in both Britain and the US, representations of blackness cannot escape, but rather are the results of, their colonial past (Hartmann and Husband 1973: p.270). In Britain especially, images of ethnic minorities have occurred against an historical backdrop of hostility to immigration (Pines 1992: pp.9-12).

If media images necessarily articulate the histories of racisms, then one could speculate that the Web may be the logical successor of these traditions. Given the Internet has historically been populated by mainly white, Western participants, there needs to be more attention paid to the kinds of representations of ethnicity they are creating and the racisms they are perpetuating. These insights can be gained through in-depth discursive analysis of content (Mitra and Cohen 1999: pp.180-181). For example, Ow (2000: 54) accuses the white producers of the computer game 'Shadow Warrior' of ignorance over irony in their deliberate parodying of East Asian culture. Similarly, Nakamura's (2002) study of LambdaMOO finds that while the majority of its members are white males, stereotypical Asian ethnicity is adopted and enacted:

> The links between the history of the media and the history of racial stereotyping are strong. The romantic, inaccurate and sometimes overtly racist visions of the oriental that circulate in contemporary film, video, games, television and other electronic media are part of a vocabulary of signifying practices that are redeployed on the Internet by identity tourists. (ibid: p.59)

Simultaneously, LambdaMOO members are discouraged from declaring their actual ethnicities in the interests of maintaining racial harmony in the LambdaMOO space. This definition and elimination of non-whiteness from a white viewpoint illustrates LambdaMOO's connection with and reflection of media histories. It is precisely these racialised 'ways of seeing' which have been interrogated in older media that Nakamura argues have not been challenged in cyberspace.

But what about the progressive possibilities for representing ethnicity on the Internet, particularly its capacity to encapsulate the shifts and advancements that have been made in conceptualising and depicting non-whiteness? Zurawski (1996) says that the Web offers new possibilities for self-determination and self-representation whereby ethnic minorities can construct their own identities in their own image. This is reiterated by Cisler (1998): 'One of the strongest reasons for having a presence on the Internet is to provide information from a viewpoint that may not have found a voice in the mainstream media'.

However, Zurawski (1996) does acknowledge that it is inevitably the privileged 'techno-elite' within those communities that have access to and, subsequently, representational power in cyberspace. In the last years of the twentieth century, less than 2% of the world's population were online (Hamman 1998), yet in 2004 few countries can claim the majority (that is, more than half) of their populations are Internet users (ClickZ 2004). Therefore, those with access to the Internet are still a minority. Within this minority are the minority (44%) of Internet users who have created online content (Pew Research Center 2003; Greenspan 2004). Against this backdrop, the potential for misrepresentation is tangible considering it is only a select few have access to the technology (Arnold and Plymire 2000). But control over representation extends beyond those who are simply using or even creating on the medium; it ultimately depends on those who manage the distribution and flow (rather than the production) of information. Zurawski (1996a) cites as an example AOL's censorship of sites and newsgroups deemed offensive, which apparently included those not using the English language. Where the broadcast media are concerned, it has been those at the helm of both production and distribution, which are traditionally more closely aligned, that have influenced images of ethnicity in popular culture.

Historical critiques of images of blackness in the media have suggested that one of the main forms of racism has been the lack of black visibility. Even considering the involvement of black people in the media industries throughout their histories, it has been found that their appearances have been exceptional (Silk and Silk 1990: p.128). The prevailing mode of representation of black and ethnic peoples in the media has been absence, which implies non-existence, or at least a distant existence – 'out of sight, out of mind'. Black absence in US film signifies their absence from the ideal America constructed by Hollywood (Diawara 1992: p.11) and implies whiteness as the object of desire (hooks 1993: p.291). As Tunstall (1977: p.90) puts it: 'One of the simplest but most important values of the Anglo-American media is the status given to the north European physical appearance'.

The prestige accorded to white presence has its own manifestation on the Internet. Nakamura (2002: p.47) argues that ethnicity is 'whited out' in LambdaMOO. White is the default ethnicity because anything otherwise is seen as bringing the divisions of real life into the virtual world. Declaring ethnicity online implies a notion of the body, which violates online etiquette (Nguyen 2001: p.187). Mason (1999) calls this absence of ethnic minorities 'erase-ism' in that it ignores, rather than liberates us from, the issues of race and ethnicity that continue to resonate in everyday life. Instead of it being perceived as a problem as it has been in relation to the media, it is celebrated as the end of discrimination based on ethnicity, gender, religion or sexuality.

When ethnic diversity isn't made invisible, it is stringently controlled through 'cybertypes', racially stereotypical representations that serve to define white identity by what it is not (Nakamura 2002: p.5). Indeed, Zurawski (1998) claims that inherent in the concept of the global village, which the Internet is said to epitomise, is the constraint of ethnic difference to the level of food, folklore, and traditional dance and music.

So there are two main, sometimes conflicting, lines of argument when it comes to the representation of ethnicity in the media and in cyberspace. One is that film, television and the Internet are inevitably products of the racist societies in which they operate: as Gajjala (1999) says, they replay the discourses that circulate in real life. The second is that film, television and the Internet are entirely unrepresentative of ethnic minority communities, their heterogeneity and the realities of their daily lives: as Nakamura (2002: p.28) says, the consuming public are 'hoodwinked' by such representations.

But both trains of thought miss a crucial point because to criticise the media for ethnic cleansing and bringing up all its characters 'white and bright', is to ignore the range of representations of blackness which have existed. Indeed, this can be said of the research that has been undertaken about the Internet thus far: the preoccupation with its possibilities for the transcendence of race (Nakamura 2002: p.xii), as well as the lack of participation from women, certain classes and corners of the globe, shifts the focus away from those minority groups who are actively engaged in the medium. Media researchers have been vigilant in noticing the times when black presence has materialised on television – Hall (1995: p.20) observes that it is like a rainbow in that it comes and it goes – just as researchers of the Internet need to be when it appears in cyberspace. According to Zurawski (1998), it is not actually rare or elusive: there are resources devoted to issues of culture and ethnicity which are not only readily available but regularly used. However, instances of black presence are not necessarily those which are positive or have been created from within black communities. Rather, the majority of images of black people that have been studied have been found to have been created from a 'white gaze' and have depicted blackness negatively. Unfortunately, this has not been balanced with critical analyses of self-produced representations of ethnicity.

The dilemma with the extraordinariness of black visibility on the screen is that, by inference, it signifies a problem or impending danger when it emerges. Therefore, studies of representations of blackness in popular culture have concentrated on the negative portrayal of black people and concluded that the majority of albeit scarce images of blackness are overtly racist. This extends back beyond media depictions to the history of literature and poetry, where as Hoch (1979: p.43) describes, the story of the conflict between white hero and black beast is inscribed in Western civilisation.

Hoch's (1979: pp.44-46) white hero/black beast dualism refers to white Europe, the civilised West which embodies intellectual and moral purity; as opposed to the latter, dark Africa which symbolises barbarism and base instincts. It illustrates the binary oppositions by which black people have been represented as the antithesis of a dominant and superior white population (Hall 1981: p.41). 'The white man is sealed in his whiteness, the black man in his blackness' (Fanon 1967: p.9).

Associated with these mutually exclusive representations of race are hierarchies, whereby blackness is depicted in a less powerful position to whiteness (Diawara 1993: p.11). Such images articulate the biological constructions of race discussed in the previous chapter. They are also translations of the 'white gaze' which have predominated in the British and US media industries, whereby the authority to define has resided firmly with white people.

Nonetheless, it should be acknowledged that these dichotomous renderings of race are not as simplistic than they might initially seem, partly because of the dynamic ideology of racism which has resulted in different portrayals of non-whiteness over time (Silk and Silk 1990: p.viii). Hence, historical analyses of black presence in the media and popular culture demonstrate a range of representations of blackness. But despite such transitions, how much has actually changed?

At the height of imperialism, African society was portrayed as anarchic and in need of law and order, with the European Empire having the responsibility of civilising indigenous populations in a manner similar to the training of animals (Pieterse 1992: p.78). From this historical period emerged depictions of black people as 'noble savages': exotic, primitive, subhuman, physically and sexually aggressive by nature, but could be tamed through social control (Hoch 1979: p.48; Silk and Silk 1990: p.viii). Such images have been reconstituted for more contemporary contexts: on the Web, in cyberpunk movies and books, as well as advertisements for telecommunications companies, Africa is still constructed as exotic (Hall 1998a, Nakamura 2002: pp.xv-xvii). Both offline and online, ethnic minoritites continue to be represented as 'primitive'.

Both Silk and Silk (1990) and Tunstall (1977) agree that in the early days of US film, there were sympathetic portrayals of black people, such as during the 1930s Depression and World War II. In emphasising national unity, black people were represented as productive and useful, although mainly as entertainers or as 'mammy' figures.

Across the Atlantic, however, the situation was somewhat different. In post-war Britain, exclusionary strategies and anti-immigration rhetoric were important in (re)constructing and (re)affirming its national identity. The political climate was one which sought to restrict immigration, and this was manifested in the BBC's programmes through the depiction of black people as 'problems' (Tulloch 1990: pp.143-144; Pines 1992: pp.9-10).

A historical perspective highlights the extent to which the representation of race within media and popular culture is also part of the broader representational strategies of national discourse (Hall 1993). Conversely, it demonstrates that racial dualisms have been sustained throughout history by the structures and practices of nationalism (Said 1993). Such dichotomies are not only evident in biological notions of race, but also in the oppositional construction of the West and Orient.

According to Said (1995: pp.1-3) European identity was forged in diametric opposition to the Orient. The latter was represented as the 'cultural contestant of Europe' and the embodiment of all that Europe was not. These essentialist categories, invented by Europe, therefore gave rise to certain ethnic stereotypes such as the humorous Chinese servant and passive Filipino houseboy (Berelson and Salter 1973: p.117).

The notion of the Orient as an homogenous entity can be successfully interrogated on the Internet. In one sense, the myth of 'one China' (Buruma 1999) is dispelled in cyberspace, which has become a platform where debate from a diverse range of Chinese groups, communities and factions has raged. Mitra's (1997: p.69) and Mallapragada's (2000) studies of the Indian diaspora in cyberspace found similar divisions and differences over Indianness, with the Internet offering space for discussion, disagreement and challenges to the ways in which Indianness is depicted in the Western media.

At the same time, the myth of unified ethnicity, is also perpetuated from within. Buruma (1999) notes that visitors to Chinese Web sites are sometimes addressed as 'brothers and sisters' as though all Chinese were part of one family. Foreign voices are often not welcome either.

The representation of difference through the mutually exclusive divisions of West and Orient, black and white, is also intersected by gender. That is, the depiction of black masculinity and femininity has fulfilled particular functions in relation to their white counterparts. On the one hand, as Hoch (1979: p.44) has observed, black masculinity is often associated with sexual potency, in direct contrast to the high morality and intellect of white masculinity. But because this has symbolised a challenge to white men's virility, there are also instances where black men are represented as asexual (Pieterse 1992: p.188), as seen in the 'ebony saint' character of the 1960s: superhuman, self-sacrificing and sexually abstinent (Silk and Silk 1990: p.158).

In comparison, the representation of black women has been much more uniform than their male counterparts. Black women have been consistently eroticised, depicted as promiscuous and as sexual objects, with black female sexuality represented as controlled by higher forces (Jones 1993: p.253). hooks (1992: p.62) contends that the black female body has been portrayed as a site of sexual deviance in order to 'normalise' white sexuality. Therefore, if black women are inherently sexual, white women cannot fulfil the role of 'slut'. hooks suggests the emphasis on black sexuality serves to dismember black bodies by representing them as a series of parts, and works as part of a wider strategy for fragmenting and disempowering black identities. Indeed, Gonzales' (2000) case studies of the UNDINA and Bodies INC web sites show how body parts are devalued in the process of shuffling, recombining and selecting racialised and gendered 'appendages' to create online identities.

Although the consideration of gender and blackness in relation to the Internet has been spartan, these observations are supported by Nakamura's (2002) study of LambdaMOO. Her findings show gendered portrayals of Asian characters in LambdaMOO, with Asian females eroticised and depicted as sexually submissive. Nakamura attributes this partly to the under-representation of women in cyberspace, resulting in much computer cross-dressing, or male users adopting female characters. In other words, the production of such images is from a 'male gaze', in the same way that the depiction of women in popular culture also has been. These conclusions need to be explored in other areas of the Internet, especially given the huge array of sex-related material available on the Web.

The historical patterns detected in representations of black and white masculinity and femininity, race and Europeanness, suggest that ethnic minorities have served a specific purpose in media and popular culture. The function of their limited visibility has been to define whiteness through their difference from it. They have been depicted according to the 'white gaze' which has pervaded popular culture from the colonial era to the present, through the structures of the US and British media industries and beyond.

The notion of the 'white gaze' is based on colonisation, whereby the non-white 'other' was spatially distant, and travel to exotic destinations was time-consuming. It has now evolved, according to Zurawski (1997) into something no longer separated through space and time: the 'white gaze' has perhaps been translated into what Nakamura (2002) calls 'identity tourism'. The 'white gaze' suggests a distant relationship between the white spectator and the black subject, whereas identity tourism implies a closer proximity between them. Tourism suggests a position of privilege and entitlement on the part of the white spectator, who is able to live vicariously online as and through the black subject: 'The vacation offers the satisfaction of a desire to fix the boundaries of cultural identity and exploit them for recreational purposes' (Nakamura 2002: p.42). In LambdaMOO, for example, it is where a white player enacts a character who is non-white: that is, they adopt the behaviours and language they believe characterises a particular ethnic minority. By contrast, on television, white people rarely play black characters, so the relationship is not one of empathy. However, the stereotypicality of ethnicity on television and in a medium like LambdaMOO remains on a par: the latter is no more progressive than the former. Identity tourism is merely the contemporary cousin of colonialism (Nakamura 2002: p.98). There is no transformation of the black subject who is still 'sealed in blackness' (Fanon 1967: p.9): rather, it is the white spectator who has the opportunity to take a break from his/her own identity.

Likewise, Spender (1996: p.118) has found evidence in one area of the digital domain, CD-ROMs, that colonial legacies of racism remain long after empires have been dismantled. The 'white gaze' infiltrates the CD-ROM 'Pilgrim Quest', aimed at children, in which the players are English pilgrims undertaking the task of colonisation by bargaining with the 'natives'. So it seems that as historical change takes place in the representation of race, things are not necessarily lost or even superceded, merely transposed.

The extent to which the prevalence of the 'white gaze' in the media has shifted has been tested through research (including this study) that has attempted to complement these historical studies by examining a cross-section of contemporary representations of race and ethnicity. Studies which focus on the depiction of ethnic minorities in media and popular culture at any one time include Berelson and Salter's (1973: pp.110-124) content analysis of US magazine fiction. Across 200 short stories, 900 characters were identified, with ethnic characters appearing in lesser proportions than their presence in the general US population. Non-white characters tended to have minor, stereotypical and functional roles in relation to white characters, who occupied central, privileged and powerful positions in the stories. This type of study has been reproduced for television, with similar results.

Jhally and Lewis' (1992: p.58) analysis of black characters in US television from the 1970s to the 1980s revealed that black people were over-represented in roles as criminals: there were comparatively few instances where such roles were played by white people. Also, representations containing other ethnic minorities did not increase during this period.

The situation in Britain was equally slow to change (Pines 1992: pp.9-10). While the 1950s and 1960s saw black settlement represented as 'invasion', the 1970s still represented black people as a 'problem' but attempted to do so with humour. The spate of situation comedies in which black characters were part of and subject to racist jokes were regarded as a way of managing race relations in Britain, but of course, from a white perspective as such programmes were directed at white audiences.

The evidence in the literature on representations of race in the British and US media seems conclusive in finding that ethnic minorities have been negatively portrayed in the history of broadcasting through to the present day. This negativity is due precisely to the depiction of race in terms of biological, hierarchial and essentialist categories of black and white. However, it has been acknowledged that there have been token occasions when blackness has been depicted positively.

Generally, instances of positive black representations cited in media studies come from the US. Silk and Silk (1990: pp.163-164) regard the 1970s as the 'black is beautiful' decade in which the visibility of black people in film and television increased in response to the black nationalist movement. Jhally and Lewis (1992: p.58) provide some qualification of this: while the proportion of major US television characters – those in main roles – increased, those who were portrayed as working class declined to the point of disappearance. This trend continued into the 1980s until the majority of principal black characters were represented as middle class.

Despite that such 'unreal' representations transformed the previously dominant mode of depicting black people negatively (Crane 2000: p.92), they attracted much criticism because such images of black affluence presented a stark contrast to the growing poverty amongst the black US population during that time. Between 1988 and 1991, the net worth of American households dropped an average of 12%, with the median annual wealth for white households being US$44 408, compared with US$4608 for black people and US$5345 for Latinos (Alkalimat 1996). Therefore, television portrayed an extraordinary situation which did not accurately reflect the experiences of black people in the US and reinforced the American Dream of a society without racism, crime or poverty. It suggested that positive black role models were ones which were middle class. The extent to which a particular representation of blackness could be regarded as positive was determined by the upward mobility of the characters. The show inspired the coining of the term 'Cosby-isation' (in reference to the popular sitcom *The Cosby Show* of the 1980s), also known as 'coconutting', which referred to the process of substituting white characters for black characters in television so that while they were brown on the outside, they were actually white on the inside (Hall 1995: p.22). The issues surrounding lack of black representation in the media were addressed cosmetically by depicting black characters in a way which white audiences found acceptable and non-threatening. The elimination of any signs of difference, social or ethnic, was perceived as kowtowing to the white structures of the US media industry. It was seen as an example of the internalisation of colonial ideology as described by Fanon (1967: p.11). That is, the black subject accepts the dichotomous rendering of white superiority/black inferiority and is then determined to prove that s/he is incongruous with this stereotype. The black subject decides to become as much like the white coloniser as possible which necessarily entails a deviation from his/her own history, a complete renunciation of his/her native culture and mother tongue, the adoption of the colonial language and the wholesale appropriation of European etiquette and values. Such criticisms have been standard to television programmes which have featured black, middle-class characters.

Thus so-called positive depictions of blackness were dismissed as token gestures from a white media industry. The 'white gaze' still existed as the structures of media institutions remained fundamentally unchanged, but perhaps it was no longer imperialising. It had merely been transformed into one which was more sympathetic or even remorseful, whereby the inequalities of race were rectified through media representations because they were so slow to be addressed in real life. What this implies is the difficulty, even inability, the media industries have had in representing *ethnicity*, that is, dynamic configurations of different aspects of identity.

These tendencies to find any representation of race forever problematic suggest several possible explanations. Firstly, the conclusion that the majority of depictions of ethnic minorities in the British and US media are negative seems logical given that it has been established that the media industries are primarily a white domain. Indeed, similar statements have been made about the Internet on the same basis: Lockard's (1999) findings that the Web's representations of race and ethnicity lack diversity were due precisely to cyberspace being monoculturally white. So perhaps the images of ethnicity will never be satisfactory until the structures of production are representative of the ethnicities they seek to depict.

Alternatively, maybe no image can ever adequately represent the multi-dimensionality of ethnicity. It is possible that too much emphasis has been placed on the text, and the ways in which the media's institutional and cultural production inscribes preferred readings of race into it. If the aim is for perfection in the representation of ethnicity, then it seems as though the struggle can never be won. But certainly, the Web's capacity to accommodate ethnicity has simply not had enough attention. As Ross and Greaves (2001: p.75) argue, there is no cyberspatial equivalent to *The Cosby Show*, although there are Web sites which are aimed specifically at African Americans such as BlackPlanet.com, AsianAvenue.com and NetNoir (Nakamura 2002: p.9). It would be interesting to see if the same arguments made of *The Cosby Show* are also relevant to these sites: are they representative of their wider ethnic minority communities, or do they speak to the advantaged, young, affluent, educated ethnic Internet user?

Another approach would be to concentrate on the multiplicity of meanings and interpretations that can be generated by a representation; to look at the active consumption of these texts by ethnic minorities, those who are excluded from the structural/institutional power of the media, focusing on their strategies for resisting and negotiating these preferred meanings of race (Ang 1996: p.138). Indeed, Hall (1995: p.13) theorises that it is their consumption, and not the texts themselves, which form the critical interface between black audiences and television as an institution that will tell us more about the implications of the portrayal of race and ethnicity in the media and elsewhere. But how can this be studied in relation to Web audiences? Jones (1999: p.15) and Sosnoski (1999: p.131) both recommend qualitatively studying what the Internet means to users, in part, by looking at Web 'surfing' as a form of reading.

Research thus far has shown the following about ethnic minority Web users: they are marginal, almost invisible (Lockard 1999), but this is because they choose independent, rather than mainstream, spaces on the Internet (Melkote and Liu 1999: p.14). However, Berry and Martin (2000: pp.74-81) contend that the Web is used also to make their offline identities proudly public. But either they frequent Web sites which are produced by ethnic minorities for ethnic minorities to strengthen diasporic ties with 'home' (Mallapragada 2000), making their presence in cyberspace seem peripheral; otherwise, when they are in more populated areas of the Internet, they purposely render their ethnicity invisible (Nakamura 2002: p.47). This suggests two possible strategies for investigating ethnic Web consumption: one is to examine the spaces of production, consumption and representation ethnic minorities have forged away from the 'white gaze'; and another is to consider how ethnic minorities engage in mainstream consumption and with texts for whom they are not the intended audience. Both approaches have already been explored in relation to black audiences and the media.

Reid (1993: p.135) argues that there is a need to look at the ways images of blackness which have been created by white media industries have been reappropriated by black people. Audience studies have shown that black viewers have derived heterogenous meanings as well as enjoyment from televisual and cinematic texts. Reid's (1989) study of the television viewing habits of young black women in London found that although there was a consensus that there was a scarcity of black people on British TV, there was diversity in consumption based on age, education, occupation and time available. Soap opera was a popular genre amongst the research subjects, indicating that they have been able to derive positive viewing experiences from television despite being dissatisfied with its lack of representations of blackness.

Similarly, in relation to cinema, hooks (1992: pp.291-393) says that most of the black women she has encountered in her research were aware of the absence of black women in film, but still appropriated representations of black womanhood which could be considered negative. They were able to suspend their acknowledgement of racism and sexism in these images in order to derive pleasure from the cinematic experience.

This confirms Diawara's (1993: p.219) thesis that the black spectator is also a resisting spectator, offering active criticism of representations of blackness in film, which are constructed from the 'white gaze' of the media industries and exist for the pleasure of white spectators (ibid: p.215). Bobo's (1993: p.272, 285) study of black women's responses to the film *The Color Purple* demonstrates that even with a film made by a mainstream male, Hollywood director, they extracted images of power and related them to their own lives. This suggests that while apparently negative representations can be transformed in the interpretive process, the issue of who is behind the camera and the image is also important. It could be argued that this sort of active consumption on the part of ethnic minorities is even more prevalent on the Web because any snap judgment about the political correctness of a particular representation is hindered by the opacity of who produced it. Furthermore, it is necessary because the hypertextuality of the Web necessitates the conscious processes of filtering and skimming (Sosnoski 1999: p.35).

When the perspectives of black audiences have been considered, it becomes difficult to generalise about the so-called positive or negative connotations of representations of ethnic minorities in the media. But what is crucial, according to the research subjects in Reid's (1989: pp.118-119) study, is an increase in the number of black people in the media, so that there can be more programmes aimed at and which feature black people. Effectively, the representations of *race* which have been constructed from the 'white gaze' need to be balanced with representations of *ethnicity* that have been self-constructed. There have been spaces for this in the media industries, although they have been somewhat marginalised ones. Such spaces have also been created on the Internet but what is their scope and how do they compare with, for example, the independent black film sector?

Mainstream vs Independent Production, Representation and Consumption

The problem with the overwhelming amount of research which has concluded that representations of ethnic minorities have been negative is that they have focused on the popular media. Histories of black people in cinema have tended to focus almost entirely on commercial films (Reid 1993: p.2) and corresponding television studies have been mainly undertaken prior to the proliferation of cable and satellite, thus concentrating narrowly on programmes broadcast on terrestrial television networks. It is possible that this distinction between mainstream and independent forms of representation can be made in relation to the Web in terms of commercial and non-commercial content.

Research on ethnic minority media has highlighted the stark contrasts between objectified representations of race and self-constructed depictions of ethnicity in the qualitative differences between the mainstream media and the independent ethnic minority media sector. It is proposed that as the popular media industries have been white domains, images of black people have been in their 'protective custody', constituted by white sensibilities and expectations of blackness (Guerrero 1993: p.239). Even token or positive depictions of black people constructed from a 'white gaze' do not depict the nuances and complexity of black life because they are not produced from a position of 'experiential authority' (Diawara 1993: p.11; Clifford 1988: p.35). They tend to resort to racial dualisms to represent blackness rather than portray it as a dynamic and hybrid ethnicity. They purport to 'speak for' black communities in a way which parallels the tactics of the West when it invented, colonised and subsequently claimed to represent the Orient (Said 1995: p.3).

In contrast to this, black films offer a perspective which is not Eurocentric, but self-conscious (Ross 1996: p.167). For Diawara (1993: p.4-5), black independent US cinema and Hollywood parallel the relationship between blackness and Americanness. The former provides a point of contestation for white mainstream cinema through alternative representations of blackness. Its search for new possibilities of representation means that it conceptualises blackness in terms of ethnicity rather than race. But the notion of a 'black film' also suggests a redefinition and reappropriation of race. Instead of it being a signifier of biological or physiological difference, it is used politically to highlight the socio-economic difference and disadvantage black people have experienced in relation to white people – it is an example of Spivak's (1993: pp.3-5) concept of 'strategic essentialism'.

Black films are produced through different media practices to conventional or mainstream cinema in that they position the viewer or reader differently, that is from a black perspective. Ross (1996: p.154) and Reid (1993: p.2) agree that black films are those that include black characters; whose content is concerned with issues of race and ethnicity, and focused on black communities; and which are written, directed and produced by black filmmakers. Reid (ibid: p.111) goes on to describe a sub-category of black films, known as black womanist films. These attempt to address various facets of black women's oppression, as well as the sexism and phallocentrism of black films produced by men. This consideration of difference *within* black identity means that the self-produced images of the independent film sector are better able to articulate ethnicity than the mainstream media's orientation toward race.

Within the parameters of these definitions, it could be said that there are black Web sites, such as Jet, Ebony, Essence, cafelosnegroes.com and BlackPlanet.com (Ross and Greaves 2001: p.67; Morrissey 2003), which have been developed by ethnic-specific media companies. However, these have been created in response to market demand: that is, they are commercial Web sites for ethnic communities. Therefore, they straddle the commercialism of mainstream media and the independence of minority media. Hill (2001: p.25) claims that there are no independent non-profit Web sites aimed at ethnic minorities which can compete with these larger scale sites. But there is evidence to suggest that an independent ethnic sector on the Internet is thriving. Melkote and Liu (1999) have examined what they term a 'Chinese ethnic Internet', which diasporic Chinese students and scholars depend on heavily for learning about news of the Chinese community and China. They argue that where these communities are concerned, the Internet has a fragmenting tendency similar to cable television and satellite direct broadcasting in that it allows people to 'opt out' of the mainstream, just as the independent black media sector has its own audiences outside the major media institutions.

There are particular parallels between independent media and non-commercial Web sites. An example of the latter are personal home pages, which are produced by authors using the Web as a means of presenting themselves (Chandler and Roberts-Young 1998) and as a space for emphasising who they are (Miller and Mather 1998). Personal home pages are concerned with the construction of the author's identity, and primarily centred on class, age, gender and ethnicity so as to appeal to others 'of a like mind' (Chandler and Roberts-Young 1998). These declarations are attempts at seeking out virtual communities of shared identities and interests, similar to the ways in which black films concentrate on the common experiences of black communities. But Chandler and Roberts-Young contend that the potentially global audience of personal home pages makes the Web more comparable to mass media. Unlike the independent media sector with its niche audiences and classification as minority media, the Web integrates the features of a mass medium through its worldwide accessibility with the capacity for individual self-representation in a non-commercial context. Jones (1999: p.3) defines it as 'personalised' mass media.

One of the aims of the empirical research was to locate the equivalent of an independent black sector, similar to that which exists in cinema, on the Web. That is, it sought and found, amongst other things, self-constructed representations of ethnicity. Furthermore, as all the research subjects, including myself, were women, and the objective was to find Web texts which articulated our particular ethnicities; sites and pages which were commensurate with black womanist films in their content were especially significant. There is evidence confirming that there is such content on the Web, although it may take longer to find. Delgado-P. and Becker's (1998) study of indigenous Web sites showed that they are generally not inclusive of indigneous women. Miller and Mather's (1998) comparison of men's and women's home pages on the Web showed a ratio of 15% of home pages constructed by women, to 75% produced by men, with 10% being gender unidentifiable. Just as black womanist films address their audiences differently to black films produced by black men, there was a distinction of styles between men's and women's home pages. Generally, women's home pages were longer, more focused on people, feelings and relationships; and subsequently had more links. They were more community-oriented in their connection with other sites, individuals and organisations, and inclusive of the reader in their direct addresses to the visitor.

Conclusions

It important to remember Gilroy's (1995: p.34) comment that each televisual zone configures race and representation in a different way. Perhaps this may be extended to apply across other media zones, so that depictions of race and ethnicity from television can be considered distinct from those on film, which in turn, can be distinguished from those on the Web.

But while the representational practices of each medium differ, they also borrow from each other. As Bobo (1993: p.273) says, the racist representations of the print media were inherited by radio, and subsequently, by film and then television. Therefore, the Web might be the logical successor in this lineage, acquiring the frameworks for constructing race from its historical antecedents.

If media images of race are informed by the racism of their time, as media research has found, then there is every reason to believe that this will be evident on the Web as we continue to live in social contexts which are pervaded by racism. Media studies have investigated the operation of racism in the media using a variety of strategies which could be adapted in the much-needed further empirical research on race and ethnicity on the Internet.

Historians of the Western media have concluded that as the structures of the media industries have been primarily white domains, the images of race and ethnicity produced by them have inevitably been from a 'white gaze'. Both the structural and visual representations of ethnic minorities in the media reflect and inform a social history of imperialism and racism. This chapter has discussed contemporary examples of media representations which contain legacies of colonialism, as well as those which have been found in new media. Contrary to much optimistic early speculation about the absence of racism on the Internet, later empirical research on the different aspects of the medium has highlighted the need for closer scrutiny of its constructions of race and ethnicity.

While access to and participation on the Internet has shown a similar historical pattern to that of the British and US media industries in that they are predominantly territories of white people's expression, media research confirms that this does not mean that representations of ethnic minorities are completely absent. Rather, depictions of race and ethnicity are mostly produced from a white viewpoint and serve the ideological function of reinforcing white identity as unified (Hall 1993). This usually means that the visibility of ethnic minorities is ephemeral. But there is much that is yet to be explored empirically on how the 'white gaze' permeates and manifests itself on the Internet.

The hefty amount of scholarly work undertaken on the political correctness of representations of race and ethnicity in media and popular culture has only begun to be attempted in relation to the Internet. But it is clear from media studies that this becomes a somewhat redundant exercise when the process of consumption is not considered. The meanings that black audiences make of the ways they are portrayed in the media is an equally important area of inquiry which also needs to be pursued in relation to the Internet.

The range of black presence both in the mainstream media and independent minority media sector has been another avenue of investigation for researchers of the media. Such studies have regarded the media as a space which negotiates the tensions between objectified representations of race that marginalise ethnic minorities, and resistant representations of ethnicity produced by ethnic minorities themselves. It seems that the Internet, too, could be considered a place where this sort of mediation occurs.

These are approaches which I use as starting points for studying the World Wide Web as a form of ethnic minority media as well as a 'racialized geography' (Lockard

1999) which is informed by wider social, economic and cultural contexts. The empirical research analyses the meanings made of representations of ethnicity on the Web by a group of ethnic minority women who are the research subjects. In the Web texts selected and interpreted by them, we explore similarities and adaptations of representational themes and strategies used historically in media and popular culture, including possible presences of the 'white gaze'. Of particular interest are Web pages and sites which have been created from within ethnic communities and demonstrate the ways in which they are using, engaging with and mobilising around the medium.

Whereas this chapter has attempted to make connections between the broadcast media and the World Wide Web, the next chapter discusses the unique qualities of the Web's mode of operation. It is concerned with the capacity for the Web to be a form of alternative media and accommodate participation from ethnic minorities. Therefore, it will attempt to deconstruct the Web's systems of production, representation and consumption; juxtaposing them with those of other technologies which have been accessed and appropriated by minority groups.

Chapter 4

Tactics and Technologies of Resistance: The Web as Minority Medium

This chapter extends upon the previous one'e exploration of the ways in which ethnic minorities have appropriated and translated media representations of race and ethnicity. But whereas the last chapter analysed representation from a top-down perspective, looking at how the depiction of ethnic minorities has been informed by the structures of the media and Internet industries; this chapter approaches it from the bottom up. Specifically, it discusses the grassroots consumptive and productive strategies marginalised groups have deployed to participate in technologies of representation, such as film, television, telecommunications and music. These resistant practices are examined in relation to the contexts and modes of those technologies' consumption and production: where are the spaces which enable such technologies to become minority media? Where are the gaps and margins which make this agency possible? (hooks 1993: p.289) More importantly, are these tactics transferrable to the Web?

The chapter aims to situate these struggles in cyberspace within competing discourses surrounding technology. That is, to what extext have claims made about the Internet also been made about other technologies (Sterne 1999: p.277)? These perspectives can be historically located, beginning with the emphatically evangelical and dystopian speculations of the Internet's 'utopian moment' in the last years of the twentieth century; through to the more modest conclusions emerging from empirical studies of particular aspects of the Internet conceptualising the Web as a site of both resistance (by ethnic minorities) and power (of dominant forces). Such studies have shown it is not useful to generalise about the Internet, as there is no one culture of the Internet, but rather a multiplicity of existing, emerging and overlapping cultures (Kendall 1999: p.70; Crane 2000: p.8; Nakamura 2002: p.xiv): '...cyberculture is a far-flung loosely knit complex of sublegitimate, alternative and oppositional subcultures...' (Dery 1994: p.8)

Equal Opportunity: The Necessity of Structural Intervention?

As I have illustrated in the previous chapter, media institutions have tended to be white domains and the lack of black representation, both in their structures and in the images they produce, has been challenged by independent minority media. This is not to say that the whiteness of the media is monolithic and static, but ethnic participation has only really increased marginally through policy.

The disadvantages experienced by ethnic minorities seeking careers or promotion in the media industries has been acknowledged in the implementation of equal employment opportunity and affirmative action policies. There have been attempts to address the 'industrial racism' inherent in the underfunding of programmes for black communities (Pascall 1982: p.7), through the establishment of multicultural programming units (Young 1995: p.46). Hall (1995: p.19) is certain that black visibility in the media would not have increased without these dedicated funding initiatives. However, despite the existence of such initiatives, changes have been slow to materialise.

Such projects are not the result of media institutions' benevolence but of much lengthy campaigning by minority groups (Phillips 1995: p.66). But it seems that the efforts of this black intervention – the monitoring committees, the codes of conduct, the ethnic minority programming departments – have not altered the (white) organisational culture of the media industries (Ross 1996: p.167, p.177). At best, the mainstream media appears to follow the lead set by the independent minority media sector, long after pioneering representations have been put forward by the latter.

The black independent media sector emerged in response to an identifiable lack of black visibility in film and television, resulting in projects aimed at increasing black media production through training in film and television companies and schools, as well as grants which allowed black media practitioners to avoid studio conventions and be experimental (Reid 1993: p.2, 125). In relation to the Internet, this sort of structural intervention may be located in, for example, educational institutions' information technology courses for ethnic minority students; initiatives such as community technology centres (CTCs) and Free-Nets which promote online access and participation beyond home computer ownership (Johnson 1996: p.92; Lillie 1999; Hill 2001: p.21). In turn, this is translated into the grassroots production and consumption of ethnic community-based Internet resources.

It would be tempting to conclude that measures like those used in the media industries to increase and improve black representation in film and television, are not necessary for the Internet. Because the Internet embodies a system which is outside government structures and State influence, its lack of accountability makes it possible for minority voices to be heard: for example, in totalitarian countries, exiled dissidents are able to broadcast via satellite and the Internet into their mother countries (British Broadcasting Corporation 1996). For Marriott (1998: p.1), it is also the relative anonymity of the Internet which attracts and facilitates a diversity of viewpoints. As minorities have freedom to express their opinions in cyberspace, perhaps the sort of institutional racism found in the media industries does not exist, or even is not possible, on the Internet. Without these structural biases, the Internet is arguably not subject to the kind of dichotomisation that has occurred between the mainstream and minority media.

Mainstream vs Independent: Never the Twain Shall Meet?

In terms of the media industries, black independent film is a political rejection of commercial cinematic content, production, distribution and exhibition (Reid 1993: p.5; Diawara 1993: p.6). However, where black filmmakers have forged their own path through independent production, there has been the additional difficulty of getting their films distributed. The dominance of major studios meant that even films that were independently financed could not be distributed widely (Silk and Silk 1990: p.144). Thus, divergent media practices appear to have ensued from corporate as opposed to independent contexts of production and distribution, a split which originates from the early days of the film industry: as it moved away from small independent producers to a more standardised structure to what was to become the studio system, the range of black representations became more uniform (ibid: p.122).

By contrast, the Internet has clearly not avoided corporate influence: Schiller (1996: p.95-96) contends that the electronic information superhighway is 'privately constructed and owned' for the benefit of corporations rather than individuals; that essentially, cyberspace is market-driven. One of the by-products of this is 'roadkill' as the high cost of building information networks means that some, mainly the poor and ethnic minorities (Nakamura 2002: p.xii) are run off the highway. This gives large corporations enormous advantages in dominating the Internet. Indeed, the private sector has made its presence felt on the World Wide Web with the advent of sponsorship as a major form of electronic advertising (Shields 1996: p.2). In this sense, the Internet operates similarly to the commercial mainstream media industries, and the lesson learnt from the latter has been that it is problematic for ethnic minorities to contest racism from within this context, particularly if people of colour are under-represented as producers of cyberspace (Nakamura 2002: p.115).

In addition, the complete independence of sites from corporate and mainstream ones seems improbable on the Internet and particularly the Web for ethnic communities. The distribution mechanism is the same for corporations as it is for ethnic minority groups. As Hall (1998a) argues, anyone, anywhere with a computer and an Internet service provider can publish a Web site. The struggle for black representation occurs within the same space where the 'white gaze' prevails. Unlike the separate entities that the mainstream and independent media sectors have necessarily become for the latter to agitate the former, the Web is an arena where the confrontation between objectified and subjective depictions of race and ethnicity can happen from within.

Lockard hints at the problems of distribution and audiences when it comes to ethnic representation on the Internet. He suggests that while ethnic minorities may occupy the same representatative arena that is cyberspace as the 'white gaze', they don't actually compete with or challenge each other. Rather, they confine themselves to the gaps and margins of cyberspatial activity. These virtual ethnic ghettoes are likened by Mitra (1997: p.62) to ethnic neighbourhoods in large metropolitan areas. They are on the peripheries of a dominant online culture and discourse (Carstephen et al 1998: p.124), similar to the kind witnessed in the media industries which pushed ethnic producers and consumers out of the mainstream into, amongst other things, the independent minority media sector. The censorship of non-English newsgroups by some Internet service providers (Zurawski 1996a) demonstrates the institutional fears surrounding minority activity arguably driving ethnic communities into their own virtual enclaves.

Discourses of Independence: Invisibility, 'Ghetto-isation' and Notions of Freedom During the 'Utopian Moment' of the Internet

Given the anxieties that the presence of minority groups generate online, it is no surprise that ethnic users have often deliberately avoided any reference to their ethnicities, as seen in Nakamura's (2002) study of LambdaMOO. Such a tactic could be considered an act of resistance on the part of ethnic minorities in that ethnicity is present without being declared. However, it is also a double-edged sword in that the ephemeral nature of representation on the Internet, amplified by the sheer quantity of material which 'remains unfinished, unfixed, and adaptable' (Landow 1994: p.198), problematises the process of identifying and addressing black (in)visibility.

This dilemma was reframed by some theorists in the late 1990s as a virtue of the Internet, arguing that this ability to 'switch off' race (Kolko et al 2000: p.5) should be celebrated as the ultimate act of resistance, that is, to not be defined by markers of race or ethnicity which have been historically utilised for discriminatory purposes. According to Nguyen and Alexander (1996: pp.103-104), everyone is subject to 'virtual equal treatment' on the Internet, at least in its text-based areas such as chat rooms, MUDs and MOOs. Because users are developing new and unique identities for themselves, acquiring pseudonyms and creating 'fantasized personae' (Argyle and Shields 1996: p.59), traditional forms of identification, particularly notions of race predicated on physiology, were no longer relevant. Instead, users represent themselves through keystrokes and mouse-clicks, describing their physical body in any way they choose (Nakamura 2002). Consequently, commentators focused on the possibilities for losing, transforming and/or performing one's identity in cyberspace (Turkle 1996: p.222; Donath 1998) and the apparent unlimited choice in this 'identity buffet'. If race and ethnicity supposedly disappeared on the Internet, then the simple deduction was that racial discrimination cannot exist. But Hall (1998a) goes as far as saying that this is an ideal environment for racism to flourish, for the very same reasons that make it apparently immune from racial prejudice: freedom of speech, anonymity and easy mobilisation of self-interested groups.

However, this approach of ignoring race and hence racism is hardly liberating according to Nakamura (2002: p.xv). Rather, it only serves to further fragment ethnic minorities. It makes the objective of increasing black visibility in cyberspace seem superfluous: because black presence on the Internet is less conspicuous, it is not obvious whether it is there and further, if it is, where it can be found. McPherson (2000: p.120) says this conspicuous absence of race is somewhat ironic given that the Internet is celebrated as a place where new identities can supposedly flourish. Thus, ethnic minority groups are confined to either self-imposed invisibility in mainstream online culture, or languishing in the 'independent' virtual ethnic ghettoes of cyberspace. As Lockard (1999) comments: 'Even as ethnic/race-defined user groups establish themselves on the Internet, they disappear from public view, accessed only by those interested.'

Nonetheless, subcultural activity has greater possibilities on the outskirts, the 'out -of-the-way corners of cyberspace (Nakamura 2002: p.117). Indeed, Phillips (1995: p.72) argues that the changes and challenges to the whiteness of media institutions and the images they create have been forged away from those very organisations, in the 'nooks and crannies of broadcasting'. The independent black media occupies some of these outside, in-between spaces. It is from these locations, where control over production can be exercised, that racism in the mainstream media has been effectively attacked, according to Morris (1982: p.79).

Likewise, there are 'nooks and crannies', gaps and margins for black media production to occur on the Internet, but such spaces seem to operate outside of the commercial or private sector. Indigenous groups are using the Internet as a community resource, to give them a group identity and as a means of resisting assimilation into the mainstream (Zellen 1998): 'They use it for communicating in their own and other languages, and between tribal members, members of other indigenous groups and members of the general public' (Cisler 1998). For Cherokee Indians, the technology facilitates and is central to debate about how to preserve indigenous cultures (Arnold and Plymire 2000: pp.186-193).

Melkote and Liu's (1999) research also shows that for Chinese students and scholars studying and working overseas, the Internet (specifically the China-Net bulletin board service) is a tool for rejecting the mainstream cultural values of their host society because it provides them with their own sense of community. According to Buruma (1999), the instant communication offered by e-mail allows groups to mobilise, and indeed conceptualise, themselves in ways that were never before possible. These imagined connections extend beyond their immediate communities to encompass nations and diasporas (Mitra 1997: p.60) and serve to strengthen their ties with 'home' (Mallapragada 2000: pp.179-185). This is seen in the virtual ethnic neighbourhoods of newsgroups like soc.culture.indian (ibid: p.56), e-mail discussion lists like SAWNET – the South Asian Women's Network (Gajjala 1999) and Web sites such as Indians Abroad Online. These were not only sites of commonality, but of struggle over what made them common in terms of Indian identity (Mallapragada 2000: pp.179-185).

Lockard (1999) warns of the dangers of black communities believing that the abovementioned ethnic ghettoes on the peripheries of cyberspace can achieve the kind of representation that they have not been able to gain in other areas. But at least here, the Internet can be equated with the independent minority media sector in that not only can control be maintained over production and representation, but distribution as well. In terms of the media industries, the independent sector has been a vital avenue by which ethnic minorities have gained access to and participated in technologies of representation. This tactic of 'strategic essentialism' (Spivak 1993, pp.3-5) in which ethnic communities organise to resist circumstances working against them has also been adopted in relation to technological predecessors of the Web with similar criticisms about the lack of structural intervention to enable equitable access and true independence.

Like an Old Record: Replayed Notions from Older Technologies

As Dovey (1996: p.109) says, it is often difficult to resist the 'utopian moment' of each new technology in which popular expectations and aspirations for it are at its peak. It is when the belief that technology can be a catalyst for changing the balance of power is at its strongest (Mulgan 1996: p.1). Certainly, the claims about the revolutionary potential of the Internet, echo those made about previous technologies, such as cable and satellite television and video camcorders.

For example, the concept of community is the current metaphor for envisaging online social relations, whereby cyberspace is constructed as a virtual town hall, public sphere or agora (Fernback 1999: p.204). Yet in the 1970s and 1980s, cable television was hailed as the new medium of 'democracy and interactivity' (Johnson 1996: p.94-95). With its technological convergence of telephone and broadcast systems, there were attempts to use it in a similar manner as the Internet, as an 'electronic meeting hall'. Images of each viewer's living room could be broadcast simultaneously for the cost of local telephone rates, which were usually free. The proliferation of independent cable and satellite channels in the US offered the chance of having 'a wider range of voices on the air' (Murdoch 1989), some of which could be those belonging to ethnic minority groups.

Likewise, the video camcorder held the hope for many of realising the global village democracy by increasing the possibility of representation through its accessibility and interactivity (Dovey 1996: pp.114-125). The advent of the camcorder offered the viewer the opportunity to participate in production.

The diffculty of endowing technology with this civic responsibility is that it assumes the technology alone has the ability the develop its own solutions: all it needs is to be presented with the problems. It is premised upon a technological determinism, an insistence that a particular value (whether this be a sense of community or greater democracy) is enabled by the technology. This has also been evident in relation to cyberspace with claims that the 'power of the Internet' will always be victorious: 'Those that struggle against it are going to fall by the wayside. The Web is too big to fight against' (Kleiner 1997: p.31).

But just because it was technically possible to have more self-constructed representations and channels of distribution through video camcorders and cable television, the whiteness of the media industries was not fundamentally altered. Such macro-level changes could not be achieved solely through the technological medium itself. According to Johnson (1996: pp.94-95), cable television's struggle to become a universal medium failed because it became dominated by the private sector: 'We were sometime political actors who had stumbled in the midst of an enormous communication land grab and we preceded (sic) to place ourselves in the public right-of-way just as one corporate juggernaut after another full of big money and lawyers, hit town.'

For Johnson, the ideals of freedom and democracy which were promised of cable television were constrained by capitalism. Instead, the technology became a site of contestation between different interpretations of freedom – market freedom versus freedom of expression – with the latter succombing to the greater power of the former.

There has also been much lament over the camcorder's adaptation for profit. The use of home videos has been extremely beneficial to the television industry, extremely cheap in terms of royalties and dispensing with the need for crews or equipment: 'The prophets of the "camcorder revolution" were certainly quite definite about the utopian future of that medium, which in reality ended up splattered messily somewhere between Jeremy Beadle and Rodney King' (Barry 1996: p.173).

The respective fates of the video camcorder and cable television have given critics with techno-dystopian tendencies much ammunition. As Schiller (1996: p.87) points out, technology will only magnify inequality through commercial exploitation and information abuse, eliminating any sense of community, public service values, social responsibility and distorting democracy in the process. Once services are privatised and require payment, divisions are exascerbated between rich and poor, the 'haves' and 'have nots': those who are 'information rich' are also financially rich and those who are 'information poor' are also financially poor (Johnson 1996: p.90). These binary oppositions constitute the notion of a 'digital divide' (Nelson and Tu 2001: p.2) which depicts people of colour as its victims, and sets up fundamental contradictions between the discourse of market freedom and those of individual liberty, social democracy and freedom of expression.

Within this dichotomisation, the freedom of the market is perceived as mutually exclusive to the freedoms which allow marginalised groups some space to participate in new technologies. It adopts a cultural imperialism thesis, in which the powerlessness of minorities fall victim to the 'unrelenting, all-absorbing, linear process' (Ang 1996: p.152) of global capitalism. To Ang, this perspective hints at the now debunked 'hypodermic needle' theories of the media which resort to simplistic 'cause and effect' explanations. Just as this stance was once prominent in relation to media technologies, it was also reiterated in debates about the Internet during the late 1990s:

> The potential for cultural imperialism, for propaganda and indoctrination, is enormous and insidious...Not only might there be just one version of the news in the global village (CNN); there might also be only one version of cyber-education; white, male and Californian in priorities and perspective (Spender 1996: p.118).

The fear that corporate power and influence will eliminate diverse perspectives on the Internet is one derived from the historical outcomes of other technologies, where the precarious balance of (corporate, democratic and expressive) freedoms has only been maintained through government regulation and protectionist policies. Schiller (1996: p.xv) contends that ensuring universal benefit of new technologies can only be achieved through public community-based services, which in turn, require government funding and support. Cable television in the US is a case in point: its public dimension was successfully protected only by First Amendment legislation (Johnson 1996: pp.94-95). On this basis, Johnson (ibid: p.92) argues for Internet regulation, proposing that cable access centres, universities, community computing networks, Free-Nets, media arts centres, libraries, citizen's advisory groups are only some of the types of organisations that would be threatened by the unhampered commercialisation of the Internet.

> There is ample evidence to show that the benefits of universal access to the new services provided by cable, digitalisation, signal compression and the Internet will only come if there is substantial public investment and regulation in the sector (Campaign for Press and Broadcasting Freedom 1996: p.10).

The argument being made here is that government intervention and specific initiatives, similar to those which were intended to increase the number of black people working in media institutions and encourage the development of independent black media, are required in order for a space to be maintained for minority access to and participation on the Internet. These would include publicly funded programmes in libraries, community centres and housing estates (Lillie 1997). There are a couple of assumptions underlying this position: firstly, minority representation can only be sustained through structural intervention and establishing an alternative infrastructure; secondly, the activities of minority groups are somehow incongrous with and diametrically opposed to those of commerce.

As mentioned previously, this sort of approach, which attempts to address an identified lack through policy, has had limited success in the media: equal opportunity and affirmative action projects in media institutions have not substantially increased ethnic minority representation in the industries' structures or content; and this has only been counter-balanced by external activity in the independent media sector with alternative modes of production, distribution and consumption. Another kind of strategy, one which is more localised and emanates from the ethnic communities themselves rather than outside of them, has been deployed in relation to other technologies and arguably been more effective in ensuring their access to, participation and representation in them. This tactic does not necessarily situate the needs of minority groups as mutually exclusive to the corporate sector: while technologies may be quickly adapted for the purposes of capitalism, this does not mean their progressive possibilities cannot be realised.

Local Activity vs Structural Change: The Role of Technology in Ethnic Minority Struggles

By looking at the micro-level, 'everyday spaces' of ethnic participation in a technology (Nakamura 2002: p.134), it is possible to find an alternative narrative to the 'digital divide' which depicts race and technology as incongruous (Nelson and Tu 2001: p.2).

However, this does not propose that ethnic minorities necessarily apply technology in ways that are any different or more progressive than others. But it does give a contrasting viewpoint to pervasive notions that a technology is inherently liberating or disadvantaging. Rather, it may be used creatively and meaningfully, and simultaneously in ways that are not always well-meaning: for example, the introduction of electricity and indoor plumbing in France was the basis of its post-war modernisation, while in Nigeria, they were instruments of torture (Verges 1996).

Furthermore, looking locally provides an indication of how minority groups negotiate structures in which racism is embedded and are not amenable to change. There is evidence to suggest that users, particularly those for whom a technology was never meant, constantly reinvent the language of technology, appropriating it for their needs: '...People are going to do what people always do with a new communication technology: use it in ways never intended or foreseen by its inventors...' (Rheingold 1992). This has resulted in new technological and cultural practices and politics, which are instrumental in new formations of ethnicity (Gillespie 1995: p.10). According to Alkalimat (1996), this has often produced contradictory relationships to technology for black people, as they are involved in the struggle to participate in a technology on their own terms while simultaneously trying to free themselves from enslavement by it. Alkalimat cites, for example, the invention of the cotton gin and mechanical cotton picker which effectively liberated African-Americans from slavery. But the efficiency with which these technologies replaced human labour also evoked mass black unemployment, rural-urban migration and displacement. The economic forces influencing the application of a technology can be as detrimental as potentially exploitable to ethnic minorities.

Contrary to Johnson's and Barry's arguments that the video and camcorder revolution was annihilated by its wholesale commercialisation, these technologies have been popular with marginalised groups. Ang (1996: p.11) claims that video cassette recorders (VCRs) have enabled those who have been traditionally poorly served by the television industry, such as ethnic minorities, to 'opt out' of the broadcast media by giving them more choice and control in their media consumption through time-shifting, still-framing, fast forwarding, rewinding and repeat playing. This explains why passive, play-only video technology has not been successful with consumers (Halleck 1991: p.217). Likewise, the camcorder has provided the opportunity for this choice and control in media production and representations. It has narrowed the gap between professional and amateur images (ibid: p.219). These technologies have facilitated connection across the Indian diaspora, as seen in Gillespie's (1995: p.7) ethnography of Punjabi families in Southall, which shows correspondence taking place through video letters and the exchange of taped Bollywood movies. These global transactions, which have been enabled by the widespread availability of video and camcorder technologies, are localised challenges to the centralised power of the broadcast media industries: '...Third World cable, satellite and video cassette recorders have begun to destabilize and decentralize the institutional and technological arrangements of TV provision which had been in place for decades' (Ang 1996: p.10).

Ethnic minority engagement with the VCR and camcorder has taken place even further away from the media industry than the independent minority media sector, at a more micro-level and without an established infrastructure. For example, the camcorder has been used by African-Americans and Latinos as a self-defence against excessive police force (ibid: p.227): that is, it has been deployed specifically in an anti-institutional manner.

Likewise, Gilroy (1987: pp.157-158) notes that books and records have been vital in carrying oppositional ideologies and philosophies across the black diaspora. This informal process of distribution hints at the history of black exclusion from educational systems and music industries, as well as the ongoing endeavour to address the structural disadvantages confronting black people in these areas. At the same time, it establishes networks of knowledge and culture which are not provided by institutions. But institutional distance is not imperative to this process of resistance and nor does it necessarily involve subversion of dominant economic forces; in many cases, it has borrowed from the innovative forces of commerce.

Hall (1996a, 1996b, 1998b) observes young black British people's appropriation of the mobile phone as symbolic of a peculiar combination of the black 'jive-walking hustler dude' stereotype and that of the post-Thatcherite entrepreneurial individual. This contrasts with traditional portrayals of young black people as counter-cultural renegades or as 'victims of imperialism', and emphasises their embracement of free enterprise culture, not only through their adoption of state-of-the-art technology but also in their shaping of contemporary fashion and street style. The mobile phone has become a part of the redefinition and representation of black Britishness.

Nevertheless, the mobile phone is only a technology of resistance for particular sections of black communities, namely those who are young, the arbiters of street fashion and live in cities. As Nelson and Tu (2001: p.5) suggest, people of colour do not all have the same relationship to technology. Dery (1994: p.192) argues that urban, black youth live in a digital culture of hip hop, Nintendo, beepers, Walkmen, Discmen, ghettoblasters, samplers and drum machines. It is also this contingent which has exploited the potential of dance and music technologies as a space for high black visibility. Nonetheless, it has been through interaction with such technologies that black youth subcultures have undermined the disadvantages confronting them in everyday life (Gilroy 1987: p.163) to the extent that young black identity is now equated with oppositional cool, street resistance (Crane 2001: p.120). But even within this demographic there is exclusion, as the informal collectives through which DJs learn their craft tend to marginalise women (Rose and Coleman 2001: pp.150-151).

The turntable, a commonplace technology of consumption has been reconditioned to become an instrument through which music can be produced (Dery 1994: p.211). The use of turntables, speakers and electronic synthesizers in dance music signifies an 'alchemy of poverty', whereby African-Americans have created new enterprises through the wilful desecration of technocommodities (ibid: p.185). The inner city as site of decaying industry is reclaimed and represented as a location for a different mode of production. The places where black people were exploited as labourers and slaves have been transformed into factories of creativity for various kinds of music

(Hesse 1996; Williams 2001: p.158). Hip hop developed in response to the displacement of R&B by disco, so the latter's two turntables were embellished with the technical addition of a beat box, heavy amplification, headphones and handwork. Rather than blend one disc into another like disco DJs, hip hop DJs actively manipulated the discs, selecting and sampling a few seconds of tracks and weaving the sounds into one another (Baker Jr 1991: pp.198-200). The fundamental principles underlying the constitution of this music include borrowing from a diverse range of sources, and 'mixing it up: socially, racially and musically' (Gilbert 1997: p.3). Technology is key to this process of ethnic and technological hybridisation, even when it is alluded to rather than physically manifest: this is seen in the early days of hip hop, when vocals were used to emulate electronic drums and turntable scratching; as well as in the 1970s fad of 'robot-dancing' which eventually developed into breakdancing (Dery 1994: p.187). In both cases, the black body becomes integrated with technology, mimicking whilst simultaneously satirising the labour exploited in industrial manufacturing (Williams 2001: pp.158, 161). Audio cassette tapes of hip hop music were sold at breakdancing competitions in the parks of New York City, where the objective was to attract more buyers/listeners/spectators than your opponents (Baker Jr 1991: pp.198-200). Thus, the relationship between industries, technologies and ethnic minorities is not necessarily an uncomfortable one. In this sense, ethnic minorities are cyborgs as defined by Haraway in that they are 'seizing the tools to mark the world that marked them as other' (1985: p.94). Cyborgian politics uses technology as a basis for unlikely hybridity and affiinity, and as a means of taking control over and responsibility for representation (ibid: pp.65, 73, 89).

However, while the particular industrial and productive practices generated by ethnic minority use of technologies may be new forms of enterprise, they may also undermine the tenets of capitalism. So although hip hop music has now become a mainstream industry, it is a genre which is contemptuous of copyright (ibid: p.204): records are deprived of their 'artistic authority' and instead, are reorganised and reworked by improvising DJs (Gilroy 1987: p.165). This undermining of restrictions imposed by copyright poses a direct challenge to capitalist systems of managing intellectual ownership, property and profit (Cubitt 1996: p.55).

Where technology is concerned, it seems that minority groups position themselves ambiguously in relation to the industries and organisations which exclude them. The relationship is more often one of negotiation, whereby marginalised groups employ technologies to locate spaces on the peripheries of institutional economies and forge alternative modes of production, consumption and representation.

The Way of the Web

To what extent can the Web be considered a minority medium or a technology of resistance? How does the Internet, and the Web in particular, work in ways which parallel the technologies discussed above that have been effectively reappropriated by ethnic minorities as tools of representation?

As Gillespie (1995: p.11) argues, media and cultural consumption is key to the construction of ethnic identities and communities. In our examination of video, mobile phone and music technologies, it is clear that it is through the act of consumption that ethnic minorities have been able to undertake forms of self-representation, and in doing so, dispute prevailing constructions of race and ethnicity. There is a close association between consumption and production in these technologies, a feature which can also be ascribed to the Internet. In addition, it is a characteristic which is suited to the work of cyborgs such as ethnic minorities as it transcends the dualistic and hierarchical status of production and consumption (Haraway 1985: p.65). As Mitra (1997: p.60) says, there is no Internet user who is not empowered to play an active role in the production of texts. To Mitra, a consumer of Internet content can just as easily be a producer of Internet content. This is somewhat supported by the finding that 44% of American Internet users have contributed online content, including maintaining their own Web sites, uploading images, filesharing and posting to newsgroups (Pew Research Center 2003; Greenspan 2004).

Where the Web is concerned, the technology that is required for consumption is also that which is required for production and distribution: that is, browsing, creating and publishing your own Web pages requires a computer, a Web browser, a modem, and Internet access. However, there are varying degrees of status attached to each of these activities, as those that can 'surf' the Web may not necessarily be able to 'author' Web pages: this is suggested by the statistic showing that less than half (44%) of users had created any online content (ibid). Web browsing requires basic skills in computer usage, such as navigating with the mouse and familiarity with doing database searches; while Web production requires a higher level of technical proficiency (Barry 1996: p.144), although the development of Web building tools has meant that knowledge of HTML is no longer necessary to create Web pages. As Dery (1994: p.9) says, the roles of reader, writer and critic are quickly interchangeable on the Internet: indeed, the reader is writer (Mitra and Cohen 1999: p.182).

Were the majority of users not able, or simply did not want to create online content? Kendall (1999: p.58) contends that the desire to be online depends as much on ability and equipment as age, class, gender and ethnicity. McDonald (1995: p.538) suggests that the activity of consuming the Web – using menus, pushing buttons and clicking on hot spots – is more demanding than for other media. Therefore, Web consumption could be considered a kind of production in itself, or at least closely aligned with it. This distinct but linked relationship between Web production and consumption is perhaps asymmetrical, but is certainly not one of 'master and slave', as Mosco (1982: p.7) suggests of any technology where there is a gap between those who control production and distribution and those who do not. Rather, the Internet enables the disintegration of these dichotomies, facilitating interconnectivity and 'unprecedented levels of compatibility between areas and things which were once carefully separated and clearly demarcated' (Plant 1997). It is precisely this intimate connection of production and consumption which seems to characterise technologies that have been embraced by ethnic minorities. As this is a feature of the Internet, then a noticeable black presence is unsurprising.

In terms of the global Internet population, the number of Internet users in the East, particularly China and Japan, is rivalling the US (Greenspan 2002). Research has also shown that Asian Americans who speak English are more active and experienced Internet users than their white counterparts (ClickZ 2001). As early as 1998, Hoffman and Novak's research suggested there was a significant amount of black participation on the Web. They estimated that there were more African-American Web users than the popular approximation of 1 million derived from market research. Together with the more recent estimates of 10 million African Americans and 15 millions Hispanic Americans online (Morrissey 2003), this demonstrates that although the Internet is an affluent technology, this does not mean that the population of cyberspace is monolithically white, Western and male. There are a number of factors informing ethnic minority Web use and ultimately, its reappropriation: African-American computer users are more likely to be both newer and less frequent users of the Internet (ibid; Hoffmann and Novak 1998: pp.6-7), which suggests that there are constraints on their access to the Web. According to Hoffman and Novak, the main issue is computer ownership: white Americans are more likely to have a computer at home and therefore more likely to use the Internet (ibid: p.2; Hill 2001: p.17). The probability of owning a computer increases with income; as access to computers increases with level of education (Hoffman and Novak 1998: pp.3-4; Robinson 2001: p.141). The research implies that there is more white participation on the Internet because white Americans generally earn more and are educated to a higher level than African-Americans. If this is the case, then it may indicate that African-American Internet users, too, are typically affluent and highly educated. For Lillie (1998), this is reflected in the prominence of US Latinos on the Web who are mostly middle class and therefore presumably own their own computers. The difficulty with much of the research on Internet usage is that it is premised on home computer ownshership: could the results of such research be read differently to mean that African-American, Latino and other ethnic minority computer and Internet usage might be located outside of the home, in places such as educational institutions, work organisations and libraries, that it is a more community-based activity? Similarly, African Americans and Hispanics are less likely to use email, but more likely to use chatrooms and the Web for research purposes than white Americans (Greenspan 2004a), illustrating that they are engaging in alternative forms of participation on the Internet. The possibility of this different mode of production and consumption would be similar to those realised in black appropriation of video, camcorder and music technologies.

Certainly, if ethnic minorities have resisted the dominant or intended use of such technologies, instead employing them to make links across the diaspora, then the Web's 'selectivity' (Feldman 1997: pp.4-5) probably appeals in a way not unlike the VCR's capacity for choice and control. Just as the VCR has seen ethnic minorities tune out of the broadcast media, the Web has been a significant replacement for television (Lillie 1998). The user selects sites and pages of interest, disrupting the linear patterns of consumption of the broadcast media in ways similar to the VCR. With the appropriation of the VCR, together with the camcorder which enabled do-it-yourself production and representation, came new methods of distribution (as seen in the transnational to-ing and fro-ing of video letters), the formation of new audiences and the fragmentation of old ones. In this sense, the Web really is a minority medium as it is not suited to mass marketing and consumption, so its audiences, if they can be called that, are 'demassified' (Nguyen and Alexander 1996: p.110). Mitra (1997: p.73) and Melkote and Liu (1999) contend that the Internet has a segmenting tendency where it is difficult to locate the dominant, as opposed to media texts which have a centralising orientation. Thus notions of audience derived from broadcasting seem dated and irrelevant to the Web, in part because of the comparably smaller numbers of people involved, but also because it implies a degree of passivity. As much 'active consumption' as media audience theories allow (see for example Lull 1990; Buckingham 1993; Morley 1993), the distance and dichotomy between media audiences and producers remains. A site called 'Race Relations in Black and White' constructed in February 1998 as part of America Online, was inundated with a total of 3600 messages over the course of a month, posted by people of diverse ethnicities (Marriott 1998: p.1). As an 'audience' in media terms, this seems negligible, but as a 'virtual community', it is considerable. Being part of a community implies an obligation to contribute through both consumption (reading other people's messages) and production (posting one's own messages). The Web's facility to 'pick and choose' not only applies to consumption (in terms of which sites and pages to browse), but also to production (in terms of which communities to participate in).

The capacity for community development has been an important attribute of technologies of resistance. In this respect, the much-celebrated community-building (as seen in Rheingold's work on virtual communities) which occurs on the Internet defines it, in part, as a minority medium. It offers the facility to 'pick and choose' which particular communities of minority interest to join:

> The electronic communities produced by the diasporic people are indeed imagined connections that are articulated over the medium of the Internet, where the only tangible connection with the community is through the computer, a tool to image and imagine the group affiliation' (Mitra 1997: p.58).

On the Web, hypertext and links automatically position the author as a node within an extended community beyond the realms of the site (Miller and Mather 1998; Mitra and Cohen 1999: p.182). This illustrates a use of the Internet whereby ethnicity is made explicit and which undermines it as a space where 'people go to be someone else' (ibid). According Miller and Mather (1998), the Web, in particular, seems to be where people are emphatic about who they are. This is supported by Berry and Martin's (2000: pp.74-81) work showing online identities to be extensions of offline ones. Chandler (1998) agrees that Web sites and pages are comparatively more honest than text-based forms of communication on the Internet: 'Personal home pages are thus not the favoured medium of those who wish to adopt identities which would be completely unrecognizable to those who know them in RL' (sic).

Chandler contends that the Web is not just being used to publish information, but to actively construct identities, to ask and answer the question 'who am I?'. Hence many sites are frequently labelled 'under construction'. Such issues of identity have been central to ethnic minority engagement with technologies: indeed, as we have seen in the technologies of music, independent black film and mobile telecommunications, blackness is stated loud and clear. The Web enables these statements of identity and ethnicity to be made in the text iteself and beyond it. Hyperlinks can map the connections which exist in what Gajjala (1999) calls the 'cyborg-diaspora', virtual online imagined ethnic communities.

Self-constructed representations of ethnicity on the Web may be able to contest the objectified depictions of race from the 'white gaze' that still resonate in popular culture. As Benjamin (1992: p.302) once said, the wide availability of a work of art to the masses inspires a diversity of interpretation, which in turn, changes public attitudes to art: 'The reactionary attitude toward a Picasso painting changes into a progressive reaction toward a Chaplin movie' (ibid).

Certainly, self-(re)presentation on the Web is unparalleled by conventional print publishing and other traditional mass media in terms of globally accessibility (Chandler 1998). Digital media has transformed the economics of media distribution by allowing more texts to be dispersed more extensively and cheaply (Feldman 1997: p.6). On this basis, the Web is capable of transforming prevailing constructions of race and ethnicity simply through its pervasiveness as a medium.

According to Benjamin (1992: p.300), the process by which public attitudes and consciousness shift is not only through the mass reproduction and diffusion of images, but also in the removal of notions of 'origin' that this incurs. This has been demonstrated in technologies appropriated by ethnic minorities, for example in music, where the corruption of origin is illustrated in digital sampling and breaches of copyright and codes of 'professional courtesy' (Baker Jr 1992: p.204). It is also particularly relevant to the Web, because as it is a digital medium, questions of authenticity are never far away. A Web page can be produced simply by copying the HTML code from any other page on the Web, then inserting new and/or tailoring the existing text and graphics. The reliability of information contained on a Web page is always open to suspicion because it is not necessarily verifiable, particularly if the author does not list contact details. The address of the Web site or page may or may not give some indication of its location: for Web addresses without a country suffix (such as .uk or .au) like those ending with .com, their geographical whereabouts cannot be determined unless it is stated in the Web page itself. Furthermore, Web pages can easily reside on servers in countries outside of where the author lives: 'where a piece of information is on the Internet is a little hard to describe. It is on some computer somewhere (maybe even on one's own), but it is available anywhere the Internet is' (Costigan 1999: p.xxii). The elusiveness of any sense of originality in Web production is also reflected in the idea of ethnicity being 'not where you're from', but 'where you're at' (Gilroy 1990/1: pp.13-16). Therefore, technology and ethnicity parallel each other as both have been redefined, reconstructed and put to work by minorities in ways never intended and imagined, undermining any sense of static purpose or foundation.

There is 'bricolage' in the production of personal homepages in the inclusion, allusion to, omission, adaptation and arrangement of information (Chandler 1998). The ethnic 'bricoleur' also partakes in these activities when representations of blackness are wrested from the objectifying 'white gaze' and reconstituted, whether it be on the Web, in music, film or through other technologies of resistance.

Conclusions

This chapter has highlighted the spaces on the Internet and other technologies where ethnic minorities are present. It has examined the variation of strategies used to encourage greater ethnic minority participation in technologies, comparing the outcomes of structural intervention with self-organised grassroots activity.

The Web is comparable with a minority medium like independent black cinema in that it is being used as a tool of representation by ethnic minorities for ethnic minorites. But while black film has a particular relation to the mainstream film industry, addressing racism from outside it, the Web makes problematic those centre/periphery, inside/outside, majority/minority relationships that have manifested in mainstream media industries.

However, the Web parallels other technologies that have been appropriated by minority groups in that its modes of production and consumption are intertwined, similar to domestic uses of VCR and video camcorders. Its distribution process is devolved enough to allow ethnic communities to produce, disseminate and consume their own representations of ethnicity without the mediation of institutions and which are not contingent upon market forces.

Because the Internet has facilitated this subcultural activity amongst minority groups, it has been subject to a pervasive rhetoric which suggests that it contains abundant possibilities and infinite diversity. This was explored with some reservations given that such claims had been made about older technologies but had never been realised accordingly. Although ethnic minorities have engaged with film, video, music and Web technologies as a means of subverting prevailing discourses of race, ethnicity and authenticity, as well as resisting prescribed structures, it is often in the wider context of their under-representation in those industries.

The empirical dimension of this book further explores the particularities of the Web. It examines ethnic minority production of Web pages; how the Web is being appropriated by and used to mobilise ethnic communities; as well as how the Web is consumed by a group of ethnic minority women. In short, it is concerned with how dominant constructions of race and ethnicity are being contested on the Web through ethnic minority participation, production and representation. It concentrates on the ways in which ethnicities are being declared (rather than hidden) on the Web, and as such, how the Web is being utilised as a tool of resistance.

The next chapter introduces the empirical research including the research subjects, their relationship to me, and our positions within the wider educational context in which the research took place. It is particularly concerned with the methodological issues involved in studying the Web, such as adapting and experimenting with tried and tested research traditions.

Chapter 5

The Matrix: Interdisciplinary Methodologies for Internet Research

The relationship between the previous chapters and this chapter, which discusses the empirical research, requires some narrativisation. Briefly, the grand narrative which I have illustrated thus far shows that certain social and institutional structures prevent ethnic minorities from participating and being represented in media industries and technologies, yet these obstacles have been and are actively resisted in heterogenous ways. This chapter begins to localise the narrative by grounding it in a concrete setting and introducing characters and players who have assisted me in exploring whether this narrative is repeated in newer media technologies such as the Web. Of course, it needs to be made clear that underlying all research is the interpretation of experiences which are then expressed via a realist narrative as 'facts' according to Clough (1992: p.3). That is, the process of describing the empirical research involves active construction on my part. It does not merely reflect or report events as they happened. Usher (1996: p.35) calls this narrativisation in research 'world-making'. As deceptive as this inventive quality of research may seem, it is a means of making sense of the world in which the research took place. That is, the practice of writing about one's research constructs a certain reality and creates its own kind of world: '...writing dissolves the opposition of fact and fiction...' (ibid).

Indeed, in the context of this study, such narrativisation is useful in bringing some order to what Said (1995: p.93) calls the 'disorientations' of research. Said argues for the chaos of research to be made explicit over its sanitisation. Certainly, I have learnt, as with any piece of research, no matter how precisely it is planned, there is always an element of methodological improvisation and this was especially the case with this study due to its interdisciplinarity. Interdisciplinary research inevitably creates new knowledge because it adapts traditional or 'normal' forms of enquiry (Leicester 1993: pp.77, 79; Jones 1999: pp.x, xiii), which provide a framework and point of departure for narrating the research.

Therefore, the chapter aims to describe and construct a narrative for the empirical research, without ignoring the methodological complexity and innovation that was an inherent part of it. I liken the research to a matrix because of the array of contexts in which it occurred and the subsequent mesh of ideas and issues that it engendered. Like the movie of the same name, this takes place across online and offline worlds. A matrix gives this some degree of organisation while highlighting all the possible relationships between them. This chapter examines these in detail, the particular methodological approaches chosen and the difficulties encountered as a result. It seeks to situate the research environmentally, institutionally, disciplinarily and methodologically.

Firstly, it discusses the social, economic and cultural environment of east London, where the research was formally undertaken and where the research subjects resided. It is where the university is located, where I was employed as a lecturer and researcher from 1996 to 1999, as well as where the research subjects studied. As a region which is regarded as socially deprived, the research focuses on the experiences of marginalised social groups, which in this case were those of women from ethnic minorities. In this respect, it follows, in part, the methodological principles of British cultural studies in combining ethnography, auto/biography and textual analysis (Sterne 1999: pp.269-170).

Secondly, the chapter looks at how my research operated within the larger research framework of Project @THENE, in which there were other researchers involved apart from myself and which was underpinned by an explicit feminist praxis. While @THENE was concerned with women's under-representation in computing and technology-related higher education, my research, although informed by this feminist praxis, is oriented more towards ethnicity and technology.

Thirdly, because I was a Tutor/Researcher on Project @THENE and my students were research subjects for both @THENE and my research, the study is, in many senses, ethnographic. The research took place in a well-defined environment (that is, in an educational institution), in which I occupied a role other than that of a researcher. So the research context was not artificially created for the sole purpose of the research. Also, it is ethnographic in that it is concerned with the study of ethnicity, of a particular group of people who have in common ties to an imagined 'ethnos' or homeland (Hall 1992), which, in this case, were women from ethnic minorities who were also all mothers and students on the same course. The consideration of ethnicity, class, gender, personal situations and access conditions in Internet research allow the relationship between online and offline contexts to be be explored as recommended by Kendall (1999: p.57).

Fourthly, the study required the research subjects to collect data from the Web, on their computers at home, in their own time and at their own pace, so it drew upon their experiences of interacting with the technology. Therefore, the students themselves were researchers which meant that an autobiographical approach was needed in order for each research subject to report and comment upon her findings from the Web.

Fifthly, given that in 1999 the Web was a new area of study for which there were no methodological conventions (Jones 1999: p.x), there was a degree of improvisation involved when designing the research tasks. They provided the research subjects with instructions for searching the Web and a series of questions to answer. But while they were similar to questionnaires in this sense, their distribution over the Internet posed challenges to how questionnaires are conventionally used in research.

Sixthly, interviews which were conducted as part of Project @THENE helped to gain a better insight into the conditions under which the research tasks were performed and provided an opportunity to discuss the students' written responses in the research tasks.

The methodological issues which arise from the empirical research stem from: the different institutional roles that I played in the research; the ensuing relations of power between myself and the research subjects which this created; and finally, the study of a new technology and the subsequent need to draw from a range of academic disciplines and research traditions to gauge how it may be investigated in the future. The chapter attempts to acknowledge the particular challenges presented by the empirical research and more broadly, offer a constructive critique of the methodological approaches used.

British Cultural Studies, Working Class Communities and East London

The empirical research continues, in part, British cultural studies' examinations of working class communities and subcultures (Turner 1990: pp.169-195), as well as those excluded from legitimate institutional power (Ang 1996: p.138). It is located in east London which has been a site of previous (see for example Robins and Cohen 1978; Cohen 1997; Hobbs 1989; Holme 1985; Cox 1994; Butler 2000) and ongoing investigation because it is an area which is underdeveloped and deprived compared with the relative affluence of the south east of England (Rix 1997: p.119).

While my research is informed by the environment in which it takes place, it is not about east London *per se*. Nonetheless, it is necessary to outline the features of this socio-economic context. The economic disadvantage of east London has resulted from its 'de-industrialization', the transition from an industrial to a post-industrial economy throughout the 1980s and early 1990s. This has particularly affected the docks industries, which have diminished considerably, and manufacturing which has been increasingly transferred to developing countries. With production having been globally restructured (Kennett 1994: pp.20-22), east London was left with a labour force which did not have the skills required for post-industrial high-tech occupations, such as social work, teaching, law, science and computing (Rix 1997: p.119). By 1994, 45% of London residents were employed in these post-industrial service sector-based occupations whilst east London experienced high employment: in the boroughs of Hackney and Tower Hamlets, the rate of unemployment was 25% compared with 12.5% in Kensington and Chelsea (HMSO 1995: pp.51-53).

East London's long history of immigration has meant that its ethnic minority communities have been particularly prone to high unemployment, because of racial discrimination in the labour market and lack of English language skills in addition to economic disadvantage. In 1994, more than one third of all unemployed people in London were from ethnic minorities: the unemployment rate amongst non-white ethnic groups was 24% compared with less than half of this for the white population (HMSO 1995: p.52). The 1991 census showed that more than 42% of the borough of Newham's population were non-white or of ethnic origin, of which over half were South Asian (that is, Indian, Pakistani and Bangladeshi). Black ethnicities include black Caribbean and black African. Unemployment is exceptionally high amongst Bangladeshi (over 40% in 1991) and black African (nearly 40% in 1991) ethnic groups in Newham and

Tower Hamlets (HMSO 1991). In 1985, people of Bangladeshi origin comprised the largest single linguistic minority in inner London (Khan 1988).

As a result of economic restructuring, there has been a decline in the number of women in certain inner city boroughs of east London participating in the labour market, despite a general increase in London and Britain as a whole (Rix 1997: p.131). Tower Hamlets, the borough adjacent to Newham where the research subjects live and study, had the lowest proportion of working women of all London boroughs and the highest rate of female unemployment in east London in 1991.

The empirical study has as its research subjects, women from ethnic minorities, a group which is particularly marginalised by east London's social and economic dislocation. Despite it taking place within a specific geographical area, the research avoids defining ethnicity in terms of fixed boundaries. It acknowledges the research subjects' gender and ethnic minority status in the socio-economic environment of east London as a factor in their limited access to higher education as well as to information technology (IT). If we take Terranova's (1996: p.72) view of Internet users as basically not including 'the terminally unskilled and unemployed, single mothers on welfare, the old and the poor', then the research subjects fulfilled most of criteria for omission from the 'wired' population. Effectively, this classified the research subjects as 'have nots' (Mosco 1982: p.7), or the 'roadkill' of the information superhighway (Nakamura 2002: p.xii): those do not have access to new technologies.

However, in spite of this apparent exclusion resulting from their socio-economic and geographical positionings, the research subjects were 'have-nots' who became 'haves'. They challenged their educational marginalisation by gaining entry to higher education, albeit as non-traditional students. Furthermore, they undermined their isolation from IT by becoming students on a new technology degree programme. That is, the general profile of the research subjects indicates that they were not typical of the population which occupied cyberspace in the latter half of the 1990s: they were neither white, male, or middle-class home computer owners (see Apple 1992: p.118; Johnson 1996: p.98; Spender 1996: p.118; Hoffman and Novak 1998: p.3; Interrogate the Internet 1996: pp.125-127; Kendall 1999: p.63; Pastore 2001; Greenspan 2003b); nor were they North American (Pastore 2000a; ClickZ 2004, 2004a). They were part of the minority of UK households with Internet access.

Although the research subjects seemed to be atypical in many respects, their existences prior to being students were characterised by disadvantage. Their transition from members of the 'have-not' to the 'have' community did not necessarily preclude their ability to represent the former. Certainly, their gender and ethnic minority status remained the same, as did their location in east London, and with it, the probable experience of marginalisation and discrimination. Their identities as students meant that while they had access to education and technology, it was in the absence of affluence.

It is also important to recognise that the research subjects came to be part of this study through a larger educational research project aimed at widening access to higher education for women from ethnic minorities. Project @THENE, unlike cultural studies' investigations of working class communities, actively attempted to address educational disadvantage by providing access to opportunities and technologies that ethnic minority women have been shown to be denied. It could be described as an antiracist educational initiative (Leicester 1993: p.21) in its concern with combating institutional and structural racisms by providing access irrespective of socio-economic status and promoting ethnic participation in a white-dominated digital culture (Hill 2001: p.21). It was an educational access programme similar to others taking place in corresponding regions of social and econonic deprivation. But it also followed in the mould of initiatives which sought to encourage women's participation in IT. Because of the focus on women, such projects (including @THENE) are generally underwritten by a feminist praxis.

Feminist Praxis, Ethnic Minority Women and Project @THENE

Project @THENE was similar to initiatives such as the Women and New Technology project at Leeds University (Pillinger 1988), the National Council on Educational Technology's 'Attracting Girls to IT' project (NCET 1996b) and the Cyber Sisters Club in the United States (Lichtman 1998). All were established in response to the well-documented under-representation of women and ethnic minority groups in technology-related education and occupations.

Karpf (1987: p.159) argues that women are mainly consumers of technology and absent from producing, defining and creating it. Despite the dot.com boom of the late 1990s, according to the National Council on Educational Technology (NCET 1996a: p.3), women constituted only 17% of students of Computer Science, 22% of the IT profession and 4% of IT managers. This was above the findings of the Department of Trade and Industry which stated that as little as 13% of students of Computer Science are female while an even lower percentage enter the IT industry. It was estimated that up to one third of female Computer Science students changed to another degree course at the end of their first year (DP Connect 1997). As at 2001, only 39-43% of UK Internet users were female (Pastore 2001) and by 2003, only 45% of all UK women were online (Greenspan 2003).

This lack of access and participation has clearly been acknowledged for some time (given Leeds University's Women and New Technology project began in 1986) and as a transnational phenomena (as seen in the North American Cyber Sisters Club). In relation to Project @THENE, it was also recognised institutionally. The University of East London (UEL), where the project was conducted, has in its mission statement a commitment to providing access to higher education for non-traditional students. These include mature students (over the age of 21) without conventional academic qualifications, which constituted 55% of new enrolments in 1994/1995. In the same academic year, 50% of new students were women, 45% were from ethnic minority backgrounds, 40% were from the immediate locality and 10% were from outside the UK (UEL 1997a). This policy of integrating non-traditional students into mainstream higher education was supported and enacted by @THENE through its recruitment of 14 mature women from ethnic minority backgrounds residing in east London.

According to Leicester (1999: p.9), this sort of integration is fundamental to 'enabling education' for women, ethnic minorities and the disabled.

@THENE was a research project centred on a one-year foundation course which prepared students to specifically enter a new technology degree programme within the Department of Innovation Studies of the University of East London. This provision for the needs of ethnic minority students was an example of a departmental antiracism strategy in action (Leicester 1993: p.29). But both in its research and educational delivery, @THENE was also explicitly feminist in its orientation: it focused on women's experiences and attempted to understand *as well as address* women's exclusion from participation and representation in IT. It challenged the traditional association of technology with masculinity by giving women technical competence (Karpf 1987: p.138; Faulkner 1996) in a women-only setting. It investigated the 'condition of women in a sexist society' (Stanley 1990: pp.12-15) but also acknowledged this condition as oppressive and struggled against it.

The learning gained from @THENE was derived directly from the experiences of the students. The female teaching staff were also key contributors as role models, who helped students overcome the anxieties many women feel with regard to technology (Wacjman 1991). Therefore, the production of knowledge was grounded in material activities. That is, theory and practice were collapsed: Stanley (1990: pp.12-15) calls this *praxis*.

Although my own study foregrounds ethnicity rather than gender, it is inevitably informed by the feminist praxis of @THENE. In any case, research which focuses on ethnicity can also be feminist: as I argued in Chapter 2, ethnicity cannot be examined in isolation from gender (or any other aspect of identity), as they are reflected and refracted in each other (Brah 1992: p.131). Furthermore, I identify myself as a feminist and locate my own experience within the research, as a tutor on the @THENE Year Zero and as an ethnic minority woman. I, myself, am a subject of the research in that I undertook the same tasks of collecting empirical data from the Web as I set for the students. The research tasks themselves, which are discussed in more detail later in this chapter, are grounded in the experiential through the use of autobiography, an approach commonly employed in feminist research. In many senses, my research methodologies are similar to that of Chan's (1997), also a Chinese feminist who examines her personal experiences of working in an institution. Likewise, it parallels Chung's (1990) occupational ethnography on gender and ethnic relations in a Chinese restaurant, especially as she, too, identifies herself as a Chinese feminist researcher and uses herself as a primary source of data in her research. Being a collaborative study which implicates my professional experience as an educational practitioner, and which involves me as both a subject and object of the research, it can also be classified as action research (Zuber-Skerritt 1996: p.3). Action research shares with feminist praxis, the principle of instigating change, but is more commonly applied in educational and organisational research.

While the feminist principles of @THENE form an appropriate and inextricable foundation to my research, its focus on ethnicity and technology posed challenges to their wholesale application. While one of the principles of feminist methodology is to minimise discrepancies in power, within the context of this research some of these are inherent. Firstly, although the research took place within a group of women, including myself, who shared a collective identity as women from ethnic minorities, there were clearly unequal relationships of power which existed within the group. The fact that the group was constituted by women of diverse ethnicities highlighted differences rather than similarities. With the majority of research subjects being of African/ Caribbean ethnicities, their experiences of ethnicity were considerably different to my own, as well to the other students in the group who did not identify themselves as such. Indeed, Gillespie (1995: p.68) found in her study of British Asian youth in London's Southall, being a different ethnicity to her research subjects was a disadvantage in that it was difficult to avoid treating them as 'exotic'. At least Gillespie acknowledges the implications of this difference: black feminists have long argued that black women have been oppressed within feminist theory and practice because difference amongst women has not been taken into account, and ethnicity has been considered independently of gender (Brah 1992: pp.134-136). If, as Ackers (1993: p.210) claims, all research is hindered by the operation of racism within it and the relationships of power which exist between white women and black women, then it was certainly present in this study given the differences in defining blackness that existed between the research subjects and myself. But as discussed in Chapter 2, the question of who is included and excluded from blackness remains unresolved: while 'black' is a signifier of solidarity amongst communities subject to racial discrimination (Hall et al 1992: p.308), it also retains currency as a term which refers to biological or physiological characteristics (Hernton 1988: p.xii). So while I, as a person of Chinese heritage, might identify myself as black, some of the research subjects may have found this contentious, as the term's reference to Britain's Asian communities has been (Brah 1992: pp.127-128). However, I may be overstating this concern, as according to Luttrell (1988: pp.249-254), black working-class women, because of their marginalisation, have a community-oriented consciousness. Nonetheless, the dynamics of power between myself and the research subjects, and amongst the research subjects themselves, were contingent upon this perception of solidarity or difference. Thus, the extent to which common ground could be found between us and the appropriateness of feminist methodologies was challenged by the intersection of other aspects of our identities with our gender.

Secondly, in addition to the differences in power inscribed in ethnicity which, in turn, is inflected by gender and vice versa, another facet of myself (as their tutor) excluded me from their experience (as students). My role as their tutor enabled me to influence their educational experience and lifespan as students. This position of privilege overrode any overall sense of commonality the students felt they had with me as an ethnic minority woman: this was articulated in the struggles I had with some of the students in the classroom and over the research tasks. Such conflicts were not only challenges to my perceived power as their tutor, but were also a result of its intersection with ethnicity, class and 'different ways of knowing' (Luttrell 1988: pp.249-254). Luttrell contends that black working-class women regard themselves as potential sources (as opposed to receivers) of knowledge. So where there were differences in our constructions of knowledge, my academic 'authority' was often disputed. Brown (1997: pp.70-74) argues that the outcomes of any teaching situation are influenced by the ethnicity and gender of the tutor, whereby being the same ethnicity or gender as one's students does not necessarily result in a sense of camaraderie. In addition, my occupation as Tutor/Researcher meant that my relationship to the students was socio-economically unequal. My gainful employment and relative financial security, a result of having already obtained higher educational qualifications, contrasted sharply with their vulnerability to unemployment and financial hardship. Having already done what they were doing (a degree), and having done it in a different way (via the more traditional route of going to university immediately after completing secondary school), outweighed any notion of all of us being part of a community of women of diverse ethnicities. This contrast in socio-economic status was not only an issue of class, but also of ethnicity in that it highlighted differing experiences of racism (Hernton 1988: p.xi). Walkerdine and Lucey (1989: p.4) say that these contradictions of power and powerlessness that are inherent in discourses of class, gender and ethnicity should not be silenced. The operation of these power/knowledge discourses in research are what Usher (1996: p.46) calls its sub-text, what lies beneath the research text.

The socio-economic and cultural differences highlighted amongst this group of ethnic minority women constituted by the research subjects and myself show this research to have a black feminist orientation. It is feminist research based on Yuval-Davis' (1997: pp.203-206) notion of transversal politics, whereby universal constructions of ethnicity or womanhood are rejected, difference is respected and self-reflexivity is given primacy. 'We should develop research methods and practices that acknowledge and take as central the class, race and gender relations in which the researcher and research subjects are situated' (Mashengele 1995: pp.118-123).

Relationships of Ethnicity/Ethnography, Tutor/Student and Researcher/Researched

This transversal politics coincides with other methodologies within the research. In addition to feminist approaches, the study also employed ethnographic methodologies. According to Clifford (1988: pp.25, 34, 38), ethnography is about the process of translating experience into textual form and acknowledging the use of interpretation in this 'textualization'. In this respect, ethnography utilises the reflexivity that characterises transversal politics. Hammersley and Atkinson (1995: p.1) define ethnography as 'the ethnographer participating, overtly or covertly, in people's daily lives for an extended period of time, watching what happens and listening to what is said, asking questions – in fact, collecting whatever data are available to throw light on the issues that are the focus of the research'. Like feminist research, it too attempts to address the question of whether or not anything can be known by trying, doing and accounting for the unexpected rather than debating. It is from this empirical basis that theory is developed (ibid: pp.22, 25). Gillespie (1995: p.54) suggests that ethnography demands an 'embeddedness' on the part of the researcher in the lives of the research subjects. In my research, I had at least weekly contact with the research subjects over one academic year as their tutor on a course which was arguably the main preoccupation in their lives. While my ethnographic persona was overt, Ackers (1993: p.221) advises that access to research subjects should be gained by the researcher fulfilling a powerless, passive, non-threatening role. The institutional context of my research restricted the extent to which discrepancies in power could be minimised as they otherwise ought to be in an ethnographic study. Leicester (1993: p.84) argues that there is a particular ethical responsibility on the part of the researcher when research on race is conducted in an educational context due to the unequal power relations.

Nevertheless, in accordance with the principles of transversal politics, the empirical research and indeed ethnography, not only respects, but is primarily concerned with difference. Traditionally, ethnography has studied oral cultures and the social behaviours and practices of a community of people (Hammersley and Atkinson 1995: p.168), a group in their 'ethnos' or homeland (Hall 1992) or an ethnic group, but from an outsider's position. Ethnography has also contributed to the study of diasporas (Gillespie 1995: p.1). The preoccupation with ethnicity in this study and its attempt to address inequalities confronted by ethnic minority women demonstrates what Mashengele (1997: pp.311-315) calls 'Africentricity' in its concern with black issues. It is as much an 'Africentric' as a feminist ethnography.

Ethnography can range from observational study to 'experiential fieldwork' (Williams 1990: p.254), which attempts to understand others through one's own experience. The empirical research is more appropriately classified as the latter as my own ethnicity and experience are located within and integral to it. More specifically, it may be called 'retrospective ethnography' (Greed 1990: p.147) in that it draws from the past experience of both the researcher and the researched. In the context of this study, the research subjects describe their experience as women from ethnic minorities and as consumers of technology. It is this concern with offline data about the research subjects that classifies this study as form of cyberethnography (Wakeford 2000: p.38).

Despite ethnography's emphasis on difference, the research has attempted to facilitate and locate the features which characterise the group apart from that of gender. The research subjects, apart from myself, constituted a definitive population with its own culture or 'we'-feeling (Miller 1993: p.185) in that they were all students on the @THENE Year Zero. This is in accordance with Miller's (ibid: p.180) recommendation that reference groups should be small, self-chosen with a shared identity. This established clear boundaries around the research and it also situated me distinctly outside this community. So there is an incongruity here with feminist methodologies, which require a perspective from within (Roseneil 1993: p.188). As discussed above, the notion of me being an 'insider' based on my gender and ethnic minority status was problematic in itself, but was further complicated by other relationships within the research.

The externality of my roles as tutor and researcher in relation to the students/ research subjects suited the methods of ethnography. While this was a disadvantage in some respects, this 'outsideness' allowed me the isolation necessary to reflect upon the research. As both a tutor and researcher, I occupied a position of power in direct relation to the students, but this was overt. Hammersley and Atkinson (1995: p.103) confirm that in settings which are familiar to the researcher and in which her research role is known, there is a tendency to be identified as an 'expert' and this was certainly the case because of my combined role as tutor. From an ethical standpoint, it could be argued that my position as a tutor was being exploited for my own gain as a researcher. Certainly, the research could be regarded as opportunistic (Roseneil 1993: p.188) in that access to the field was convenient. However, it is common practice in educational research for tutors to use their students as research subjects, not only because of the ease of access, but also because the research environment has not been artificially created (see Gillespie 1995: p.68; Preece 1996: pp.158-161; Lichtman 1998; Luttrell 1988: pp.249-154; Brown 1997: pp.70-74). As Roseneil (1993: p.188) points out, this familiarity with the research subjects and their environment (or 'empirical literacy') allowed for an 'in-built face-level trust' to exist between the researcher and researched; it enabled the research subjects to be comfortable with being part of the research and accept my role as a researcher.

The fact that my intentions as a researcher were declared openly was perhaps the best means of preventing exploitation of my power as a tutor, as there were constant tensions between and within these roles: between meeting the demands of teaching and keeping an ethical commitment to the research subjects (Ackers 1993: pp.223, 235); between comparative involvement as opposed to comparative detachment; and between being a participant as observer or observer as participant (Hammersley and Atkinson 1995: pp.104-124). There were occasions when I struggled to prevent my interests as a researcher from affecting my teaching.

For example, when some of the research subjects did not complete the research tasks in the timeframe I had given, I reminded them more frequently and forcefully than I would have done as a tutor who was simply concerned about the late submission of an assignment. Because the research tasks were incorporated into the coursework of the @THENE Year Zero, my Tutor/Researcher roles were especially difficult to disentangle. As a researcher fearing the prospect of having only a minimal amount of data produced from the research tasks, I emphasised to the research subjects the importance of their contributions to my personal research, but I also used my influence as a tutor to regularly ask students who had not completed the tasks to submit their findings as soon as possible. Here we can see the operation of what Bernstein (1975: p.116, 125) calls an 'invisible pedagogy'. That is, regardless of my attempts to distance my roles as tutor and researcher, the educational context in which the research occurred inevitably afforded me a degree of implicit or invisible control which I exercised over the students' experiences: as a tutor, I had the authority to arrange and construct the context of their learning to the requirements of my research. The significance of the research was communicated through my actions as a tutor: being disguised in this way, the underlying motivations of the research are made invisible.

But obviously, this relationship of power was not monolithic. As with any control imposed from above, there was also resistance in that it was just as problematic to distinguish their actions as students from their actions as research subjects. It was not apparent whether the research subjects did not complete the research tasks in the given timeframe because they found it hard managing their study time, or they were reluctant to co-operate in the research. As Thomas (1998: p.135) comments, in similar instances where respondents are asked to complete a mailed questionnaire at their own convenience, any obligation to do it is diminished and it may then be indefinitely postponed. Witmer et al (1999: p.47) say that the level of participation in email questionnnaires is particularly low: where a 50% response rate for a traditional survey is acceptable, it can be 10% or lower for online surveys. Also, as the research tasks were designed to be done on their home computers, the conditions and demands of the domestic environment impacted on the time they were able to spend on them: this is discussed in greater detail in the next chapter. In a couple of instances, there seemed to be an active resistance to participating in the research tasks: I was still having to follow up one of the research subjects, Teti, about the non-completion of the tasks after teaching on the @THENE Year Zero course had officially ceased! The fact that the research tasks were not assessed pieces of coursework contributed to this: as Boud (1988: p.35) argues, students' practices and approaches to learning are overwhelmingly driven by assessment: '...assessment methods and requirements probably have a greater influence on how and what students learn than any other single factor' (ibid).

Therefore, the research tasks may have been regarded as extraneous and secondary to the work that was absolutely crucial to passing the course. This was confirmed in the late submission of the completed research tasks by the majority of the research subjects. Most did not complete the tasks in the designated weeks (Weeks 12 and 19). Late submission was common with other aspects of coursework: as students on a foundation course which prepared them for higher education, many of the research subjects found it difficult to manage their time and meet deadlines. Perhaps because my research agenda had been made explicit to the research subjects, there may have been the perception that they were unnecessarily doing my research for me (when I should have been doing it myself). Traditionally, it is the ethnographer who collects the research data, who lives the research. But in this study, the students were co-opted as 'theorising informants' (Roseneil 1993: p.202) or an 'interpretive community' (Gillespie 1995: p.74) of their own findings from using and collecting empirical data from the Web under varying conditions.

Therefore, the study does not conform entirely to conventional ethnography, but Hammersley and Atkinson (1995: p.189) confirm the need to adapt accordingly to new technologies in ethnographic research: 'The Internet affords new ways of doing ethnographic research. For example, cyberethnography collects data offline about users and producers' (Wakeford 2000: p.38).

This particular study seeks to add this new dimension to ethnography, whereby the World Wide Web is not only the means for gathering research data but also the subject of the research itself. It is scrutinised as a site of social texts and practices, based on a rationale that the offline world cannot be studied in isolation from the online, other media or experiences (Sterne 1999: p.270). Nevertheless, with this in mind, the general principle of ethnography of searching for the universal in the local as well as 'giving voice' to marginalised people remains the same. New technologies such as the Web force ethnography to explore new 'spatial practices', to no longer study subjects in geographical isolation and regard them as distant or 'exotic' (Clifford 1988: pp.4,7,9). The research tasks were a means of examining the technological universe of the Web for its capacity to represent local ethnicities as embodied in the research subjects.

Experiential Learning, The Research Tasks and Autobiography

The research tasks were embedded in the @THENE curriculum so that the resources provided by the course could also be utilised for this study. Each @THENE student was loaned a computer with Internet access for use at home. The @THENE Year Zero had a flexible means of delivery which involved the use of computer-supported distance learning. Although the course was regarded as full-time, students were required to attend face-to-face classes for a maximum of three days a week. For the equivalent of two days per week, students learnt at a distance, in their own time and at their own pace using their home computers. Therefore, the students had immediate access to the technology required to produce and collect empirical data from the Web.

Not only did the @THENE Year Zero provide access to the equipment necessary to complete the course and participate in this study, the central concern of the course was new technology. @THENE provided students with the practical skills to interact with multimedia technology in addition to the critical and analytical abilities required to understand the social context in which technology is produced, managed, used and consumed. The @THENE Year Zero consisted of four units: Unit A Technology in Society focused on the relationship between technological change and social, economic and cultural change. Unit B The Computer, Inside and Out taught the theory and practice of computer systems and applications. Unit C Learning to Learn developed students' communication, research and study skills. Unit D Exploring Technology: Bringing It All Together combined aspects of all the units but was delivered entirely at a distance using the Internet. It adopted a more experiential approach in its teaching and learning, encouraging students to explore and reflect on their own relationship to technology and its effect on their self-identity (UEL 1997b).

Students were acquainted with me as their tutor for Unit B The Computer, Inside and Out. However, the tasks that they were asked to do as part of this research were built into Unit D Exploring Technology: Bringing It All Together, with the tutor's consent. The research tasks were not appropriate for Unit B because of its focus on the theory and practice of computer systems and applications. Unit D assessed students through the use of reflective analyses of their experiences on the course and this was more consistent with the self-exploratory nature of the research tasks. Unit D was also studied at a distance, which allowed students flexibility in the amount of time and effort they wished to devote to the research tasks. This would otherwise have been constrained in the face-to-face context of Unit B.

The tasks employed autobiography and technology, with technology being the subject matter and means through which the autobiography was told. Clough (1992: p.2) says that narrative and technology are not mutually exclusive: there is a story behind every technology and vice versa. The combination of the former and latter is evident in realist cinema and novels, television soap operas and computerised simulations. In this case, the stories were about the Web and told via e-mail.

E-mail was chosen for the research tasks because it was already the primary medium of communication between students and their Unit D tutor. Within the unit itself, students already had six weeks experience of learning and using e-mail by the time they were due to tackle the first research task, having previously been taught skills in the use of the mouse, keyboard and the general Windows interface in Unit B. While the latter unit was concerned with the development of IT skills, those related to e-mail were introduced in Unit D because of its relevance and necessity to the distance learning activities. Therefore, their familiarity with the use of e-mail meant that students could concentrate on the content, rather than the execution, of the research tasks. The students were also provided with various avenues of telephone and face-to-face support as part of the unit as a whole.

The first task was assigned in Week 12 of the course by which time the research subjects knew me for some time as their Unit B tutor. However, the activity was part of Unit D which, at that point in time, was exploring technology and identity. The distance element of Unit D provided students with the time to think about their answers in a way in which they could not in an interview situation. Because the responses provided were in a written form, they had the opportunity to carefully construct them to avoid any 'off-the-cuff' remarks that might arise in interviews.

The task was explained in the Unit D handbook as follows: 'Think about your own ethnic identity, about how you would define yourself. Try and cover all aspects rather than use a blanket term or generalisation.' Students were then required to compose an e-mail reply to their Unit D tutor, structuring it according to the following headings:

Real name:

Alternative name:

I would describe my ethnicity as:

Explain why you chose to identify your ethnicity in this way. Provide some personal history if necessary to elaborate on your reasons.

Are you satisfied with your description of your ethnicity? If not, why not?

These first few questions were intended to endow the subjects with the responsibility of their own self-definition and identification. It was also intended to fit within a model of multicultural education by emphasising cultural diversity (Leicester 1993: p.22). It gave them 'experiential authority' (Clifford 1988: p.35) by acknowledging that their conceptualisation of themselves was crucial to the research. To give my own description of their ethnic identities would have been disempowering to the research subjects, continuing racism's tradition of naming from without and marginalising through the imposition of markers of difference (Werbner 1997: p.18; Solomos and

Back 1996: p.131; Lippard 1992: p.168; Hernton 1988: p.xii; Bottomley and de Lepervanche 1988: p.33). For the research subjects to use their own words was to articulate themselves autobiographically.

The questions that were asked of the students may have oriented responses into a realist narrative framework. This linear process of storytelling (where I was born, where I have lived and where I am now), according to Clough (1992: pp.3-6), has its limitations. The experiences of the research subjects were translated and articulated to fit a chronology, which in turn were reinterpreted by myself.

While the research sought to give the research subjects their own voices, at the same time it was necessary for them to provide alternative names in order to protect their privacy should the research be published. Thomas (1998: p.134) suggests that participants in research tend to be more candid if they are confident that their identity will not be revealed in the event of publication. Therefore, the research subjects were requested not to divulge their alter-ego to others. [Evidently, there was a degree of insecurity with the use of e-mail, which is vulnerable to viruses and hacking (Akeroyd 1991: p.99). However, this risk is comparable to the use of mailed questionnaires which can be lost in the post.] So the research subjects were stripped of their identities in one sense. They were anonymised while my identity remained exposed.

The first research task continued by exploring the ethnicity/technology relation and asking students about the ways their ethnic background might have influenced their relationship to technology:

> What technologies are usually associated with your ethnicity?
>
> How do you think these associations between certain technologies and your ethnicity have affected your feelings about computers?
>
> If you were to surf the Internet for Web sites that best represent your ethnic subjectivity, what do you think you would find?

Having composed their responses, students were instructed to send them by e-mail to their Unit D tutor, keeping a copy for themselves as they would need to refer to their responses again before completing the second task.

The questions were intended to move from the general to the specific. When they were asked to do the second research task seven weeks later in Unit D, that is searching the World Wide Web for a site that could accurately summarise the different facets of their ethnic identity, the findings were interpreted in relation to their general feelings towards computers as well as their expectations of the what the Internet could offer.

This subsequent activity was again embedded within the Unit D curriculum in a block which explored technology and identity and followed their introduction to the World Wide Web in Unit B. Students were experienced in the use of a Web browser, having used this to send and receive e-mail messages as well as to 'surf' the Web.

Students were asked to refer to their responses to the questions posed in the first research task, particularly their answer to:

I would describe my ethnicity as...

As argued in Chapter 2, ethnicity is not static, but a dynamic state of diversity and hybridity which is constantly transformed and reinvented (Ross 1996: p.xi). Therefore, it is probable that in the seven week duration between the tasks, the research subjects' descriptions of their ethnicities changed. But for the purposes of reflection, they were asked to complete the second task on the basis of the first.

Based on this self-definition, each research subject listed keywords that could be used when searching on the World Wide Web for sites which embodied this conception of themselves. They were given as an example keywords that related to the description of my own ethnicity as 'Australian-born Chinese':

Australian
Chinese
Western Chinese
Australian Chinese

Using the keywords they listed, the research subjects then searched the World Wide Web employing one search engine only. They were encouraged to visit the sites which seemed to represent their ethnicity as they defined it, noting the actual number of sites visited and the ones which were relevant. If there were no Web sites which were appropriate, they repeated the process using another search engine. Where there were Web sites which a research subject felt were representative of her ethnic identification, she was asked to nominate the best one and give its URL. If she was not entirely satisfied with her chosen site, she could attempt to select a better one using another search engine.

The research subjects were asked to record their findings in a table noting the following:

Search engine used for each Web search
Keyword/s used for each Web search
Number of Web sites found with this keyword and search engine
Number of Web sites visited with this keyword and search engine
Details of the relevant Web sites using this keyword and search engine, including the URL and % relevance:

The completed table was then submitted to the Unit D tutor together with feedback on the following:

URL (the Web address) of the site or page/s which best summarised your ethnicity
Search engine used to find this site
Keyword used to find this site
Why this site was better than the others that you also thought were appropriate
Whether the site summarised your ethnic identity sufficiently and, if not, why not?
What was missing from the site?

> How the content of this Web site compared with the images of your ethnic identity that you see on film and television, giving examples of representations of your ethnicity that you have seen on film and television.

In many respects, the research tasks were like questionnaires, in that they were designed to be done at a distance, the questions asked were in written form and they required written responses from the research subjects. But questionnaires are often employed to collect data from a large number of respondents, such as in a survey (Thomas 1998: p.13), where there is usually and literally a distance between the researcher and the researched: that is, there is no personal relationship between the two and the people surveyed would be anonymous to the researcher. Evidently, this was not the case in my research. There were 14 research subjects whom I knew personally and who all knew me. If they had any questions about the research tasks, they asked me face-to-face when they came to my classes. Also, their responses were not anonymous. So if the research tasks can be considered to be like questionnaires, they did not employ them conventionally. However, they did attempt to exploit the use of the Internet and the distance learning context in which it was applied. That is, there were educational considerations underpinning the design of the research tasks. Nonetheless, the tasks also capitalised on the familiarity between myself and the research subjects by highlighting and sharing personal experiences.

Autobiography was important to this research, and indeed the course overall, because of the general neglect of personal experience in formal education (Stanley 1997). It is a rejection of the notion of 'objective' or 'certain' knowledge. Instead, it offers a connection between the individual and the social rather than regarding them as mutually exclusive. While it has been criticised as subjective and unreliable (and subsequently not academically valid), how else is it possible to address questions of difference, identity and ethnicity except subjectively? Stanley argues the academy makes the problematic assumption that subjectivity cannot be analysed from within, insisting that knowledge must always be produced from a position outside the subject. But theories are just other ways of telling stories, but do so by removing any sense of agency and divorcing themselves from lived experience. The research tasks use autobiography as a tool for theorising about the experiences and representations of ethnicity in different media in which the theorising is done by the research subjects as well as myself. Educationally, the focus on personal experience is classified as a form of 'radical pedagogy' by Leicester (1999: p.13). In relation to both teaching and research, the use of autobiography is also consistent with feminist praxis in making the personal explicit in the production of knowledge and giving voice to the marginalised.

> An anti-oppressive ethic/methodology demands an understanding of personal values and the connection of these personal values to life histories of people. (Mashengele 1995: pp.118-123)

The autobiographical approach of the research tasks also correspond with principles of an antiracist curricula in terms of encouraging students to recognise racist stereotyping (Leicester 1993: p.14, 23), as well as those of experiential learning, which acknowledge difference in the ways students learn:

> Every day, we are confronted with problems and challenges which we address by drawing on our experience and by using this experience to find ways of learning what to do in new circumstances...We rarely enrol in a course or take a class or consult a teacher as part of these learning projects. Learning through experience is the normal commonplace approach to learning, and we take it for granted. (Boud and Miller 1996: p.3)

Beaty (1992: p.13) argues that an effective method for making the most of students' experiences is through the keeping of diaries, which help develop a practice of reflection through which they can learn. Reflecting on one's own experiences in a diary is, in essence, autobiography. The research tasks encouraged students to record their experiences of using the Web, albeit as a one-off written reflection, but overall, Unit D was assessed according to the regular submission of diary entries.

Similarly, autobiographical approaches are evident in media audience studies. Audience research has traditionally relied on the diary in which members of households record their viewing behaviour and their opinions on programmes watched (Ang 1996: pp.56-58). There are definite parallels with this study in that the research subjects followed much the same process, but as users of the Web rather than viewers of television. But as Ang remarks, this method has been increasingly ineffective for audience studies because of the proliferation of channels, leading to participants getting confused or simply forgetting about the programmes they watched, which in turn, is reflected in their diary entries. These issues also arose in relation to the research tasks, as each student visited numerous sites. Consequently, there were some anomalies in the completion of the second research task: Web addresses were noted down incorrectly or it wasn't always clear to which Web site reference was being made.

Some research subjects also seemed frustrated by the means through which they expressed their autobiographical voice. The fact that the vast majority of the research subjects submitted the research tasks physically rather than electronically (as instructed) suggested an uneasiness about the technology they were using to tell their stories. The technological medium through which they produced their responses disguised the processes of production: vital information may not have been given because some research subjects did not feel confident using a keyboard and subsequently omitted anything which required lengthy explanation. Despite attempts to prevent this apprehension through training in all the necessary technological skills before the research tasks began, it needs to be taken into account when considering the research subjects' responses and indeed, at any time when autobiographical approaches are employed. The differences in how the research subjects express themselves according to various media are examined in the next chapter.

While most research subjects were seemingly open and non-plussed about the personal information they revealed in the research tasks to the Unit D tutor and myself, as mentioned previously, one of the students, Teti, was especially reluctant to participate in the research. In the process of discussing with her why there was such a delay in her completion of the research tasks, I asked if she was having any difficulties with them.

She said she did not see the purpose of exploring ethnicity, particularly as her own was so complex, and that she did not know what I wanted. This indicated to me a clear discomfort in discussing ethnicity and a distrust of me as a Tutor/Researcher who she perceived as 'judging' her work and even her identity. This is true in the context of Clough's (1992: p.3) claims that all research interprets and narrates experience: Teti challenged the balance of power tipped in my favour as the ultimate narrator of her experiences. This resistance to the research is reflected in her responses to the tasks, which are discussed in Chapter 7. It points to the much larger question of whether the research overall was affected by them being compelled to look for sites about their identities, as opposed to seeking them out of their own accord. Teti's experience was the most prominent case of misgivings.

Nonetheless, measures had been taken in an attempt to avoid this reluctance to explore personal experience. I undertook and completed the research tasks prior to the research subjects in an attempt to mitigate and prepare them for any potential difficulties. In order to encourage self-disclosure and dispel any unease that the students may have had in revealing information about themselves that was highly personal and emotional, an example was provided of the completed first research task using myself as the subject. I hoped that this would generate a curiosity about my personal history (which I think students generally have about their tutors) and subsequently, an interest in the issue of ethnicity and technology which would inspire them to be open and detailed in their responses. It was also to declare my position as a kind of participant observer in the exercise, that is to negotiate what Blumer (1992: p.30) calls 'mere perception' (simply making my thoughts and opinions known in the same way that is expected of the research subjects) and 'scientific conception' (remaining somewhat detached in order to be able to extract common themes from the experiences of the research subjects). It must be acknowledged that this instance of participant observation had an inherent power differential, given my role as a tutor to the student research subjects and also because my participation in the research task pre-empted theirs. The answers that I gave for the research task may have been viewed by the students as an 'ideal' model on which they should base their own responses. Thomas (1998: p.135) confirms that it is not unusual for respondents to answer according to what they believe will please the researcher. It was hoped that any such effect would have been diffused by the fact that the research task was not an assessed part of the unit. But Usher (1995: pp.178-183) is, nevertheless, wary of the compelling influence of the tutor/student relationship:

> ...what concerns me is the possibility that as educators we are (implicitly) telling students the story they must tell – and the story whether it be located in a pedagogy of individual self-realisation or one of personal and collective empowerment, is still emplotted through the narrative of development which educators find virtually impossible to critique as narrative.

The 'invisible pedagogy' (Bernstein 1975: pp.116, 125) of the research tasks, whereby my motivations as a researcher are unconsciously transmitted in the manner in which I conduct myself as a tutor, inevitably remains in spite of the measures taken to make the tasks more methodologically robust. However, I would argue that my participation in the tasks was more desirable than maintaining a distance from them in the name of 'objectivity'.

Eliminating my input in the research tasks would have bypassed an opportunity to demystify and democratise the research by incorporating the personal experience of the researcher (Stanley 1990: p.320) which is crucial to any robust research methodology. It is through publicising what is private (Becker 1992: p.62), making explicit what is implicit, that events underlying the research could be 'unpacked': my responses to the first research task provided an insight to my interest in the ethnicity/technology relation and the rationale behind this study. For the research to be non-participatory on my part would have given me the sole responsibility of categorising the experiences of others without making relevant references to my own (Miller 1993: p.178). Therefore, the inclusion of my personal history and responses in the research meant that it encompassed both the personal and the professional. It meant that, ethnographically speaking, the research was not only woven into my job, but my life became woven into the research (Ackers 1993: p.223). This examination of a world in which one is part can be a rich source of data but also carries the risk of making oneself vulnerable. In this instance, the exposure was not to my peers but to my students.

In completing the research tasks myself, I consciously avoided the use of any esoteric, theoretical terms and attempted to write in a relatively colloquial style with an informal autobiographical voice. The intention was to engender a sense of camaraderie between myself and the students so that participation in the research tasks was seen as a collaborative but 'polyphonic' effort (Clifford 1988: p.51), a kind of plural authorship (Gillespie 1995: p.74), as utopian as it may sound. That is, I wanted to make clear that the expectation was that each person's approach and responses to the research tasks would be different and it was likely that there would be marked contrasts between them. But despite my attempt to share my experience with the students, the revelations may have had a contrary effect of alienating them through the content and/or the way in which it is written. According to Ackers (1993: p.215), researchers have often been 'handicapped by their approach, manner, accent, vocabulary and image'. I completed the research tasks as follows:

Real name: Linda Leung

Alternative name: Mai

I would describe my ethnicity as: Australian-born Chinese.

Explain why you chose to identify your ethnicity in this way. Provide some personal history if necessary to elaborate on your reasons.
I was born in Sydney, Australia to immigrant parents. Both my mum and dad grew up in southern mainland China and emigrated to Australia as teenagers after living for some years in various places like Hong Kong, Macau and the Solomon Islands.

Are you satisfied with your description of your ethnicity? If not, why not?
I'm slightly uncomfortable with calling myself Australian for several reasons:

1. My parents emigrated to Australia during the White Australia policy which meant that it took 15 years before they were allowed to become Australian residents. For anyone who was deemed 'white', it was only 3 years. Therefore, because the Australian government were very wary of giving my family the right to be called 'Australian' I am hesitant about identifying myself as such. It's really for want of a better term.

2. Australia has an extremely racist history. What is being Australian anyway? Australian Aboriginals are probably the only ethnic group that can be legitimately called Australian. I'm sure they didn't call the land 'Australia' before the British arrived. So to call myself Australian is associating myself with a colonial history which has imposed itself on Aboriginal people as well as my family.

It gets complicated calling myself 'Chinese' as well. It's not entirely suitable because my parents are really more Chinese than I am. At least they were born there. Yet how can they be Chinese when they've lived in other parts of the world for most of their lives? Therefore how can I legitimately be called 'Chinese'? I've only been to China (including Hong Kong) for holidays.

The term 'Australian-born Chinese' (or ABC as it's abbreviated) doesn't really refer to other ethnic and cultural influences in my life such as having lived in the United States and being married to an Englishman and living here for the past 5 years.

What technologies are usually associated with your ethnicity?
Chineseness is usually associated with working hard at the expense of a social life. I think this rubs off on Chinese kids who typically spend a lot of time in their parents' restaurants trying not to be bored stupid. To compensate, the parents buy them the latest toys. Chinese boys are invariably playing computer games (Sega, Nintendo etc) and end up engrossed in playing their Gameboys at the expense of socialising with other children.

Most Chinese men I know are either cooks or accountants. The older generation who are cooks I associate with kitchen technologies: woks, butcher's knives, chopping boards made out of tree trunks. Young Chinese men are more likely to have a profession, so I often link them with computers. Typically, they're a bit dweeby, clean-cut (never with long hair) wear digital watches and carry mobile phones.

I find it much more difficult to associate young Chinese women with any particular technology although it is very 'Chinese' to appear affluent and have a nice car and a mobile phone. But there are very few popular images that resonate when I think of Chinese women and technology.

How do you think these associations between certain technologies and your ethnicity affect your feelings about computers?
I probably would have been a lot less exposed to new technologies if I was an only child or had a sister/s. I think the fact that my younger brother was given a computer when I probably needed one more for my schoolwork influenced me to think that such things either were inappropriate or too complicated for girls. But I don't think that I quite believed what was being inferred as I was always really interested in the computer. Maybe that made me determined to show my parents that girls can use computers too at the expense of being thought of as not very feminine.

I still feel like computers are very much a masculine technology even though they are central to my work and study. Certainly I think the Chinese see any high technology as better in the hands of men and boys, and are surprised by any woman who knows a bit about it. So I'm not sure whether my perception of computers as masculine stems from my upbringing and/or the fact that the industry is male-dominated. That sort of outlook is probably not constructive and I would like it to change.

If you were to surf the Internet for Web sites that best represent your ethnic subjectivity, what do you think you would find?
I imagine there may be quite a few sites which relate separately to China and Australia, their populations, geographies and so on. But I expect very few, if any, may combine the two. There may be a site for an Australian Chinese association or something similar which attempts to reach out to Chinese people living in the West. And if I were to find these sites, I suppose most of them would be produced by men (rather than women) of Chinese ethnicity bearing in mind what I said about computers being a male domain in both perception and practice where the Chinese are concerned. So I think anything relating to Western Chinese women will be produced for men and quite likely to be pornographic. That is, I suspect that women will be the objects of consumption rather than behind the production of Web sites.

The technique of autobiography was central to locating and making myself explicit in the research. Autobiography was not only a means to reconstruct and rationalise the past and relate it to the present, to chart my own experiences while comparing it with the other research subjects; but it also allowed me to see their perspectives while simultaneously being aware and critical of my own (Miller 1993: pp.37-38).

As a tutor, the timeframe which I set for myself to complete the tasks was perhaps freer than for the students, who were supposed to do them as part of their coursework. That is, I was not working to a particular deadline, although I had to finish the tasks in order to include them as examples in the learning materials for Unit D, which was quite some time before the research subjects began doing them. My process of searching on the Web was sporadic, continuing over many weeks, whereas the intention was for the research subjects to complete each of the tasks within a week. The differences in timescales for completing the research tasks between myself and the research subjects does somewhat explain the discrepancies in the quantity of findings and in the detail of the interpretation, with comparatively fewer findings and more abbreviated analyses produced by the research subjects.

Issues in Web Research

The research tasks employed methodologies that have been widely applied in other kinds of research, ranging from media audience studies to educational research. In part, this is because in 1999, research on and using the Web had not yet developed its own methodological conventions (Jones 1999: p.x). In response, Lockard (1999) calls for research methodologies for the Web to be developed, involving more in-depth engagement with the Web and its contents, for Web sites to be analysed as texts, similar to the ways that films are studied as texts.

The research considers Web sites and pages to be official documentary sources (Hammersley and Atkinson 1995: pp.159-161) in that they are published texts. However, their official status is often called into question because, as discussed in Chapter 4, the origins of Web sites and pages are not always apparent: the author may not declare his/her identity or contact details; the Web address does not necessarily indicate the whereabouts of the site's location or where the author resides. As the research tasks effectively required students to analyse these texts of dubious authenticity, several methodological issues were raised.

Firstly, the transient quality of Web texts meant that some of the sites and pages found by the research subjects could not be located again. Either the texts had been moved to another site, or removed from the Web altogether. According to Kahle (1997), the average Web page is only online for 75 days, so there is considerable turnover. In a few instances, the Web addresses had not been recorded properly by the research subjects. In other cases, the site had changed. Therefore, the status of the text itself was unpredictable to the extent that it was impossible to ascertain whether it existed at all, was out there in another location or in another form. When research subjects submitted their completed second task, I visited the sites they had listed soon after and printed the pages. While this gave a fixity to the text, it also removed it from the context in which it was intended to be seen. That is, it became a printed text rather than hypertext.

Secondly, if the authority of Web pages is questionable, then there are implications of how we think about representation. As Lockard (1999) says, one of the problems of Web research is the difficult comparison between representation and reality. Representation implies a relation to an objective truth, but this study was not concerned with verifying the information on the Web texts found. It was more preoccupied with how ethnicity was represented, accurate or otherwise, on the Web; the claims being made for those representations and most importantly, the meanings made of them by the research subjects. It is in the process of consumption that texts become meaningful (Mitra and Cohen 1999: p.182). It became apparent during this study that there are, inevitably, unknown variables and that there is a certain imprecision involved in Web research. This was particularly exemplified in the act of 'surfing'.

Searching on the Web is generally assumed to be an objective, technical and autonomous process (Ruhmann 1997). Search engines, according to Baginski (1997), have a 'sort of life in the net'. But they are biased in a number of ways: like any piece of software, they construct 'a set of ways of sensing, knowing and doing in the world' (Fuller 1999a); they structure the user's experience of the Web (Yahoo alone directs 30 million Web users a month – Patelis 1999), yet there is no system of organisation in the same way that libraries, for example, use the Dewey Decimal system: '...search engines and the arbitrary quality of wandering amongst hypertext makes coherent organization particularly daunting' (Franck 1998).

Search engines are dependent upon the use of language to articulate what the user is seeking: in my search for heterogenous representations of Chineseness on the Web, my keywords simply did not adequately express this. A search engine will generally only find Web sites and pages containing those keywords, but this is not a guarantee of relevance. So even where there may be sites related to those keywords, if they are not present on the site, they would not be retrieved (Fuller 1999b).

> The search engine is absolutely unable to treat a word or any collection of symbols entered into it in a contextualised manner, there are ways of refining or narrowing down the search for sure, but the core of what it has to act upon is the string of characters that it has just been requested to find matches or correspondences to (ibid).

That is, search engines are only able to assist the researcher in distinguishing between those sites which are relevant and those which are not through quantitative means. They cannot articulate the subtleties of language – allegory, irony, metaphor – and instead, operate on the premise of its universality and the standardisation of meaning (ibid).

It is not only the inability of search engines to critically and qualitatively discriminate Web content which skews the results of Web searches. Search engine companies sell keywords to willing buyers, so that advertisements for the buyer's services are displayed whenever a search is done using one of those keywords (Dawson 1999). Also, Yahoo and Excite receive a commission for each sale when advertisers sell products on their sites (Eisenberg 1998), which are, therefore, strongly commercially oriented. In addition, Web sites can increase their relevance rating by linking to the search engine's site: AltaVista, Excite and Infoseek do this (Fuller 1999b). Indeed, the top 10 domain names in the UK are predominantly search engine portal sites, such as Yahoo and MSN, which reach 19-41% of the total number of individuals using the Web in any given month (Pastore 2001b), indicating that search engines actively direct users rather than objectively locate sites for them. These issues are critical in Web research given that search engines are so relied upon to find more sites and pages than is possible for any researcher to analyse in-depth.

Each search engine selects from an unknown quantity of texts, from which the user then selects. The full online environment cannot be simulated because, as Kahle (1997) argues, the information collected by search engines does not encompass all the information that can be seen on the Internet, with much of it being restricted by publishers or not available to the 'crawlers' used by search engines, even though it may be accessible on the Web. ('Crawlers' are programmes used by search engines to collect data from the Internet.) Searches are made more complicated by new texts being generated constantly on the Web and makes any kind of generalisation from the search results problematic. In 1997, there were an estimated 50 million Web pages with the number doubling each year (ibid). In comparison to this, Kelly and Wolf (1997: p.71) estimated 150 million Web pages in 1997, increasing to 1 billion in 2000. Therefore, the accuracy of the results of searches are impossible to assess because search engines mask the ways they are programmed: they are what Fuller (1999b) calls 'black box' technologies.

But while the reliability of search engines and the formulae they employ to seek data is questionable, I used the same set of keywords with four search engines (Yahoo, Excite, Infoseek and Lycos) in order to generate a larger sample and compile a more satisfactory collection of sites. The research subjects, however, used approximately two search engines each to undertake their searches. If, as Fuller and Lovink (1999) say, search engines reach a maximum of 15% of content on the Web, then the searches undertaken in this research did not thoroughly select from all the possible material on the Web. The sites and pages discussed in this study were only taken from 'a thin slice of the Web'.

The research tasks themselves did not ask the research subjects to consider and reflect upon the range of results given by different search engines. So the responses did not contain any indication of the problems the research subjects encountered when undertaking their Web searches. Furthermore, there were varying conditions under which this empirical data was collected. As the researcher, I was not present during this element of the research because the tasks were done in each student's home. Therefore, there was a degree of mystery to this part of the study which I have attempted to enlighten by drawing on @THENE interview material.

Media Audience Studies, Domestic Spaces and the Interviews

Interviews with the students were done as part of Project @THENE's research element. The interviews were conducted as part of an evaluation of the course and not intended specifically for my own research. The principal purpose of the interviews was to collect data on the students' experiences of distance learning. However, the topics upon which students were asked to comment were both directly and indirectly relevant to my research.

While the interviews were not administered for the sole purpose of my own research, they provided an ideal forum to individually explore students' responses in the research tasks. It was particularly fortunate that the interviews were conducted after the research tasks were scheduled to be completed. Specifically in relation to the research tasks, the students were asked their opinions on them, whether they enjoyed or disliked them. Students were also asked to discuss the sites that they found and the process by which they found them. Although students were required to do this in writing as part of the research task itself, their interview responses were beneficial in clarifying, elaborating and/or confirming their written responses. As Keats (1993: p.18) argues, interviews are entirely appropriate where data collected from questionnaires needs to be enriched, where there is much variation in the responses and this requires feedback, cross-checking and verification.

Although my use of interview material can be regarded as opportunistic (Roseneil 1993: p.188) in that I have taken advantage of convenient access to the data, they provided students with an alternative means of expression and me with a secondary source of data from students who had not completed the research tasks yet, or only gave brief written responses. This additional information was particularly crucial given that as pre-university level students who had been out of education for some time, many lacked confidence in their writing skills, so the interviews were another strategy for incorporating their own voices. They also gave me an opportunity to resolve any queries I had about a student's findings. So they formed a framework through which the findings of the research tasks were interpreted.

The interviews compensated for what the research tasks missed. For example, the research tasks did not account for the conditions under which the data from the Web was collected and how these subsequently affected the outcomes. Nor did they consider the amount of time that each student spent on each research task and the implications of this for the findings. There was also no way of ensuring that the replies given were solely the work of the student herself or part of a collaboration with others (Hammersley and Atkinson 1995: p.221). As I was not present, there was no opportunity for the research subjects to ask for clarification on the instructions. These are some of the disadvantages of using a questionnaire, or such like, for data collection (Thomas 1998: p.169).

Certainly there were disparities in the ways that the data was collected which are explored in the next chapter. The interviews enabled these experiential differences in the doing of the research tasks to be explored. The interviews contextualised this by gaining an insight into the personal circumstances of the research subjects and the physical environments in which they worked. Their interview responses as well as the act of interviewing the students in their homes, were able to confirm whether their domestic spaces were amenable or otherwise to doing the research tasks and helped account for the variations in the amount and detail of their Web findings. They showed another dimension of the students' lives beyond what was recorded in the written responses, and provided the offline backdrop against which their online artefacts could be examined (Jones 1999: pp.xi-xii).

The use of interviews in this study follows in the tradition of ethnographic television audience studies, but in this case, the research subjects were users of the Web. According to Gillespie (1995: p.55), ethnography has come to be associated with in-depth, semi-structured, open-ended interviews, which Project @THENE employed. Likewise, ethnographic audience studies are usually undertaken in the home: in their examination of the microprocesses of daily life (ibid: 1), they consider the context and the relationships of power within the domestic environment (see for example, Lull 1990; Buckingham 1993; Morley 1993). Just as the interviews revealed the conditions under which the Web was consumed and the research tasks conducted, similarly Reid's (1989: p.120) interviews with young black women in London showed their television viewing habits to be influenced by occupation, time and age amongst other factors. While the experiences of consuming these technologies might be very different, there are continuities in the ways methods can be applied to their study.

As the interviews were a group effort on the part of the @THENE project team, I did not conduct all the interviews with the students and was therefore not able to visit every students' home: in such cases, I have had to rely solely on the transcript of the interview. As Walkerdine and Lucey's (1989: p.36) rereadings of interview transcripts demonstrate, analyses can vary greatly. Thus, I am more familiar with the personal situations of some of the research subjects than others and this is reflected in my use of the interview material. My inclusion of direct quotes from the students are not intended to represent 'slices of reality' or 'facts' (Ang 1996: p.47), but has obviously been subject to selection and interpretation by me. '...as researchers we should reflect on the political interventions we make when studying "audiences": how can we develop insights that do not reproduce objectified knowledge?' (Ang 1996: p.45).

The Research Subjects: Selection and Profile

In examining the heterogeneity of the research subjects, their typicality needs to be considered (Hammersley and Atkinson 1995: pp.44-45). That is, it is necessary to combine this micro-level analysis of the research subjects and their domestic environments, with a macro-level analysis (Brah 1992: p.139) of the context in which the research subjects were selected. Or as Ang (1996: p.10) says, there should be a connection between the structural and individual, so that the research subjects are not only constructed as heterogenous beings, but also in terms of the structures which they inhabit.

As this study was framed by Project @THENE, the students were selected solely according to their suitability for the course (which stipulated certain conditions of entry) and not for my research. As a Tutor/Researcher on the course, I did have some input into the selection procedure. Admission to the course was also biased towards those who applied early as these were candidates who had clear intention, had thought about the implications of undertaking a degree and had organised their lives accordingly. Those who applied late were not only ill-prepared in themselves but external forces, such as difficulty in obtaining funding, made it impossible for them to proceed even if they were offered a place. While the @THENE Year Zero was intended to encourage women lacking confidence into higher education, the somewhat self-selective factors of the application and interview processes arguably led to the most assertive and determined of the applicants to be selected. Furthermore, within the group of candidates that were offered admission, it could be said that only those with even greater courage and fortitude accepted their place on the course and were fully prepared to confront the trials and tribulations of doing a four-year degree.

Overall, the profile of students admitted to the @THENE Year Zero were women over the age of 21 up to 50+ years of age and of either 'UK Black', 'African' or 'Caribbean' ethnic origin as stated in the categories given on their application forms. However, this did not represent the extent of the ethnically dense and diverse population of East London. No matter how conventional the process of selecting the research subjects may have been, they could never be considered to be representative of the average computer user, student or even woman. Therefore, the conclusions from the study can only apply to the research subjects in it because they did not constitute a sample that even accurately reflected the population of ethnic minority women in east London. Any claim to do this would require statistical generation of representative samples (Thomas 1998: p.102).

As students on a new technology degree, the research subjects were atypical in that they were ethnic women residing in a socio-economically deprived region, who statistically for reasons of ethnicity, class and gender, as I have acknowledged above, would not ordinarily have access to IT, let alone be found in technology-related education. Indeed, they probably had an unusually high exposure to IT, particularly to the Internet, compared to students in other disciplinary areas. But their technological literacy was necessary to the research and in assisting me obtain empirical data from the World Wide Web. To have attempted to execute this with a group of research subjects who would, in any other circumstances, have little or no contact with the Internet or who had not actively chosen to learn about technology and its social effects, particularly in relation to their own personal experience would have been both far more difficult and different in its outcomes.

Conclusions

The uniqueness of the research is only characterised in part by the research subjects. I do not wish to apologise for their extraordinariness because the study is precisely interested in what the Web might hold for those who are not at the centre of cyberspace. The inability to generalise from an in-depth qualitative piece of reearch is a perpetual issue for researchers using this approach. But it is magnified by the limitations in investigating the Web with any kind of accuracy. There seems to be a resignation to its 'unquantifiability', and this has been equated with its 'unknowability'. However, the empirical research has attempted to make a small contribution to our knowledge of it thus far. However, it has meant adopting and adapting traditional methodologies innovatively from a range of disciplinary areas.

The consequences of this interdisciplinary approach are that it results in methodological complexity. The research tasks, for example, were designed to examine some of the content of the Web. So the study undertakes a textual analysis, of sorts, with a particular focus on representations of ethnicity. It attempts to regard Web sites and pages as texts, just as media studies considers televisual images to be texts. But it acknowledges that the hypertext of the Web does not have the same fixity as film, television or printed texts: in short, it is a very different kind of text. The ephemeral quality of the Web reinforces the futility of giving its texts primacy, as textual analyses are inclined to do. That is, the interpretation of these Web texts were not based on the premise that meanings are embedded in them to be read objectively. Rather, the research is more preoccupied with what the research subjects did with and made of the Web content that they found, how they produced, resisted and reappropriated its meanings. This necessitated not only a study of the texts, but also the research subjects themselves.

The location of this study within the larger framework of Project @THENE meant that, in one sense, it was part of a piece of educational action research underpinned by feminist praxis. Its particular concern with ethnicity and how the research subjects, as ethnic minority women, consumed and interacted with the Web, gave the research an ethnographic orientation. As an ethnography, it has some parallels to media audience studies, as well as to more traditional anthropological work in that the research was conducted in a 'natural' setting where I had additional roles to that of a researcher (such as tutor, role model, ethnic minority woman) and subsequently, various relationships to the research subjects.

The negotiation of this multiplicity of roles and relationships which I inherited were indicative of ethnography as a constant movement between cultures, of dwelling and travelling simultaneously (Clifford 1988: p.9). The integration and interdependence of the numerous roles I played meant that it was impossible to portray the findings abstractly, but rather that various realities had to be negotiated (ibid: p.22). Thus, the data that has been produced has been interpreted with consideration to my compelling influence as a tutor and a researcher, but also accounts for the strategies the research subjects used in negotiating power in the matrix of relationships within the research.

The subsequent chapters are less about my relationships to the research subjects and more about our relationships to technology. The next chapter examines the practices and processes of consuming the Web by presenting findings from interviews with the students. Beyond illustrating the conditions under which the research tasks were undertaken, they explore the ways in which a group of ethnic minority women interact with computers and the Web in the context of their domestic environments and familial relations.

Chapter 6

A Computer in the Home or a Bug in the House? Ethnic Minority Women's Consumption of Information Technology in the Domestic Sphere

The previous chapter examined the structural context of this research study: the socio-economic environment, the institutions and the framework of the course of which the research subjects were part. It also outlined the tasks on the Web which the research subjects were assigned. In addition, it highlighted the several common facets of their identity as ethnic minority women, students and mothers with childcare responsibilities.

In this chapter, I draw upon interviews with as well as written responses from the research subjects to examine in more detail these aspects of identity in relation to computers and the Web. Specifically, the data was analysed with the intention of looking at the ways in which these technologies were consumed not only as part of a research exercise, but also in the context of an educational programme undertaken in domestic settings with a group of users who would otherwise not have access to them. It looks at the intersections between the online and offline (Mitra and Cohen 1999: p.269; Wakeford 2000: p.38) through a localised situation (Kendall 1999: p.57) in the process of interrogating the relationship between technology, ethnicity, gender and class. It affirms Jones' (1999: p.xii) claim that having one's life touched by the Internet is inevitable, even with an unlikely novice user group who do not own their own computers and have minimal experience of computing.

While the findings showed that the particular conditions in which the consumption of computers and the Web occurred were heterogenous, they nevertheless provided some insight into how ethnic minority women engage with information technology, as opposed to other sorts of technologies, in the home environment. Utilising the findings from the interviews and research tasks, the chapter seeks to compare the computer and Internet with other media and technologies of resistance which ethnic minorities have appropriated. But as all the research subjects were women, there is also a need to pay tribute to the considerable amount of investigation that has been done on gender and technology. In addition, this chapter attempts to identify in the responses of the research subjects, the specificities of computer usage and the qualities which characterise the Web's consumptive practices. The findings from this empiricial data contribute to the body of literature on black audiences' media consumption, as well as research into women's attitudes and approaches to computing. In this sense, it uses all three approaches to studying the Internet qualitatively as recommended by Jones (1999: p.15): as a product (what it means to its users), process (how it is used) and in terms of what is written about it.

It is important to note that this chapter discusses the responses of the research subjects apart from myself. I am excluded because the context of my computer and Internet consumption was in the workplace rather than the home; primarily for the purpose of research and not as part of an educational programme; and my longer experience and greater familiarity wth computing compared to the research subjects meant that my interaction with the technologies was considerably different.

A Technology of the Home

In media studies, consumption has been regarded as the critical interface between black audiences and television institutions (Hall 1995: p.13). Most of the study of media consumption practices has taken place in the home, such as in television ethnographies (see for example, Lull 1990; Buckingham 1993; Morley 1993). This chapter extends upon this by examining the consumption of new media, as the Internet is often called, in the home.

Likewise, much feminist research into technology has been produced by case-studying technology in a particular setting (Faulkner 1996), such as the home. But where it has been found that there tends to be a sexual division of labour surrounding technologies in the home, so that those which are predominantly used by women become associated with women (ibid; Linn 1987: p.134), this study has been conducted in somewhat unusual circumstances.

Firstly, the computers were not owned by the research subjects, although they were designated as responsible for them. As part of the @THENE Year Zero course, they were loaned the computers so they could carry out their learning flexibly and at a distance. Therefore, while the research subjects were part of the minority of the world and UK's population which had access to the Internet in the late 1990s (Hamman 1998, ClickZ 2004), they were not part of the contingent where this was due to home computer ownership. Contrary to Hoffman and Novak's (1998) suggestion that the number of ethnic minority Internet users is tied to their ownership of computers, the black population of cyberspace is probably bigger than anticipated given that their access to computers and the Internet may not necessarily be based on this. However, most Internet statistics relate to home connections: the 6.4 million households in the UK with Internet access translates to 27% of the UK population or 13.5 million people (Pastore 2000a). Taking this into consideration, the research subjects were a minority within a minority given that home connections were a relatively new phenomenon in Europe compared with the US, and were mostly the preserve of those with incomes of £15,000 or more (Pastore 2001b). In this sense, the Internet could be considered a form of minority media in that it was being used by the research subjects in a way which defies the conventional means of participating in computing and the Web: they were on the wrong side of the economic digital divide and members of ethnic communities which have been shown to spend less time online because they generally do not own home computers (Morrissey 2003).

Aside from the fact that the computers were not owned by the research subjects, the second unusual aspect of this study was that by placing computers in the homes of the research subjects and giving them responsibility for them, it automatically created an association between these women and computers. This relationship was difficult for a number of the research subjects, because it transformed the home environment into an educational one:

> I was working before I had the youngest one, I stopped when I was 8 months pregnant...it made me realise how much I hated being at home actually. I just really wanted to get back out and do something. I felt wasted at home. The home is just not for me, I don't like it (Champagne – interview).

> Giving the assignments in on time is hard especially when you have got a young child at home (Sasha – interview).

Without the distinct separation of the home from the educational environment, Sasha and Champagne seemed to struggle to integrate their studies into their family lives. Champagne regarded the physical environment of the home as incongruous with productivity. Champagne's response is curious in that research has shown that women generally perceive the home as a site of work rather than leisure (Faulkner 1996; Linn 1987: p.134; Ang 1996: p.50). However, it has also been found that women's engagement with technologies of the home centres mainly on their domestic responsibilities (ibid), so it may be that the kind of work associated with computing was perceived by Champagne as incongrous with the work that is usually done around the home.

In conjunction with this attempt to combine home and study, as symbolised by the bringing of the computer into the house, were the subsequent renegotiations of domestic power relations. Although the computers were intended for the sole use of the research subjects, members of their households often regarded them as communal technologies like the television.

> Sasha: Everyone wants to come to the house and use the computer...I don't let many people use it.
>
> Interviewer: Who's everyone?
>
> Sasha: My friends, boyfriends, family and my sister because she is using a computer at college she wants to use the Internet all the time but you just have to learn to say "no" that they are not using it...My boyfriend knows about the computer but he's never touched it yet. If it was my own it would be different.

The provision of a computer in the students' homes did not necessarily mean they had exclusive access to it. The computer was inevitably noticed by the significant others in the students' lives, and whether willingly or otherwise, it became a resource which was shared with members of her family. It seemed that when the computer entered the home, it was perceived as a technology for the shared use and benefit of everyone in that home. This complicates Kelly and Wolf's (1997: p.76) argument that broadcast media like television, radio and film tend to be consumed in communal spaces and require minimal interaction; while computers and the Internet require the isolation and intervention of the user to extract information. The social relations surrounding the use of a computer at home in the context of the @THENE Year Zero seemed to contradict this, as the computer was consumed communally:

> ...it's now become part of my everyday life and I am using it just like I use the washing machine or turn the television on or use the hi-fi... (Lorraine – interview).

Lorraine treated the computer like other technologies of the home which were used by and/or benefited everyone in the household. The likelihood of the computer becoming a communal technology depended on the extent to which the student could assert authority in the household and/or was willing to police access to the computer. In Sasha's case, she was able to impose some control over others in relation to the computer because she recognised that she was responsible for it and used this fact as a way of maintaining her claim on it over others. However, students did not always occupy a position of power in their household which would have enabled them to refuse demands to use the computer:

> ...the other drawback is because it's here [living room]...last week it was Id [religious festival] – some relatives came with children and they were just banging on the keyboard and even though I was being nasty and saying "please don't touch it", she kept going back to it... (Noori – interview).

Clearly, Noori felt that she was unable to regulate the actions of others in relation to the computer, partly because it was located in a communal area in the home. Noori had no space of her own in which to study so that she felt she had no right to insist on her privacy or claim the computer as hers. Therefore, in Noori's home, the computer became a shared technology partly because her authority over it was not recognised. But she was also complicit in allowing her children to share in the benefits of the computer:

> ...my eldest daughter is doing a project and sometimes I let her type. She did a choir project and she wanted to type out the choir one and I think she's doing one on India and I searched the Net for maps of India and printed them out so it's helping the children in that way and the boy who is seven, he doesn't like reading very much but he's written a story on it and the one after him, he is very good at reading and writing but because the elder one had a go at writing a story he did too so I've got stories saved on my hard drive and the youngest one she is very good with the Paintbrush which she knows how to use all the tools, she's really good on the mouse and she's done lots of paintings on them... (Noori – interview).

Whether it was by choice or not, the computer was appropriated as a shared resource by the students' families. Some students were openly willing and keen that their children were able to learn from having the computer in the home:

> ...My daughter, I have given her a chance to play with the mouse, mouse control and I find she is very good at that, she is really good at designing things on the computer... (Tessa – interview).

These admissions on the part of the research subjects that they were encouraging others to use the computers, meant that the conditions of the loan agreement that they were to be the sole users were not being met. Therefore, the computers were utilised as technologies of resistance, in ways which, as Rheingold (1992) says of new communication technologies, were never intended. As the computer was a technology which the research subjects would, in all probability, otherwise not had if it had not been loaned to them, there was perhaps an obligation to ensure that others were able to participate in it as well. The research subjects' homes were used as informal community technology centres (CTCs), initiatives designed to encourage access and participation, as well as to help ethnic communities 'keep up' with IT (Hill 2001: p.21). Again, this may be indicative of the way in which computers and the Web are consumed by ethnic minority groups who do not have access based on ownership, and by women whose responsibilities involve the care of others. It is certainly consistent with findings that the majority of African Americans believe the Internet has had a positive effect on their children (Greenspan 2003a).

Indeed, when asked to identify the best thing about the @THENE Year Zero, a student replied that it had benefited her son enormously, a clear indication that she prioritised his educational progress over her own:

> ...It has been brilliant for my son. He has learnt a lot educationally. He has become a lot more creative and it is something else for him to do rather than watch TV or books (Bella – interview).

The prioritising of their children's needs and wants by the research subjects could be expected. In keeping with Walkerdine and Lucey's (1989: pp.67,74,173) findings on 'women's work', it seems that the home is inextricably linked with motherhood. Home is where motherhood takes precedence over and above the research subjects' own educational commitments, as women's work in the home has become associated with children's cognitive development and mothers are held responsible for the educational success of their children (ibid). This may also explain the difficulties that Champagne, for example, experienced in using the computer and the Internet in her home: it meant doing a different sort of work in the home, work which was in addition to her responsibilities as a mother, and work which centred on herself rather than her children. This privileging of children over oneself may have been more pronounced in households where the research subject was the sole parent. It may also have been magnified within particular ethnicities where cultural expectations place the onus on women for children's welfare. For example, according to Luttrell (1988, pp.249-

254), black working-class women perceive themselves as knowledge-givers to their children. Similarly, Bandyopadhyay et al (2001) contend that Indian women are honoured in the domestic sphere and as the educators of their children.

For Gina, it was only because her daughter already had her own computer that she was able to feel ownership of the one provided to her for the @THENE Year Zero. That is, because her daughter's educational needs had already been met, she could then use the computer for her own requirements:

> ...nobody has used it by the way, just me...there's no need, if she wants to do any word processing she can use the old one to do it...we have got a computer which belongs to my daughter but not as expensive as this one... (Gina – interview).

But even where students had apparently reorganised their family lives to give their studies primacy, there were other influences which enticed them away from their coursework. Students were encouraged to explore the technology that they were given, but some made forays into various computer applications which were not necessarily in accordance with the @THENE Year Zero curriculum. Chwime said that she was using PowerPoint to produce documentation for her church group, even though the application had not yet been covered in the @THENE Year Zero curriculum:

> ...my mate showed me. She just told me about it on the phone and that is it. Once I am told something I can do it... (Chwime – interview).

Similarly, another student was using her computer for paid work:

> Having the computer at home has allowed me to do private work. I do a typing service for certain people doing their assignments... (Tessa – interview).

The extra-curricular purposes to which the computers were being put demonstrate the strategies deployed by the research subjects to resist their prescribed use as tools for research and education. It also raises related questions about their consumption of the Web: despite Zurawski's (1998) findings that ethnic community-based Web resources are frequently accessed and used by minority groups, would the research subjects have sought out the sites they found as part of the research tasks if they were not under any obligation? If their use of the computers extended beyond the scope of the course, then it follows that their use of the Web would probably be quite different to what was found as a result of the research tasks. While research shows that African Americans actually use the Internet for research more so than their white counterparts (Greenspan 2004a), can the same be said for black British Internet users?

The subversive activity of the research subjects was not of the kind of conspicuous production and consumption that urban, black youth engage in as part of their shaping of street style and music subcultures (see Hall 1996a, 1996b, 1998b; Dery 1994; Baker Jr 1991). The work that the research subjects were undertaking was clearly done out of material necessity. These were acts of resistance without political agendas (Hossfeld 2001: p.54). Whether it be religious commitments or the need to supplement their income, there were obligations, other than to their children which permeated the students' existences:

> I decided to take this course because it was the flexibility for me to work at least twice a week because with the grant...I am head of the family, I am the bread winner of this family and I couldn't afford to live on that... (Gina – interview).

> ...the work I have to do I can fit in around my family plus I am able to work as well. I do a little part-time job in the evening as well... (Lorraine – interview).

So the enterprise culture which Hall (1996a, 1996b, 1998b) sees in black British youth was also evident in the research subjects' use of the computers for procuring paid work. While this suggests that their extra-curricular use of computers and the Web was perhaps more pragmatically oriented than identity oriented, it also shows that some of the research subjects developed an affinity with the computers, not unlike the ways urban black youth have affiliated themselves with music technologies. The computers became part of the identities of the research subjects in the process of putting them to work.

Feelings About Computers

In spite of the appropriation of the computer as just another domestic technology, the responses of the research subjects also suggest that the relationship they had with their computers was different to other technologies of the household.

> ...having a computer at home has changed my life because I communicate less on the phone. I do this all the time – I put the phone on answering machine. I screen my calls, who I want to talk to I talk, so most people know me for that now – "you and that computer again" that sort of thing...I watch less TV. Before I used to do a lot of housework. I used to hoover 3 times a week. Now – I have hoovered today but most of the time I don't bother I just use a brush and pan. If I am expecting someone I will hoover the whole place. And cooking. I have to cook for my daughter but sometimes I prefer takeaway or things I can just put in the oven, so it's made me lazy...I do less writing. I prefer to type even though I am not very good at typing but the more you practise you get the speed (Chwime – interview).

Chwime confirms that having the computer in the home has transformed her lifestyle in a multitude of ways. But she implies that its effect has been more profound than, for example, the time saved by using a vacuum cleaner rather than a dustpan and brush. It seemed to take precedence over other technologies of the home. She was drawn to it more than television and the telephone, in an almost addictive manner. This is concurrent with the 40% of Internet users who claim to watch less television as a result of having access to the Internet (Sceats 2000).

Another student actually described her relationship with her computer as one of 'addiction' as she had neglected her daughter because of it:

It's negative because I am addicted...she [daughter] sees me and starts to play games and she says "oh can we play a game" and I say "sorry I have got to go on the computer". I hate hearing myself say it but I do all the time. (Roni – interview).

Here again, we can see the technology being used in oppositional ways. The precedence given to the computer over domestic and childcare responsibilities challenges the image of motherhood as martyrdom to one's children (Walkerdine and Lucey 1989). The computer becomes a tool for 'opting-out' of the imposed obligations of motherhood as well as other media technologies. Just as video and camcorder technologies gave ethnic minorities an alternative mode of production and consumption to the broadcast media (Ang 1996: p.11), the computer seemed better able to fulfil the needs of some of the research subjects than other technologies of the home.

As with other technologies of resistance, the computer was important in affirming the identities of the research subjects:

...it's like I have built up a relationship with the computer, it seems peculiar but yes I have so when I actually sit at the computer and start it's like I am talking to a friend so it's no longer in my eyes a machine, it's like my friend now (Lorraine – interview).

...I feel as if this is like a companion...I feel sometimes when I come in it's like another baby – it's like a partner the computer. I am getting too cosy with it. I feel I am actually going into a different world when I am on the machine (Tessa – interview).

...I call her Jezebelle. I kind of personify her and I talk to her and things like that... (Bella – interview).

The affirmation of the research subjects' identities seemed to occur through a personification of the computer as a member of the family, friend and/or confidante. This seems closely aligned with notions of 'virtual community', as the computer not only becomes part of the household, but a gateway to a network of friends and alliances. Mitra (1997: p.58) argues electronic communities are merely imagined connections facilitated by computers: in the case of the research subjects, these imagined affiliations extend to the computer itself – it is more than a tool of interconnectivity, rather it is integral to the student's sense of self and the communities of which she is part. The computer parallels the Web in this respect, as it provides a space where the research subjects can be emphatic about who they are, rather than pretend to be someone else (Miller and Mather 1998; Berry and Martin 2000). They do this through the act of 'surfing' the Web, travelling to exotic and exciting places in cyberspace which not only provide a hiatus from real life but define them by what they are not (Nakamura 2002: p.40).

The integration of the computer into the research subjects' identities has meant a redefinition of their subjectivities. It involved a transformation in their relationship to technology:

...I generally viewed computers as a male 'thing' (Lorraine – written response).

> ...I am not frightened of computers any more. I used to think if you press the button it might be the wrong button it might explode or something but they are a lot more robust than you think (Lorraine – interview).

> Computers really frightened me even when I first started. Maybe my course tutors would have noticed I was really frightened (Oyen – interview).

The research subjects' attitudes to computers seemed to have shifted from enstrangement to familiarity, as well as from the pessimistic to the utopian. Their initial dystopian conceptualisations of computers are reminiscent of those like Schiller (1996) and Mosco (1982), who contend that new technologies further alienate disadvantaged groups. Indeed, the research subjects do confirm Mulgan's (1996: p.1) argument that technology, especially computers, are a potent source of fear: they clearly saw computers as foreign, even dangerous; the 'maleness' of computers was somehow incongruous with and even threatening to their identities as women. But their responses also indicate that such anxieties can metamorphose. That is, the negative consequences of a technology are not absolute, in spite of what many techno-cynics would have us believe. On the contrary, those that are supposedly further marginalised by new technology, such as the research subjects, can also be proponents of the libertarian ideologies that circulate around computers and the Internet.

> ...this unit has made me realise that technology is for everybody....it is not a big deal this piece of machine, it's not a big deal, anybody can actually have access to it and use it (Oyen – interview).

After overcoming her initial uneasiness with computers, Oyen adopted an egalitarian perspective of technology whereby people's access to it was merely inhibited by personal fears: technology is open and free to be used – the only obstacle is the individual. The narrative is similar to one that has been used for the dot.com industries: 'everyone is a free agent' (Kumar 2001: p.77). The change in Oyen's view of technology from one of terror to one of optimism illustrates the complexities, contradictions and ubiquity of both utopian and dystopian discourses of technology.

The newfound affinity with computers experienced by the research subjects were simultaneously countered by the feelings of powerlessness that are resonant of 'Net Dropouts', people who quit the Internet after experiencing technical problems (Greenspan 2003b).

> Since I have had problems with my computer I have been totally lost...I haven't really managed to do the work for the past three or four weeks so now it is really catching up with me... (Sasha – interview).

> The worse thing is basically the problems you come across, the technical problems. Not everybody knows how to solve them and they don't try, they are only human and will try but at the end of the day you might be waiting two or three hours or two or three days (Noori – interview).

I have had the monitor replaced twice. I've had the motherboard replaced. I have had the floppy replaced three times. I have had a lot of problems so obviously that has interfered with my work and it's very disruptive. You have them come in and do whatever has to be done and you have to make time for that as well between everything else that I am doing and being at college, that has been very disruptive and very difficult...There is only so much you can whinge to someone else so I tended to keep it all in and not really discuss it with anyone...There was a period of about a week, I just did not want to go near it because it symbolised so much frustration, waste of time and everything else as far as I was concerned... (Bella – interview).

The worst thing is...like when you're confronted with some technical problems. For a start, with me I never realised maybe it's a kind of universal problem, that computers are bound to break down. It's like it does happen with every other person, it's not just me only. I think something is wrong with me maybe because I am not used to this thing, what am I doing wrong? From the start I say "oh no I am not going to start shouting about what is going wrong here" until I had one or two of the others say "just what is going in that computer, does it happen to you?"...Now I can talk about my problems, problems that I am having with my computer at home, it's very very frustrating. You sit in front of this computer, I know I've just started learning, you sit in front of this computer you cannot talk to her and sometimes you are not getting anywhere...sometimes you phone and you are not getting anywhere, it's just like the whole day wasted and you are just sitting their helpless (Oyen – interview).

These technical problems suggest a technological determinism in that the computer was seen as dictating whether the student could progress with her work. The computer was similarly regarded as both the solution and the problem for the research subjects: it enabled freedom to study away from institutional confines yet it also trapped them into reliance upon it.

...I don't think I can do without having a computer at home... (Oyen – interview).

The dependency on the computer demonstrated by the research subjects was illustrated in the pseudo-paralysis they felt when technical problems arose. As mentioned in Chapter 4, this encapsulates the contradictory relationship that ethnic minorities have with technology in that it is both potentially subversive and oppressive (Alkalimat 1996). The dynamics are mirrored in the role that ethnicity plays in the identities of minority groups: it is a core part of one's being, and yet it can also be a burden when, like technical problems, it is subject to control and definition by others, and gets taken outside one's own frame of reference.

The computer's location in the midst of this awkward technology/ethnicity equation raises questions about the unique qualities which characterise the research subjects' engagement with information technology in the home.

The Specificities of Computer and Internet Consumption

The gravity with which computer problems seemed to affect the research subjects suggests more than a technical or educational reliance on the technology. They imply a physical and/or emotional dependence on it: that is, the technology was somehow embodied by the research subjects. This was reflected in their statements about the computer becoming part of their identities: losing the computer was akin to the loss of a friend/partner/baby. The physical/emotional relationship the research subjects had with their computers articulates the notion of the interfaced body, as Terranova (1996: p.70) calls it.

The discourse of the interfaced body is concerned with the connection between the biological and technological. The notion of the cyborg blends this organically, so that they are no longer dichotomous or even separate (Haraway 1985: p.65). While this was evident in the research subjects' symptoms of 'addiction' to their computers, this union was also not as harmonious as the idea of the interfaced body connotes. The physical demands of using the computer and the Internet were awkward in many instances.

> ...with face to face you can use your hands to explain yourself that sort of thing. You demonstrate what you are trying to say, but here [e-mail] you can't really demonstrate, you've got to put everything in words...sometimes you want to express yourself more and you don't know how to put it in English – in any language actually. When you actually see the person you can sort of demonstrate more. On the other hand you just get straight to the point with e-mail. You don't beat around the bush (Chwime – interview).

Chwime recognised the importance of body language in communication, particularly in conveying emotion, and especially where English is a second language. Although she alluded to the lack of emotion in e-mail, she nevertheless regarded it as a more concise medium for expression. Tessa agreed that e-mail lacked the engagement of a face-to-face conversation:

> ...I like talking face to face with people because you can see their reaction, I think visual reaction is very important but the e-mail is impersonal...face to face you actually feel more involved and you actually get to participate physically, mentally, getting actual hands-on impressions and opinions. You can get to the heart of the discussion whereas you can't over an e-mail... (Tessa – interview).

Both Tessa and Chwime's responses indicated that they were perhaps more comfortable and adept at face-to-face than computer-mediated interactions, and this may have been due to certain culturally specific modes of interpersonal communication. This corresponds with Graham's (1996: p.156) argument that the Internet's environment is one where the user can easily become 'spatially decentred' and 'quasi-disembodied'. Indeed, according Tessa and Chwime, they felt physically and emotionally censored (hence their 'quasi-disembodiment') in their use of e-mail because they did not have a visual point of reference with which to communicate (or a 'spatial centre'). This is supported by research showing African Americans are less likely to use email than their white counterparts, but more likely to use chat rooms (Greenspan 2004a), where representations of the body, whether textual or graphic, are more possible and acceptable. The constraints of disembodiment seemed to be magnified by the home environment:

> I respond better working in the environment with other people...when I am there I feel the motivation (Champagne – interview).

The consumption of the computer and Internet at home 'spatially decentred' because it was a solitary activity, one undertaken somewhat distanced from the outside world. Champagne appears to have particularly disliked the isolation of computers and the Internet in that they were minority media at their most extreme – technologies of individualism. Although other research subjects seemed to be appropriating the computer more as a communal technology, the 'spatial decentering' was still evident in the difficulties the research subjects had introducing a technology they would otherwise consume in an institutional context into the domestic sphere. The camaraderie which Champagne sought but could not find in working from home was perhaps indicative of women's computer consumption.

As feminist studies of women and technology show, women tend to approach technology holistically, heterogenously and interactively (Faulkner 1997). This was displayed in the research subjects' 'bricoleur' approach of opening up access to the computer as a means of enlisting the support and assistance of others to address the range of skills required for computing. Indeed, the research subjects were aware of the array of competencies, including those of writing and comprehension, which formed the necessary basis for their computer and Internet use, but some were not confident that they possessed all of these:

> ...the instructions is very very difficult to follow. You have got to sit down and think about it again and again... (Oyen – interview).

> The task sometimes is not clear. You've got to read it over like about 5 times before I understand it (Chwime – interview).

> ...I have a tendency to maybe not understand the instructions very clearly...Sometimes there is too much reading on just one or two questions. I don't mind the reading but sometimes it just doesn't make sense... (Rosie – interview)

These responses demonstrate the necessary associated skills of reading and comprehension involved in computer and Internet consumption which are further physically inhibiting as they generally require isolation and concentration. The requirement of such skills have influenced up to 24% of the US population to decline to be connected to the Internet because they found it complicated (Greenspan 2003b). These skills are also obviously culturally specific as their importance is magnified if the user is not communicating in their native tongue. The physicality of interacting with these technologies seem more insistent than for other media, as McDonald (1995:

p.538) asserts. The particular efforts that are required of computer use also illustrate the close alignment of production and consumption: that is, in addition to the reading and comprehension of coursework activities and other students' e-mails, the research subjects were also obligated to contribute to electronic discussion by writing and sending messages as well. It meant that they were required to switch between roles as reader, writer and critic, which Dery (1994: p.9) says typifies participation in the Internet. It may have been this integration of production and consumption the research subjects found laborious, especially as it took place in the home which was already regarded as a site of work (Faulkner 1996; Linn 1987: p.134; Ang 1996: p.50).

The work involved in computer and Internet production and consumption suggests a kind of embodiment in that it is a physically and mentally absorbing activity. As Nakamura (2002) says, bodies are performed through text, so they are as much 'quasi-*em*bodied' in the act of using a computer, as 'quasi-disembodied' in the difficulties of expressing oneself solely through text. For example, Chwime, who had said that she felt unable to freely express herself (or disembodied) when communicating by e-mail, sustained an injury through her use of the computer:

> I've got a stiff neck. It's getting better now but I haven't got a proper chair. I just sit on a lot of cushions (Chwime – interview).

The necessity of embodiment in the use of computers is shown in the physiological impact on Chwime. This undermines 'postbody ideology' which asserts that the digital domain liberates bodies (Nakamura 2002: p.5). By contrast, other research subjects found embodiment liberatory, whereby the computer became an extension of the body:

> ...with the e-mail you can type it out, put it all in writing, express yourself a bit more. Some people might find it easier to express themselves by writing letters than by communicating face-to-face or by phone...Sometimes I find it hard to express myself to people face-to-face...I've always been a person that can write letters... (Sha – interview).

> ...when you're writing it down you get to say whatever you want to say and explain...I can put down exactly how I am feeling... (Sasha – interview).

Sasha and Sha believe the Internet gave them louder voices with which to 'speak'. This is redolent of the rhetoric of freedom surrounding the Internet but also important for minority groups who do not have representational spaces in other media. Clearly, Sasha and Sha felt that the Internet provided them with more opportunity to express their viewpoints, that they are more likely to receive equal treatment virtually (Nguyen and Alexander 1996: pp.103-104) than in a face-to-face situation. But to make the most of this potential for embodiment required time in which the research subjects could fully engage in their computers and the Internet:

> ...I can do my tasks in the night while my daughter is not there or when she's out with her dad (Chwime – interview).

> Sometimes it's easier to bury your head than to get on with it...it's like some of it is two hours for one thing, three hours for another plus I have got to work, look after the kids and I think 'when can I fit this in?' (Champagne – interview).

The need to absorb themselves in the technology could only be achieved in conjunction with its asynchronicity. That is, the physical demands of participating in the technology had to be balanced with its capacity to to be used at times convenient to the research subjects. But for most women shouldering most of the household responsibilities, there simply isn't enough time: this is a reason why men still dominate Internet use (ClickZ 2002) and some people remain unconnected to the Internet (Greenspan 2003b). In Champagne's case, not only was using the computer a disturbingly lonely experience, she simply did not have the available time with which to immerse herself in it. However, the technology's feature of time-shifting, whereby research subjects could log onto the Internet at any time of the day or night, similar to the ways in which video can be viewed at an alternative time to broadcast (Halleck 1991: p.217), seemed to be favoured by Chwime.

The temporal 'selectivity' (Feldman 1997: pp.4-5) offered by the Internet hints at a sense of freedom. Just as past studies have demonstrated that women will use media technologies in ways which do not disrupt their family's routines (Ang 1996: p.55), Chwime found times when she could escape her domestic responsibilities. Similarly, Tessa considered that the asynchronicity of computer-mediated communication actually saved her time:

> ...what I find is I have got more time to actually research, to actually hunt around for things (Tessa – interview).

The research subjects invoked temporal 'selectivity' by using the computer at times when they wanted to work in solitude, for example during more unsociable hours such as at night after the children had gone to bed, early in the mornings before they woke and at weekends when they were out playing. However, for some, this gave the illusion of freedom:

> ...even though it's supposed to be more flexible, maybe because you have that flexibility you can find other things to do...you say you'll do it later... (Askari – interview).

The apparent freedom afforded by the computer and Internet's constant accessibility seems contradicted by the degree of embodiment required for their use. In spite of the temporal flexibility, Askari's procrastination in using the computer and Internet may have been due to the physical absorption needed to consume them. In any case, any so-called freedom enabled by the technologies' 'quasi-dis/embodiment', 'spatial decentering' or temporal 'selectivity' were ultimately constrained by financial considerations.

Given that unlimited Internet access packages with untimed, fixed local call rates have been longer and more freely available in other countries, there is evidence to show that metered telephone charges in the UK and Europe have stifled their Internet markets (Godell 2000). Even in the US, one third of those that remain unconnected cite concern about expense as the main reason (Greenspan 2003b). Like other technologies before it, such as cable television and the video camcorder, the freedom of the market on the Internet has overcome the other freedoms (of information, expression and so on) potentially on offer (Johnson 1996: pp.94-95; Barry 1996: p.173). But anxieties like Tessa's about the financial implications of being online were mitigated to some extent by the subsidisation of online time as part of the @THENE Year Zero course: students were able to use the Internet on their computer at home for up to nine hours per week (off-peak) without incurring any additional costs or they could use the facilities on campus without the worry of the amount of online time being used.

Nevertheless, such constraints of capitalism were challenged by Sasha, who submitted an expensive telephone bill three months before the completion of the course which used nearly all her subsidy. This could be interpreted as her privileging of freedom of expression over freedom of the market. But as discussed previously, Sasha's computer was appropriated as a communal technology amongst friends and family, so this resistance to market forces may not have been a deliberate tactic on her part. However, it does demonstrate the deployment of the computer beyond the limits imposed upon it, confirming Rheingold's (1992) contention that invariably, this is how new communication technologies are used. Perhaps it also affirms what Kleiner (1997: p.31) calls 'the power of the Internet', which other research subjects alluded to in their admission of 'addiction' to it. That is,the degree of embodiment in Sasha's use of the computer and Internet was so absorbing that it suspended her awareness of the length of time she spent online.

Conclusions

In summarising the main points of this chapter, I would also like to ponder what the implications may be for the following chapters. Having examined in detail how the research subjects consumed information technology in the home environment, what might this mean for how we interpret the Web pages and sites they found, which are discussed hereafter in this book?

The consumption of the Web at home was significant in its insight into women's, specifically those from ethnic minorities, engagement with IT. Simultaneously, it demonstrated the heterogeneity of their interactions with technologies of the home. Indeed, the home was the hub of a multiplicity of activity and responsibilities for the research subjects, thus informing the amount of time and commitment they could devote to their study and to the research.

The importance of their children's learning was explicit in the students' interview responses and was manifest in the way the research subjects used their computers. The research subjects showed a deference to their children's educational well-being in their willingness to allow their children access to the computers, despite that the computers were intended solely for the research subjects. This may be an over-compensation for the lack of access to this technology that the research subjects had prior to joining the course. It also provides an explanation for the lengthy period of time over which the research tasks were completed.

Other instances where the research tasks were submitted late seemed due to the difficulties the research subjects experienced integrating an educational technology into the home and its associated relations of power. Firstly, there were evidently constraints of time as all the research subjects were mothers, many being sole parents, as well as students. Beyond possessing the necessary equipment, childcare responsibilities inevitably inform access to technology (Kendall 1999: 58). Secondly, providing the research subjects with a computer to use at home did not guarantee their uninhibited access to it: while they may have been complicit in allowing their children access to the technology, the desire to use it also came from other quarters, further limiting the amount of time the research subject could spend on it.

Nonetheless, the research subjects seemed to arrange their time on the computer around other members of their households and their extra-curricular activities. In spite of these pressures, some were able to immerse themselves in their computer and Internet consumption in the times they had available for it. During these times, they engaged intensely with the technology, usually in isolation, and in doing so, developed a passion for using the Internet. The strength of this was such that several research subjects changed their lifestyles so that using the computer was prioritised. It is fair to say that those who had this intimacy with their computers probably devoted a considerable amount of time to searching the Web whether it was related to the research or not.

Students' closeness to their computers may have been conducive to obtaining sincere written responses in the research. As they were required, in part, to send their comments on their Web findings via e-mail, perhaps it felt as though they were communicating with a friend, rather than to a tutor or researcher for more formal purposes. But the potential for students to be as earnest as possible in their written responses would have been influenced as much by their familiarity as their discomfort with the technology: some indicated that they were perhaps more at ease and adept at face-to-face communication than electronic mail interactions. While the latter allowed them the time to think about their answers, it may have not been their chosen medium through which to express themselves for both cultural and technical reasons. The execution of the tasks was dependent upon the research subjects following written instructions carefully, which for students returning to full-time study and where English was a second language did not necessarily come easily. The lack of confidence experienced by some research subjects in their writing and comprehension skills may explain the delays in completing the research tasks. Furthermore, the Web research tasks required competencies over and above writing and comprehension; they also necessitated IT skills. The research subjects needed to be able to perform keyword searches on the World Wide Web, type up their findings and send them via e-mail to their tutor. Indeed, some admitted to their fear of computers at the beginning of the course and it is not entirely clear whether such insecurities were dispelled when the students came to do the first research task in Week 12. The possibility of these anxieties are taken into account when their Web findings are discussed in the next chapters.

Nonetheless, it is also important to acknowledge the issues which were largely beyond the control of the research subjects and the consequences for interpreting their findings from the Web. For example, the cost implications may have hindered research subjects' use of the Internet. That is, they may not have have spent as much time searching on the World Wide Web as they would have liked because of the expense of being online. Also, students identified technical problems as one of the most disruptive and time-consuming factors in their completion of coursework. These disruptions were exascerbated by their reluctance to reveal such problems out of embarassment, lengthening the time taken to resolve them. The sense of powerlessness experienced by the research subjects seemed to engender feelings of negativity towards the computer which, in some cases, made them loath to interact with it.

The factors affecting student's execution of the research tasks are multifarious because of the lack of a common experience in which the tasks were conducted. Unlike in a laboratory, or even a classroom setting, there was no control over the environment in which the tasks were undertaken. This chapter has attempted to illustrate the highly individualised ways in which the research subjects participated in computers and the Internet in order to provide a foundation upon which their Web findings can be interpreted. It has discussed the many factors operating in their personal lives and home environments which may have had a bearing upon the ways in which the Web was consumed and the data that was subsequently produced from this. At the same time, these factors give a localised snapshot of the ways in which the Web is used by women from ethnic minorities in a specific socio-economic and educational context. This tension between their shared identity as students, mothers, research subjects and ethnic minority women; and their construction as heterogenous beings, was taken into consideration as their relationship to and consumption of IT was examined. It is in this context that the products of their forays into the Web are discussed in the following chapters.

Chapter 7

Continuing the Tradition: Translating the Web Through Previous Media

This chapter returns to the theoretical questions asked in the beginning of the thesis in the process of analysing data produced from the research subjects' forays into the Web – questions about ethnicity, representation and how technology mediates the two.

It begins by examining our constructions and descriptions of ethnicity: out of a group of 15 women from ethnic minorities, including myself, came 15 different conceptualisations of ethnicity. If, as I have argued in Chapter 2, ethnicity is not a fixed state, what does this mean for representation? Is representation an impossible task, irrespective of the technology which mediates it? Or does the technology make a difference? The empirical data is used to discuss these questions.

Employing both interview material and the written responses to the research tasks, the chapter continues by comparing and contrasting the ethnic representational practices of the Web and the broadcast media. That is, it juxtaposes the research subjects' relationships to and experiences of the Web with film and television. Firstly, it explores our consumption of media representations of ethnicity in the context of the media studies research discussed in Chapter 3. Secondly, it looks at the research subjects' expectations of the Web (in the first research task) in light of their comments about the portrayal of ethnic minorities in film and television. Thirdly, it examines their perspectives of the Web following their journeys into cyberspace (in the second research task), and the parallels with the utopian and dystopian tendencies, mentioned in Chapter 4, that accompany any new technology, especially the Internet.

As this chapter incorporates both written and interview responses, I have distinguished between them by stating if it was the latter at the end of the quote. Where there is no declaration, the quote was from a written response. One of the concerns I expressed in Chapter 5 was that because I did not conduct all the interviews, in some cases, I have had to rely solely on the transcript of the interview. Therefore, these interview responses have been mediated and interpreted by the transcriber before reaching me, translated to fit with the rules of written grammar. On the other hand, I have corrected spelling errors in the written responses where these are obvious. At times, when it was not clear whether they were mistakes at all, or rather deliberate strategies of naming (such as in 'Afrikan' or 'Black' or 'British'), I have left the text as it was. For the most part, I have left the grammar of the written responses as they are to reflect as much as possible how they were intended by the research subjects.

However, where additions were necessary, I have indicated these by placing them in [ ] brackets.

Interspersed with the research subjects' written and interview responses are my own autobiographical reflections on my ethnicity and its representation in the broadcast media. In the final part of the chapter, I present some of my own and the research subjects' findings from the Web, in particular sites and pages which construct ethnicity as fixed – be it culturally, historically or geographically – and investigate some of the continuities and departures between media and Web representations of ethnicity as well as their respective modes of production and consumption.

Differing Definitions of Difference

The first research task asked the 15 research subjects (including myself) to complete the following sentence:

I would describe my ethnicity as...

The responses to this produced 15 different conceptualisations of ethnicity, as follows:

British-born Nigerian
Nigerian born black African
British-Asian born in Pakistan
English-born/Jamaican origin
British-born Jamaican
British-born Afro Caribbean
Australian-born Chinese
African-born Black, British citizen
Asian-Bangladeshi
British-Caribbean
British Afro-Caribbean
African/Caribbean
Black African
black british
Chilean-Latin American

These descriptions of ethnicity, ranging from the general to the specific, confirm the difficulties of representing difference, as discussed in Chapter 2. Gilroy (1987: p.11) points to the struggle for meaning in discourses of ethnicity, to represent blackness beyond the categories of 'problem', 'margin' or 'alien'. Indeed, this was manifest in one research subject, Teti's, reluctance to participate in the research tasks. As described in Chapter 5, she said she could not see the purpose of exploring ethnicity, especially as her own was so complex. This was further articulated in her written reflection on the research task:

Week 19 was a difficult task for me in as much I am not really into discussing ethnicity just for the sake of it. I have always reflected around political issues. I also believe that gender and class are important, although I feel that my being black is the first issue for me. Having had an English education, spent three times as much of my life in England as I did in my own home country, I sometimes forget my nationality. This is except when I find some etiquette or other value totally unacceptable and so refer to my cultural upbringing and values. I am very much aware of stereotyping and racism that my thoughts are now not on just finding role-models, identity and representations but how one gets the understanding and acceptance that positive changes require less rhetoric and more action.

Teti suggests that the task of representation is futile because the intricacies of ethnicity cannot be pinned down, or as Gilroy (1993: p.2) says, it 'avoid(s) capture by its agents.' If, as Ang (1996: p.116) and Ross (1996: p.xi) argue, ethnicity is not a fixed position, but a state of transformation, reinvention and hybridity; then how can any form of representation be adequate? Instead, representation simply becomes conflated with labelling or naming, as we see in the interview and written responses of Askari and Lorraine:

I never had to think about what do I see myself as, I just am whatever. I don't wish to label. I have a problem with labelling myself as something just for somebody else's benefit. I have never had to. People like that will label you as whatever they want to see you as, it's not my problem. It's strange and I think people's perceptions are strange because they are very different to yours, very different and I found on this course there were so many different views and mine are nothing like that (Askari – interview).

I am not happy with my description [of my ethnicity] because I feel that no one should be labelled...I believe that it is the likes of this labelling (as well as other influences) that encourages racism to thrive – it displays division (Lorraine).

I do not like to 'label' myself because society says so (or because I've been instructed to). By labelling myself as British-born, it does not include the deep and rich ancestry I have inherited. I acknowledge that I was born in England, but that I am also of the Afrikan Diaspora (the dispersal of a people outside their place of Origin, that is, Afrika). Black people have been scattered around the world and whether we call ourselves British, Jamaican, Ghanaian, Dominican, Nigerian, Somalian or even Black we are all part of the Diaspora. If anyone asks me where I am from, I tell them my mother! (Askari).

I have got so much mix I cannot define my ethnicity because I would have to describe all races, so I don't see why it has to be defined (Champagne – interview).

I have never looked at my own ethnicity before...I have never really defined myself and stuck to that definition like I did on that exercise... (Roni – interview)

Askari and Lorraine imply that they have only given their ethnicities a name because they were following instructions to do so. That is, they were compelled to do so. This alludes, perhaps, to the issues surrounding doing research in an educational context, where the students are the research subjects and the tutor is the researcher, where there are inherent discrepancies in power as well as 'visible and invisible pedagogies'

(Bernstein 1975: p.116) at work, as discussed in Chapter 5. In other words, the necessity of participating in the research is communicated implicitly or invisibly, disguised by the more visible or explicit promotion of diligent study. For Askari, Lorraine, Champagne and Teti, the act of stating their ethnicity is perceived negatively, as if by declaring it, it is given a fixity which compromises other aspects of their identity. Ethnicity is seen in isolation from gender, class and sexuality rather than as a dimension of it (Brah 1992: p.131).

Indeed, Lorraine stresses in her interview that 'first and foremost, I am a mum, I think that's my most important job of my whole life'. The interview was a forum for articulating what Lorraine omitted from her written responses to the research tasks (Keats 1993: p.18), which was that her gender role as a mother is prioritised over her ethnicity. Yet the invisibility of ethnicity has been the subject of criticism within feminist debates by black feminists (Brah 1992: pp.134-146). Amongst the research subjects, there seemed to be a resignation to the impossibility of representing ethnicity and its complex permutations with gender and other facets of subjectivity.

Askari suggests that there is a particular dilemma in representing diasporic ethnicities such as her own because they are so diverse, encompassing the wide range of difference which migration has produced (Gillespie 1995: p.6). For example, Oyen refers to the African diaspora in describing herself as 'Nigerian born African' in the research tasks and 'Nigerian born black African' in the interview. The reference to the geographical dispersal of African people by force or choice (ibid) is significant to the representation of her ethnicity because her parents originate from different parts of the continent, thus her identity is dispersed. Similarly, Gina, being 'Chilean-Latin American, now British Citizen', demonstrates her membership to the Latino diaspora as the link between her countries of birth and residence. For Noori, her 'Asian-Bangladeshi' ethnicity depicts her location within an Asian diaspora even though she hasn't been back to Bangladesh in 25 years. Therefore, the multiple cultural reference points which characterise diasporic ethnicities makes their representation problematic, although they are often grounded by references to an 'ethnos' or place of belonging (Hall 1992).

The notion of a diaspora, the real and/or symbolic connection to an original 'homeland' (Ang 1994: p.5) seems to be an important element in many of the research subjects' ethnicities. This is evident where they were born elsewhere:

> I was born in Sudan...that's where I was for the first ten years of my life even though I really don't remember that much of it...my way of life now is very much different from the way my life would be if I were to be back at home right now, but I am still very proud that I am African (Sasha).

> I was born in Dominica, West Indies...Although there were white people on my island, I never felt threatened, I felt I belonged...Coming to England was a real shock to me at 7 years old...I did not feel a sense of belonging because I was not able to do what I used to do back home (Tessa).

...when I go back to Pakistan to visit my relatives I feel like a stranger in the country that was once a part of me. To them back home I am British, because of the way we think perhaps we are too westernised to them back home. To British people, I am still a Pakistani, British passport or not (Rosie).

I was born in Zimbabwe and came to England with my mother and three siblings at eighteen months of age...I still consider Zimbabwe home (home is after all where the heart is)...even though back home I am commonly referred to as 'English' (Bella).

For those research subjects who have emigrated to Britain, there seems to be a constant tension between what Gilroy (1990/1: pp.3-16) has termed 'where you are from' and 'where you are at', regardless of the length of time they have lived away from 'home'. It is perhaps this dislocation which is so difficult to represent because of its geographical, cultural and emotional complexity. As Robins (1991: p.42) argues, migration means that 'boundaries are crossed; cultures are mingled; identities become blurred'. Therefore, how can ethnicity be represented when one is no longer certain of what it is, especially if it is in a perpetual state of flux?

But this sense of displacement was not only confined to those research subjects born outside of Britain. Being a British-born ethnic minority carries its own ambivalences, similar to those I outlined in Chapter 5 about being Australian-born and calling myself 'Australian'.

Black people born and bred in England the way I was I think find it hard to explain their ethnicity if their parents were originally or are aliens in Britain (Roni).

3 years ago my husband and I went on vacation to Barbados and it felt so strange however nice to be one of the majority (coloured), than the usual minority of my birth country...I felt at home to an extent... (Lorraine).

Although Roni and Lorraine were both born in Britain, they represent much of their ethnicity as located elsewhere, part of something bigger, under the umbrella of the African diaspora. Roni constructs her ethnicity as 'British Afro-Caribbean' and Lorraine as 'British-born Afro Caribbean'. Just as I proffered 'Australian-born Chinese' as a statement of my inclusion in the Chinese diaspora but with much hesitation over my Australianness, Roni, Askari and others include Britishness in their ethnicities but similarly distance themselves from it.

I don't think of myself as British. When I think of British, I think of the Queen, blue, red, white flag and the cross, and I think of racists. I don't associate myself with Britain. I am still linked to it because that's all I know really...I haven't been anywhere else (Askari – interview).

...although I was born in the United Kingdom both my parents are Jamaican born and emigrated to Britain in the 1950's. I feel that my cultural upbringing has instilled within me certain traits which have enabled me to relate strongly to the Caribbean, sometimes more so than Britain because of the hostility and racism that exist... (Lorraine).

> I have to tag it on because I've got the accent...I don't really consider myself as true British, I don't hang on to that. The only time I am British is when I am abroad – "the British are this, the British are that – oh yes I am British". Everything good, yeh I'm British... (Roni – interview).

> I prefer to be called Nigerian but circumstances in my country has left us with no alternative...Possessing a British passport only improves my status. I do not feel [comfortable] in this country, due to discrimination in every aspects... (Chwime).

There is a reluctant Britishness in these research subjects' ethnicities because, like myself, they have experienced racism in their country of birth. Their Britishness is a 'necessary evil'. In spite of being born in London, Chwime is more at ease with being Nigerian. However, her Britishness is deployed strategically for avoiding the racism she has received as an official Nigerian: when carrying a Nigerian passport, she has been apprehended on suspicion of trafficking drugs. After obtaining a British passport, she now feels she is 'treated with more respect' and feels 'more confident when travelling'. These non-committal attitudes to their Britishness contest the conventional practice of representing ethnicity as constituted by a singular 'ethnos' or family or pure, homogenous community (Hall et al 1992: p.308).

Similarly, the research subjects who were born outside of Britain, by being 'not really' British nor 'at home' in their country of birth, reject the binary oppositions used to represent ethnicities and national identities.

> I have never on a conscious or sub-conscious level identified myself as British. I seriously doubt whether I would even if I was born here (Bella).

> I have always been there [Zimbabwe] as a tourist...I don't even speak the language, I can hear it, I can understand but I don't actually speak (Bella – interview).

> I came here when I was five and have never been back and really have no ties with Bangladesh...even though I may be Bangladeshi, I wasn't brought up like a typical Bangladeshi. I haven't been back to Bangladesh in 25 years. Any proper Bangladeshi goes back every 3-4 years (Noori).

> I grew up with totally English people. There were no other Asians, no Afro-Caribbeans, no Africans, nobody with the same skin colour as me. I was the only black girl there. In secondary school I was the only black person in that school. I grew up with two identities, at home I was Bangladeshi, at school I was British (Noori – interview).

> In years to come I felt glad that I was born in the West Indies because I knew two different lifestyles (Tessa).

According to Said (1995: pp.1-3), European identity was forged in diametric opposition to the Orient. The Orient was a European invention which was instrumental in defining the West as everything that the East was not. However, the research subjects refuse to be drawn into this cultural contest between their Britishness and the other dimensions of their ethnicity by being defined by what they are not. There is a sense of being, according to Tessa, 'between two cultures', but they are neither here nor there, in or out: Noori says she is Bangladeshi but not a 'proper' or 'typical' one, and only part-time British. This lack of certainty has led Rosie to feel that she has 'lost a part of my life', but it has inspired research subjects to seek points of anchorage in the representation of their ethnicities.

One of the ways in which the research subjects, including myself, have attempted to ground their ethnicities is through their places of birth. That is, where we were born, or perhaps as Gilroy (1990/1: pp.3-16) puts it 'where you are from', has been consistent in how we depict our ethnicities. It is more than a negotiation of 'where you are from' and 'where you are at', rather that the former actively informs the latter. It highlights the prominence of 'origins' in the representation of ethnicity and is contrary to Giddens' (1991: p.2) argument that identity is now divorced from a fixed sense of place because of the role of technology in mediating social relations. For the research subjects and I, the difficulties in articulating our ethnicities are relieved slightly with some geographical anchorage. Hence, many have portrayed their ethnicities quite specifically in terms of countries of birth, nationalities and geographical regions: Askari is 'British-born Jamaican'; Chwime is 'British-born Nigerian'; Sha is 'English-born/ Jamaican origin', and Tessa is 'British Caribbean'.

Other research subjects have used more general means of securing their ethnicities, as mentioned earlier, by positioning their ethnicities within a diasporic community. Therefore, they have constructed their ethnicities more broadly so that they are represented through their connection with others. For example, Rosie, in defining herself as 'British-Asian born in Pakistan' indicates that she shares her Asianness with Noori, who is 'Asian Bangladeshi', even though the nuances of their ethnicities are quite different. Similarly, because Teti's ethnicity was so complex and difficult to capture, she widened it to 'African/Caribbean', linking it with Lorraine's ethnicity as a 'British-born Afro Caribbean', Oyen's as a 'Nigerian-born African', Roni's as a 'British Afro-Caribbean' and Sasha's as 'Black African'. In these instances, ethnicity is represented through commonality rather than difference, even though it is apparent that each person's ethnicity is uniquely located according to its intersections with class, gender, sexuality, age and other dimensions of identity.

Another approach to depicting ethnicity through a construction of community was the adoption of blackness within the research subjects' ethnicities. Unlike African or Asian diasporic ethnicities which are defined both geographically and ideologically, black ethnicities are mainly ideological in that they demonstrate 'strategic essentialism' (Spivak 1993: pp.2-5). Spivak contends that 'strategic essentialism' is a tactic for mobilising a diverse group of people for a common political objective, for example, combating racism. When Sasha represents her ethnicity as 'Black African', Bella as 'African-born Black, British citizen' and Champagne as 'Black British', it is their blackness which unites them, although their conceptualisations and experiences of blackness are clearly not the same. As Hall et al (1992: p.308) contend, black identity is not about being the same, but about being treated as the same, as 'not white'. Indeed, many of the research subjects have illustrated the racial discrimination they have encountered, so their blackness is a symbol of their both their resistance to the binary system of representing race and ethnicity which has marginalised them, as well as their reappropriation of it for the purpose of solidarity (Ross 1996: p.viii; Silk and Silk 1990: p.viii). Even though her ethnicity is 'Asian Bangladeshi', Noori refers to herself as black to illustrate her isolation in growing up with 'totally English people' and with 'nobody with the same skin colour as me'. Thus blackness is deployed strategically:

> I identify myself not as a black person, I am black but I identify myself as a person, I don't really attach a black tag to it, I am just a person (Champagne – interview).

> If I don't confine myself as a geographical black person, if I just consider myself as part of the diaspora, of the spread of black people, yes that is useful for me (Roni – interview).

> I resent the sense of inferiority Whites instilled in my people and the divide and rule tactics used, which unfortunately are still evident today politically, socially and economically possibly more so than other colonies as we were one of the last members to obtain independent status in 1980 (Bella).

Blackness, as a representation of ethnicity, is embraced where necessary. In certain circumstances, it is chosen on ideological grounds, as Bella does, to distinguish between the structural inequalities between the colonised and colonisers. In other situations, it is not even mentioned: for example, Sha makes no reference to blackness when portraying her ethnicity as 'English-born/Jamaican origin'; nor does Rosie, despite that like Noori, she defines herself as Asian. As Brah (1992: pp.127-128) has pointed out, the use of the term 'black' has been contentious in Britain because of its inclusion of people of Asian descent, when many British Asians do not consider themselves to be black. It is also seen as problematic because it still resonates with biological notions of race. Yet it is clear that some of the research subjects do use race and ethnicity interchangeably, as both are conceptualised in physiological terms:

> ...I just do not like how others choose to define me based on the colour of my skin (Champagne).

> My great-great grandfather was white, he was from the borders of Scotland. I have a white surname. That's the name that I have, my grandmother was an orphan so we are not sure but going from history and going by her features, we can tell she has red indian. She has the features of the Arawak Indian, she has the same defined features and you can tell but I can go back to my dad's family which I know, my grandmother's grandmother was white French. I have got Scottish, French, African, there might be a bit of Chinese. I have got everything. I have people asking 'is your mum Chinese or something?'. I even used to get, when I was working as a hair stylist there was this Japanese girl, who said to me that 'you are Chinese' and I said 'no' and she said 'you must be, your skin it is very yellow, your skin and your features' and even my manager he said that somewhere along the line he could even tell by the way my hair is (Champagne – interview).

> I look of African origin...Both of my parents were born in Trinidad. We are all of African descent. My father and his family believe that they are purely African. My mother's family, besides being African, have a mixture of both Carib and Arawak as well as Irish and German (Teti).

For Champagne, any representation of her ethnicity is an attempt to define her racially, based on the colour of her skin. Race is substituted by and for ethnicity, which may explain, to an extent, the resistance to participating in the research tasks. The concerns which Champagne, Askari and Lorraine expressed about being 'labelled' may have been based on a perception that the meanings of race and ethnicity can be easily exchanged, that in being asked to articulate their ethnicity, they believed they were required to classify themselves racially. This highlights Gilroy's (1987: pp.154-156) claim that such terms are problematic when switched because of the distinct historical conditions under which each emerged.

Despite the notion of race being a construction of imperialism, premised on symbolic markers of the body such as skin colour, facial features, hair and physique (Hernton 1988: p.xii), it seems to be embraced by Teti. She describes her physical appearance as of African origin. Her emphasis on being 'purely' African on her father's side suggests a kind of 'ethnic absolutism' (Hall et al 1992: p.308) in its preoccupation with origins. Her family being 'all of African descent' attributes an authenticity to her ethnicity, which Yuval-Davis (1998: pp.138-139) argues is often used to engender community amongst ethnic minorities. Perhaps Teti has appropriated racial identifiers to represent her ethnicity visually given that it is so difficult to articulate through language. In using the discourse of race, which still retains a privileged position in defining difference (Ifekwunigwe 1998: p.91), Teti gives the enigma of her ethnicity a certain stability as geography similarly does. This visible manifestation of race is also a means of creating a sense of belonging: Noori implies that she may not have felt quite so marginalised at school if there had been another person with the same skin colour as her. In the adoption of race as the traditional mode of representing difference, it is transformed. It becomes redefined from within rather than from without.

It is in this way that black Britishness has developed its own 'attitude', according to Hall (1998b: p.45). Britishness is no longer an ideal to which black culture ought to aspire to or assimilate (ibid: p.40), but has been incorporated into representations of blackness. This is seen in Champagne and Sha's insistence on the Britishness of their ethnicities:

> I define myself as black british...My mother was born in Barbados and my father born in Grenada which makes them Westindian and I suppose I would be defined as WestIndian too. I personally do not [accept] this definition...it's just that I have no real bond with a country that I have never seen and probably could not fit into. All I know is my birthplace and I appreciate and love being British. I cannot love what I do not know or understand. HOME IS WHERE THE HEART IS (Champagne).

> I look at myself as being English, I don't class myself as being Jamaican because I don't really know much about Jamaica...I look at myself as being a black English woman [whose] parents [descend] from Jamaica (Sha).

Unlike the hesitant constructions of Britishness seen earlier, Sha and Champagne anchor their ethnicities through their Britishness. It is the one certainty in their ethnicities which can be confidently represented, when the other aspects of it remain so unknown, unclear and unmanageable.

Given the multitudinal, multi-dimensional ways in which the research subjects have represented their ethnicities – be it specifically or generally, with conviction or reluctance – how have or haven't these been translated via media technologies? In their consumption of film and television texts, where are the (dis)continuities between their own and the media's representations of ethnicity?

Ethnicity and Media Technologies: It's All There in Black and White

There is a distinct contrast between the research subjects' representations of their own ethnicities and those they have encountered in the broadcast media. While they struggled with attempting to articulate their ethnicities, they also challenged media images of their ethnicities. As women from ethnic minorities, they are also what Diawara (1993: p.219) calls resisting spectators in that they offer active criticism of representations of blackness, particularly as these are so often constructed from the 'white gaze'.

> ...Since doing this course I have just started noticing so much. "I wouldn't use that. Why are they showing these kind of adverts? I will never use none of those things." So there is nothing that will make me go out and buy the hairsprays, the make-up because obviously my hair is different, my skin is different... (Tessa – interview).

Tessa recognises the 'white gaze' at work in media advertising when she realises that she is not the targeted consumer for many products. As a black woman, she is both absent from the image and the ideal readership. Indeed, other research subjects too, point to a sense of invisibility when it comes to locating representations of their ethnicities in film and television:

> I think whatever is produced for other blacks also represents my ethnic subjectivity...There are not enough black films and or appearances on British TV (Chwime).

> ...you don't see many black people on TV. If you can think of a famous worldwide black person from England, I would like you to share that person with me because I can't think of one. There is no Eddie Murphy, no Oprah. OK we have Shirley Bassey...There's Trevor MacDonald he is co-founder of the mentor scheme, he is a notable black man but there is not many black people in Britain I can identify with (Roni – interview).

> I do not find a lot of representations of my ethnicity shown on the television. I can relate to the American chat shows (*Oprah Winfrey*, *Jerry Springer*) because a lot of black issues in relation to black women/men are discussed. For example; children growing up with one parent, therefore there is an increase in crime, especially with young black men, they have no role models (there is an increase in young girls getting involved with gang crimes also);
> cultural differences between black and white people; mixed relationships to name a few (Tessa).

> When Linda Carter starred in *Wonder Woman* in the 1970s, it did not take much of a leap of my seven year-old imagination to pretend that it was me. After all, the similarities were staggering. Her name was Linda. My name was Linda. She had black hair. I had black hair. And when she was undergoing her explosive spinning transformation from ordinary woman to Wonder Woman, she could easily have been Chinese...I also had my suspicions about Tin Tin from the Thunderbirds. Surely, she was Chinese. The coincidences, again, were astonishing: black hair, dark eyes; her name, Tin Tin, and my Chinese name, Ting Mai (Leung 2001).

It may be due to this lack of Australian, and in Chwime, Tessa and Roni's cases, British representations of their ethnicities that there are mixed feelings about and diminished loyalties to our respective nation states. But while it is apparent in their experiences that there are a lack of media images of black British ethnicities (which has also been confirmed in media research – see Pascall 1982, Freeth 1982, Young 1995), they settle for those which come from the US. That is, they 'make do' with images which depict their ethnicities diasporically rather than specifically. They confirm hooks (1992: pp.291-393) and Bobo's (1993: p.272, 285) arguments that black women are still able to engage positively with the few representations of blackness they come across (in my case, even when the ethnicities of the role models concerned are either different or ambiguous), even though these might not be entirely satisfactory.

> On film and television you do find it quite common to have roles for blacks that are not necessarily for black people eg *The Bill*, *EastEnders*, *Coronation Street* and other short series soaps, though there are still too few blacks filling roles that are quite suitable for them, but I have to say *EastEnders* provide quite good roles without casting blacks as WESTINDIANS. Just London born black people (Champagne).

Champagne has been able to find positive representations of black Britishness, although like Roni and Tessa, she acknowledges that there are not enough of them. But Champagne's idea of positive representation implies casting black people in roles which deny their blackness, origins and place within a diaspora. This is consistent with her own refusal to be defined by her ancestry and tendency to frame her ethnicity primarily through her Britishness. It suggests she wants a 'Cosby-isation' or 'coconutting' (Hall 1995: p.22) of British portrayals of blackness, whereby white characters are simply substituted by black characters on television, addressing lack of black representation in the media cosmetically. The need to not cast black people as West Indian demonstrates a renunciation of ethnic origins that Fanon (1967: p.11) claims is indicative of an internalisation of colonial ideology.

Certainly, this approach to increasing representations of blackness in television has attracted criticism because it has not reflected the wider social realities of black communities (Jhally and Lewis 1992: p.58); just as depicting black people in Britain as not West Indian and just as 'London born black people' would not be representative of the one million or so African Caribbean population in the UK (Mashengele 1997: pp.311-315). It is precisely the media's deviation from the experiences of the research subjects which inspires, and almost necessitates, their critical negotiation of televisual representations of ethnicity.

> ...a lot of people feel that if you [are] from Jamaica they associate with you with either drugs or violence...every time a person asks where [are] you from and if I state that I [am] from Jamaica or say I am [of] Jamaican descent some people would state that I am a yardie. A yardie is a person who dresses a particular way and...are known for dominating people, who also commit crimes and they hang around in groups (Sha).

> Black men are associated with drugs, crime and Gangsta Rap the reward of such activities being flash cars (BMWs are often referred to as Black Man's Wheels) mobile phones and other cultural artefacts – such as guns... (Bella).

> ...the stereotypical view of a Black man/woman is for them to be involved in drugs or a life of crime (eg *Cracker, The Bill, Thieftakers*) than to see a functional family living the 'good life' or as a 'normal' family (eg *The Waltons, Little House on the Prairie*) (Askari).

> ...black people in film in particular...tend to be depicted as criminals, or have low paid jobs and nurture big dreams (like Lenny and Alan Jackson in *EastEnders*). In the case of women they are usually struggling with untold children, have no employment prospects, are devoid of motivation with a violent unsupportive partner (typical storylines in *The Bill*)...with the exception of the odd mixed race character like *Coronation Street* and *Brookside*, most soaps don't even include minorities... (Roni).

> ...when I watch the television or even go out to the cinema all I see is that Black people are seen to [be] causing trouble and they are mainly young people of the same age group as me and that is not the true picture. There are many of us that do not cause trouble but we just want to get on with our studies so that we can get good jobs for our children and bring them up in a way that they do not need to get caught up in crime...there are not many Black or Asian people represented with technology they are mostly shown to be sports players, singers or dancers and I think that things have to change because there are many Black people out there with very good ideas for today's technology (Sasha).

The association of black people with danger and their depiction as 'problems' is not new in the history of representations of race in the media (Tulloch 1990: pp.143-144; Hall 1993; Pines 1992: pp.9-10). It is part of the construction of the black/white racial dichotomy (Fanon 1967: p.9; Gilroy 1993: p.1; Hall 1981: p.41), which Hoch (1979: pp.44-46) argues, also has a strong masculine inflection. The research subjects distance themselves from these representations not only as members of ethnic minorities, but also as women. That is, the images they see on television do not articulate their realities as ethnic minority women.

Roni contends that within the narrow range of stereotypical depictions of black people she has witnessed on television, the roles are also heavily gendered. Like black men, black women are not only represented as socially deviant, but are also consistently sexualised (Jones 1993: p.253; hooks 1992: p.62). In the research subjects' experiences, this is manifest in the image of the single mother, who symbolises promiscuity by having children without the desire for a nuclear family.

There is not much on the TV these days about single black women unless it's something really negative, ie single mothers, crime and such things... (Tessa – interview).

The research subjects' rejections of portrayals of black women seem to be based on the incongruities with their own realities, especially where such women are represented as powerless to higher forces, whether it be their own sexuality or to acts of God:

TV has never portrayed Bangladeshi women as positive images. The only time I have seen them on TV is when they are showing victims of flood and the women are crying because they have lost everything. The only time I have seen British Bangladeshi women on TV is when they are shopping! (Noori).

There's nothing on TV, there's nothing in the magazines. The only thing I saw was for jewellery for Asian women on the back of a bus or something. Earrings or something... (Noori – interview).

For Noori, the representations of women in Bangladesh, as well as British Bangladeshi women, are negative because they do not express their daily struggles to meet the demands of their families:

...there are [Bangladeshi] women working both at home and the factories on the industrial sewing machines. The majority of Bangladeshi women are married off but if they do work they seem to be in low skilled jobs, shop assistants, receptionists, threadpickers. The association with these technologies leads me to think that Bangladeshis seem either less intelligent than everyone else or do not realise that a good education will lead to a better future...If they have a PC it is because a "Son" is studying. If the daughter is studying then such an expensive bit if equipment is not considered important for her education. The Bangladeshis consider it wasteful to spend very much on a daughter's education because they will marry her off and she will settle down and have a family never using her brain for studying ever again (Noori).

...basically the last 13 years I have had to put a hold, a stop to my education because I have been bringing up my children and now my youngest is in nursery I feel I can go ahead and carry on with my education...I have got 4 children and a husband who doesn't lift a finger, he would sit here all day. I am in the middle of doing an assignment and he will see I'm on the computer but he has to ask for a cup of tea...last month it was Ramadan and I used to wake up at 4 o'clock, cook and everybody else used to wake up and eat then go back to sleep, I didn't go back to sleep. It was nice and peaceful and I was fresh from waking up 2 hours ago so I could get on with a lot of my assignments (Noori – interview).

Noori's criticisms of the affluent, consumerist images of Asian women are based on their discrepancy from her reality: how can Asian women be depicted as having the time and money to buy luxury items like jewellery, when her existence centres on making ends meet? This parallels the findings of Jhally and Lewis' (1992: p.58) study of US television in the 1980s which showed that principal black characters were increasingly represented as middle class, while those who were portrayed as working class almost disappeared. Likewise, Tessa's disapproval of televisual representations of black women emerges from her perception of black women, including herself, as resilient and in control:

> My mother was a very strong woman and I saw her as the breadwinner, because she made most of the decisions at home. Today I make all the decisions in my home...My mother was a machinist. My sisters and I would help our mother in the evening by clipping the threads off the slippers or skirts she was making. She had a big industrial sewing machine at home...I would say to myself that I would never do this kind of work, because of the long hours and low pay...My parents were determined that my younger brother should go to University...As girls we were expected to do the cooking, cleaning and helping our mother with her work (Tessa – interview).

The representations of ethnicity in the broadcast media to which the research subjects refer seem to be constructed from outside the realm of their experience. They are not the targeted viewer or ideal spectator in the same way that Tessa says that advertisements for cosmetics are not aimed at her. Perhaps they fulfil the equivalent function of the Orient's relation to the West (Said 1995: p.1), that is to reinforce white identity as unified, to forever have blackness and Englishness 'locked symbolically in an antagonistic relationship' (Gilroy 1993: p.1). Through these negative depictions of blackness, several binary oppositions are constructed: within the representation itself, it implies whiteness to be superior and dominant; external to the image, given their incompatibility with the research subjects' experiences, it suggests representation and reality to be mutually exclusive – or rather, it highlights the contrast between objectified depictions and self-representations of ethnicity.

For example, Bella identifies mobile phones and 'Gangsta Rap' as stereotypical signifiers of blackness when depicted from the 'white gaze'. Yet as Hall (1996a, 1996b, 1998b) has observed, black British youth have appropriated the mobile phone as a symbol of the post-Thatcherite entrepreneurial individual in tandem with the 'jive-walking hustler dude'. Other research subjects allude to the importance of these signifiers in representations of black identity, particularly the affiliation between music technologies and urban, black youth (Dery 1994: p.192):

> In England, I suspect the technologies that are associated with African/Caribbean are powerful stereo systems and sound systems that blare loud music from cars and houses (Teti).

> The only technology that comes to mind when I think of my ethnicity is domestic technology, namely 'High Fidelity', or the hi-fi as it is more commonly known (Lorraine).

> As I am an amalgamation of three cultures, I can associate with a mixture of technologies such as the London Underground in England and the sound systems of Jamaica (Roni).

> My grandfather's generation were mostly involved with public transport and this is where a lot of the men worked in the 50s and 60s. They worked as bus conductors and bus drivers. Many women from that time worked in factories or sewed for a living. A lot of

> Black women were nurses, working long hours and receiving little pay...Though sewing machines may have been associated with Black women, Black men are now very central to the whole fashion business. Many of them have started their own businesses in the fashion industry and this instantly links them to technology such as sewing machines. I think of young Black men in the studio using the latest DAT machines, expressing themselves over the microphone, whilst listening to their well thought out beats over the headphones all for the latest reggae/hip-hop/soul track. I associate young Black women with hairdressing tools, styling Afro hair into the latest style (for example, curling tongs, hairdryers, steamers, blow-dryers, etc) (Askari).

Askari recognises that the intersection of her ethnicity with other elements of identity give rise to a range of representations of blackness, so that there is not the complete discord between representation and reality which Noori perceives. That is, the portrayal of blackness is also age or historically specific, so that young black males are depicted alongside music technologies, while older black men are linked with transport technologies; similarly the sexualisation of black women applies to young black women, while older black women are associated with fashion and textile technologies. It could be said that Askari still resorts to the traditional mode of depicting black femininity, that is by eroticising it (hooks 1992: p.62), in this case through objects of preening and beautification. But the technologies Askari chooses to represent black women are the same ones which Tessa said earlier cannot be found in mainstream media images because beauty is rarely associated with blackness. It is exactly these unlikely associations, this diversity the research subjects see in their own ethnicities, which they argue media representations lack:

> ...black people are not normally depicted as intellectuals on television or films, although education is an important part of our culture (Lorraine).

> There are a lot of Nigerians educated out there. I mean this Western world, they associate them with sports (Chwime – interview).

> ...African people have been at the fore-front of many technologies but this is not widely documented – if at all...horticultural techniques pioneered by African women (ie digging sticks), which seems ironic as this continent is now primarily associated with famine and hunger...I am at present reading "Black Pioneers of Science and Invention" by Louis Haber that documents a number of exceptional and gifted Black men from as early as the 18th Century. They made a number of extremely significant contributions, their combined efforts include: pioneering electric lighting; inventing the gas mask and traffic lights; developing synthetic cortisone and other therapeutic drugs; new ways to sterilise foods and medical supplies; leading clinical anti-biotic research; perfecting techniques of preserving plasma and making blood banks possible; performing the first open-heart surgery... (Bella).

Bella suggests that there is a rich but hidden black history which is not generally known, which contributes to the continued narrow representation of black people. This is further perpetuated by the absence of control over the ways in which blackness is portrayed in the media. The review of media studies literature in Chapter 3 illustrated the under-representation of ethnic minorities in the structures of both the British and

US media industries (Campaign for Press and Broadcasting Freedom 1996: p.10; Tunstall 1977: pp.74-75; Tulloch 1990: pp.143-144; Silk and Silk 1990: pp.121-152). The research subjects demonstrated an awareness of the whiteness of film and television cultures, and the consequences for the representation of ethnic minorities:

> Watching Australian television was akin to fasting, the broadcast media industry seemed to be attempting to purify itself by undertaking its own form of ethnic cleansing. Australian television brought up almost all its characters 'white and bright', the remaining 'stains' were the minor roles which went to people of colour: in the years that *Neighbours* has been broadcast, there has never been an Aboriginal character. The producers believed they were depicting Australia's ethnic diversity when they cast an actor with dark brown hair. These images of Australianness combined with Crocodile Dundee, Sir Les, Kylie, Jason, Clive, Rolf and Skippy, make me wonder whether the White Australia policy is still in force in the broadcast media (Leung 2001).

> ...there was a girl called Sade – she sings...She's British Nigerian. I mean she's been here for ages. I know that she's British Nigerian. She must be and there's a few other ones, I can't remember their names, but I would like to see them somewhere in parliament – you understand what I am saying? It's like singing and sports that's what they're good for (Chwime – interview).

> Put a black family in *EastEnders* they are showed like – it's just like they put the hourglass on cos it's like 'how long will they last?'. They don't just move one of them, they move the whole lot, the whole family... (Roni – interview).

> There were a few black programmes on TV. Namely a comedy programme called *The Real McCoy*...and *The A Force*. These programmes covered a variety of black and ethnic issues. Unfortunately, these programmes are no longer shown on TV. The viewers rating were high amongst black people when these programmes were on, because it's not often we see black programmes on TV and when such a programme comes on the majority of black people (including myself) would tune in (Tessa).

> ...as soon as they have something really popular on, I find a lot of the viewers, mostly black, myself included, you tend to watch. After a few months they take it off and then they put something else on so it's never an ongoing thing when it comes to black viewing, black shows. It's always short-lived and I think they should put on a few more black comedy shows. Even if it's to talk about an island, not just about a holiday, going on holiday, they should portray a bit more on the Caribbean or even in Asia. They should give us a bit more ethnicity on the TV (Tessa – interview).

Chwime agrees with Hall's (1998b: p.43) argument that there are areas where black presence is the norm, sport being one. But she says that in spite of this, the 'us and them' dichotomy remains – 'that's what *they're* good for'. Difference is still represented in the media in terms of binary oppositions of black and white. Roni and Tessa suggest that this is also linked to the distance between media consumption and production, where the latter is primarily a white domain so that '*they* don't just move one of them, *they* move the whole lot', '*they* take it off and then *they* put something else on' or have the power to control the (in)visibility of ethnic minorities in the media. As Givanni (1995: p.1) proposes, access and representation are twin subjects: Roni and Tessa clearly feel excluded from the processes of media production and that they do not have access to the means to represent their ethnicity on film or television. Therefore, they speak as consumers of media images to those who produce them: '*they* should put on a few more black comedy shows'.

Other research subjects noticed the black/white dualism articulated in representations of their countries of origin. As Noori said, Bangladesh is consistently portrayed as a country victimised by poverty, famine and natural disasters.

> ...television programmes and the films...always shows the run down areas in Jamaica and bad topics are always discussed eg drugs, how many people got shot (Sha).

> I was watching a programme on the ITV called *Africa Today*, I was not feeling too comfortable about it because there were a lot of killings, and starvation... (Oyen).

> The part of the world I come from is often described as third world... (Chwime).

Again, Said's (1995: pp.1-3) notion of Orientalism is evident, but instead, developing countries are constructed in diametric opposition to developed nations like Britain. These represent the 'white gaze' or objectified depictions of national identity; and contrast markedly with the research subjects' perceptions, given that these are places with which they have a direct or symbolic affiliation. The research subjects counter these images of deprivation and deviance with their own representations of these nation states as abundant and productive:

> [Jamaicans are] dedicated workers and always....like to be in the limelight by having the latest car or the flash house and to be the first to have a gadget which just has been invented (Sha).

> Nigerian men are usually associated with farming, for example cocoa and sugarcane for export. Men used to work so hard because these cocoa plantation and sugarcane plantation were farmed manually (Oyen).

> Most Nigerians are business oriented...Young Nigerians study subjects such as economics, politics, medicine and [the] majority obtain degrees...I think hairdressing is one of our technologies, the braiding requires skill, calculation and experience. Other technologies are sewing, dressmaking, hand weaving with straws and pottery...Nigeria is rich in oil, cocoas and have the technology to extract oil from palm kernels (Chwime).

The position from which the research subjects represent their places of birth or origin is a subjective one, based on 'experiential authority' (Diawara 1993: p.11; Clifford 1988: p.35). Using tactics similar to those of independent black cinema, they attempt to contest racist media images and wrest representations of their ethnicities from the 'protective custody' (Guerrero 1993: p.239) of white media industries.

> I believe as England becomes more multi-racial, multi-ethnic and multi-cultural it will become more difficult to associate a particular technology with a particular race...Even profession-wise, it is difficult to pigeon-hole the African/Caribbean. Despite racism and the fact that the majority of African/Caribbeans are employed in the low paid unskilled jobs in factories, hospitals and hotels, their aspirations are quite high. As a matter of fact I do not have any African/Caribbean friends who do not have a computer at home or have either studied or are studying subjects linked with computer studies and other technologies such as media...I have never really associated any technology with ethnicity...I have considered it from a gender perspective. I grew up seeing women taking the lead in administration and secretarial work, many of them were given the opportunity to further their careers starting as word processing operators and moving on into computers. Although not the norm, I associated computers with women. I do believe that as with most professions technology will remain a white male dominated profession (Teti).

Teti is hopeful about future representations of her ethnicity, arguing that Britain's ethnic diversity will spawn more self-constructed and self-conscious images of blackness. But Berelson and Salter (1973: p.110) contend that racist media representations simply reflect racism in culture generally. So if the media institutions are predominantly white, the limited range of depictions of ethnic minorities that have been apparent in historical studies of popular culture will just continue: as Bobo (1993: p.273) suggests, racist media representations are merely reconstructed from previous media, from literature through film to television. As the research subjects themselves have acknowledged, both the structures of the media industries as well as the content they produce offer a white perspective of ethnic minorities, an outlook which is irreconcilable with their own experience. Considering their mostly pessimistic views of the broadcast media and yet given the 'utopian moment' of the Internet when they first went online (Dovey 1996: p.109), what did they anticipate in terms of ethnic presence on the Web prior to their introduction to it? How did they negotiate the discourses of liberation and dystopia associated with the Internet?

Techno-Phobias and Utopias: Expectations of the Web

In terms of representations of ethnicity, the research subjects mainly anticipated the Web to be much like the broadcast media. That is, they saw the Web as a continuum of television, reiterating and borrowing its depictions of ethnic minorities from the latter, as Bobo (1993: p.273) proposes. Certainly, the lack of black visibility which has pervaded media images throughout history (Silk and Silk 1990: p.128; Diawara 1992: p.11; Tunstall 1977: p.90) was expected, as was the online reiteration of issues of race and ethnicity that can be found in everyday life (Lockard 1999; Zipp 1997; Gajjala 1999).

> I don't think I would find much on the Net under the headings of British born Jamaican. If I did them under separate keyword searches, I still think there would be few results. Maybe a web site or two on Jamaica and even news on Jamaica's known reggae stars. There may be issues under the heading Black British (Askari).

Askari suggests that because there may not be an abundance of representations of her ethnicity, it is likely they would be located in the usual places where there is a black presence (Hall 1998b: p.43). As in media images, blackness would be marginalised to areas such as music:

> I think that if I were to surf the net I would find more black people on the entertainment pages, because when you look on the media that's how Black people are seen to be good at...I think that the media has to change the way it sees Black people (Sasha).

> I am really not sure what I might find if anything, but my guess would be information in relation to music or music equipment (Lorraine).

> There will a lots of sites considering I have dual nationality, of Nigeria and England. Sports is usually associated with blacks in general. There might be a few sites for music, which is one of the ways we express ourselves (Chwime).

> I imagine the internet would contain websites for artists representing African-American culture including music, literature, pictures (Roni).

> I have no idea what I would find on the Web sites. I guess I could find out about Africa, the Caribbean, Black History and Black music. I suspect a lot of it is American and probably dominated by the men, but I would not be surprised to find Black American women making an in-road (Teti).

As the research subjects viewed it, images of blackness on the Web, like in the media, would probably be consigned to the realms of sport and music. The expectation was that there would be a continuity with the usual ways black people have been portrayed throughout history as entertainers and by nature physically powerful (Hoch 1979: p.48; Silk and Silk 1990: p.viii; Tunstall 1977: pp.86-87). In addition, Chwime alludes to the dichotomies within which race is represented in the mutual exclusion of her Nigerianness and Englishness. That is, she expects to find sites about *either* Nigeria or England, rather than ones which offer a hybridised depiction of both, so that her Englishness is antithetical to other aspects of her ethnicity (Gilroy 1993: p.1). Her national affiliations, which are represented as irreconcilable, are translated into the binary oppositions of black and white (Hall 1981: p.41; Fanon 1967: p.9; Diawara 1993: p.11). As this has been the pattern of representation across various media technologies, the research subjects did not envisage that there would be much difference on the Web.

Teti refers to the constitution of the Web as a possible reason for these low expectations. Like Tunstall's (1977) view of the broadcast media as US-dominated, Teti perceives Web content to be mainly from the US. This is affirmed by statistics showing that of the 20 nations which constitute 90% of Internet users, the US makes up the largest proportion of the worlds 580-655 million online population: US Internet users outnumber those in China (the second highest) threefold (ClickZ 2004). Teti's perspective is also in accordance with claims that the Internet was and still is primarily a masculine domain (Apple 1992: p.118; Spender 1996: p.118; Interrogate the Internet

1996: pp.125-127; Squires 1996: p.200; Panos 1998; ClickZ 2002; Pastore 2000a, 2001) not only globally but also specifically in the UK (Pastore 2000a; Greenspan 2003). Therefore, the Web seemed far from able to represent the research subjects' identities as ethnic minority women living in Britain.

> I would probably find lots of Asian Web sites set up by professionals or academics dealing with things like Asian films...to Marriage Bureaux. For some of them there might be women involved but there would be a high ratio of men (Noori).

Noori anticipates the same gender hierarchies which she has experienced in the media to be reproduced on the Web. This seems astute given research showing 72% of Asian men using the Internet compared with 60% Asian women (ClickZ 2001). Furthermore, with Asians shown to be particularly active online, and users of the Internet increasingly contributing online content (Greenspan 2004), both online use and production can be deemed to be male-biased where Asian representation is concerned (Nakamura 2002: p.115). Because of the preponderance of male users of the Internet, she sees that the representation of women on the Web will be constructed for the 'male gaze', for example, as future wives for Asian men. It will be another extension of the ways in which women are depicted in the broadcast media (Jones 1993: p.253; hooks 1992: p.62): present in the image but absent at the level of both production and consumption.

Like Noori, other research subjects believed that the content of the Web would not be intended for them. Instead, it was predicted that much Web information would be for tourists planning holidays to the research subjects' countries of birth or origin:

> The Jamaican website would contain lots of information about the island's most beautiful and breathtaking landscapes, including the vibrant reggae music that Jamaican people have come to symbolise (Roni).

> By looking at the web sites it would illustrate how the island looks and what holiday resorts it might have, talk about the different types of foods...I feel that the information would be very brief... (Sha).

> I think I will find some basic explanation about my country...Copper mines and the development of copper materials...Latin American music and dance...one of the world biggest fishing fleet...thanks for the technology in refrigeration and transport we can import from Chile various product of agriculture such as fruit, vegetables and wine (Gina).

> If I were to surf the Internet, I would expect to find a lot about South Africa, which will include holidaying in South Africa, diamond, safaris, political monuments. As for Nigeria I would expect to see something about oil exploration (Oyen).

> I would be outraged if I did not find a wealth of information on Africa, from culture to demography...I assume I would be hard pressed to find a site specific to the way I describe my ethnicity. How many of us [African-born Black British citizens] are out there? (Bella).

Thus, it was presumed that representations of ethnicity on the Web would be confined to 'where you are from' (Gilroy 1990/1: pp.3-16), and shackled to geography and historical landmarks. These become the visible markers of ethnicity in much the same way as skin colour is the identifier of race: they (over)simplify the complexity of ethnic identity. They are also the basis for exoticising those places and populations: because they are holiday destinations, they are depicted as foreign to the 'white gaze' of the targeted reader/spectator, and black people are, once again, represented as alien (Gilroy 1987: p.31). As Hall (1998a) argues, the Internet extends upon the recycled traveller's tales from colonial explorations of Africa.

The pessimistic outlook of the research subjects to the possibilities of the Web echo those ideologies of cyberspace which bemoan its commercialisation (see Schiller 1996: p.xv; Johnson 1996: p.92; Campaign for Press and Broadcasting Freedom 1996: p.10). Indeed, the research subjects did suggest that the Web's representations of ethnicity would probably be limited to the commercial interests of tourism. There is also the implication that where commerce is concerned, they are not the ideal consumer because they are members of ethnic minorities. They represent niche rather than mass markets, as exemplified in Tessa's anecdote about the majority of cosmetics advertised being completely inappropriate for her. In the case of these Web images of overseas locales, such places are neither exotic or foreign to the research subjects: rather, they represent 'home' and the familiar.

Nevertheless, Tessa was one of the exceptions in terms of her hopeful anticipations of the depiction of ethnicity on the Web:

> I was basically looking for positive black women in England...British black women and a site to say there was a group of black women from the Caribbean who was born here...any organisation that dealt with black issues in the sense of children, education... (Tessa – interview).

She expected to locate a virtual community of the kind which Rheingold (1992) speaks of, or even an electronic diasporic community (Mitra 1997: p.58), whereby the connections across the diaspora are facilitated through computers and the Internet. The capacity for the Web to provide this representation to ethnic minorities is not doubted by Tessa because she does not perceive Web production and consumption as male-oriented:

> I was a tom boy at an early age, I would ride my brother's bike and would sometimes help my father with his carpentry. I was not exposed to computers until I was about 14 years old. From then on I knew I wanted to work with computers, I never saw it as masculine, because I always felt that whatever a man can do women can do it just as well (Tessa).

Like Tessa, Champagne also hints at an inherent freedom about the Web, that it is not only genderless, but classless and raceless as well. Her position is reminiscent of the upbeat discourses of the Internet during its 'utopian moment', which ignored the structural inequalities constraining access to it (see Negroponte 1995; Carstephen and Lambiase 1998: 124). It is part of the 'narrative of indifference which is inherent in the term "the global village"' (Zurawski 1997), as it suggests a world devoid of barriers.

> Technology for me has always been available as a child, as my mother worked for a world famous toy store. I had first hand in the latest games, computer chess, little handheld games and remote control games. My mother also purchased games that could improve my spelling, reading and math. We also had a music system. We could listen to the types of music we liked and teletext television to find out information. All of this was available to everyone and ethnicity did not come into it (Champagne).

Champagne's expectations of the Web imply 'virtual equal treatment' (Nguyen and Alexander 1996: pp.103-104), where ethnicity does not matter. Mason (1999) calls this 'erase-ism' because of its colour-blindness: if ethnicity cannot be seen, then it can be ignored.

Given the marked contrast between the research subjects' largely negative expectations of representations of ethnicity on the Web, and the couple that were exceptionally positive; it is worth examining the transitions in these perspectives following their introduction to the Web. How did their interactions with the Web and their searches for representations of ethnicity shift their perceptions of the technology?

Digital Disappointment and Electronic Elation: Experiences of the Web

Following their journeys into the Web, several of the research subjects were impressed by the abundance of material on their ethnicities they found. The sheer quantity of texts available formed the basis for their general optimism about the Web:

> I thought what I would find on the Web would be mostly to do with music but actually, looking inside the Web, it wasn't all to do with music (Lorraine).

> ...on the Internet, there is so much information you can get carried away. You can find out about music from your country, about your culture, about laws, you can even get food manuals and there is so many things. You can try to learn the language and sometimes bring on the sound thing, it will say the words for you. If I could afford it, I think I would love the Internet. You feel the world is so small with the Internet (Rosie – interview).

> ...going into a Web site and finding so many things about my country and about where I come from...I was amazed about how much was there. If you want to contact people, if you want to buy books from there, United States for example, in my own language. I have been completely amazed, I am very happy (Gina – interview).

> I found out other things I didn't know about my parents' homeland...about the different artists and traditions. Different types of things from the islands that they're famous for...the background and the history of what actually happened which was good (Sha – interview).

The amount of information found on the Web gave rise to new possibilities for learning as well as representation. Melkote and Liu's (1999) research shows the educational value of the Internet in terms of informing Chinese students living in the US about events in their mother country. Likewise, the amazement of the research subjects lay in their discovery of new dimensions to their ethnicity, offering the transformed and reinvented configurations of ethnicity which Nakamura (2002) did not find in LambdaMOO. Like Berry and Martin's study of gay Asian online communities (2000: pp.74-81), the Web compensated for what was not available offline. The surprise of the research subjects at content on the Web which was relevant and constructive to their ethnicities mimics my own. My analogy for the Web is that it is a veritable buffet compared with the strict set menu of portrayals of ethnic minorities in film and television.

> ...I have more recently been salivating over the new broadcast media technology that is the World Wide Web. Within it is the potential for a feast of texts and images which illustrate the hybridity and diversity of the Chinese diaspora; for catering for special requests for ethnicity to be represented in ways which avoid exclusion and essentialism; and for a taste of depictions of ethnicity which undermine traditional ones seen in the broadcast media (Leung 2001).

> ...from newspapers, it's only what newspapers want you to know but from the Internet it's the information that person has chosen to give you so that is much better than tabloid newspapers. I would prefer the Internet anytime...it's just great fun (Rosie – interview).

Rosie's preference for the Internet over newspapers lies in the different processes of production. She suggests that there are vested interests in the news agendas of the press while there is perhaps more opportunity to participate in production on the Internet than in the press. This is in accordance with claims that there is a close connection between production and consumption on the Internet (Dery 1994: p.9; McDonald 1995: p.538; Plant 1997; Mitra and Cohen 1999; p.182). But as discussed in Chapter 4, the notion of the Internet being an 'information market' (Rheingold 1992) where ideas and opinions are freely exchanged is characteristic of the discourses of liberty and freedom which were associated with it in the late 1990s. At the other end of the spectrum are the more cynical perspectives of the Internet, evident in some of the research subjects' expectations of the Web, which propose that it merely reiterates the racisms which exist in wider society (Lockard 1999).

For a number of the research subjects, their expectations were not altered after their forays into the Web. Their experiences led them to believe the processes of production on the Web to be an extension of those of the broadcast media, for example, in the overwhelming US dominance of the Web, a feature which also emerged from Zurawski's (1998) research with ethnically diverse Internet users.

> They're all African-American, there's no British Web sites. I haven't been able to find any (Askari – interview)

> On the American web sites you can find it all, there is untold web sites...A wealth of knowledge. Sometimes I wish I was a black American. I would probably feel more empowered, more at ease with my ethnicity. In America I found music web sites, not just

> music web sites because they were black specifically what I said was part of my identity, rap music, reggae music, R&B music, soul and the history of it, the key players in it, all of it. It also tells you about what effects the environment has on black people, the percentage of black people in certain occupations, the way black people have been treated. It went through all the Civil Rights, Martin Luther King, all these black people, famous black people you had never even heard of. It was fascinating. There is a black woman who is responsible for the biggest army regiment, it's the biggest in America and it's a black woman who is responsible for it. You would never find that kind of information over here. All these different programmes and all these different black influences, Oprah Winfrey, you can get her biography on the Web site. A black man who is a lawyer for the President, advisor friend, it explains all that. I could go on for ages to tell what I found on the black web sites. My keywords were Afro, obviously without the British...I put Afro Caribbean women actually, it was amazing I could have gone on forever (Roni – interview).

> I found quite a lot actually. A lot of them were African-American I found. When I put in African and did a search, a lot of them were African-American, black unity...There have been a few that are British based – like BlackNet... (Bella – interview).

> I found that most of the Web sites were from America, very little information from Britain...As much as we are all black, life in America is not totally the same as in England. The pace is faster and there are more black groups in America to cater for Afro-American. We (black women) immigrated to the States, England from our native countries, Africa, the Caribbean, we share the same economic pressures and failures/success in our lives and in our families. I would have liked to see more sites on black women in Britain on the Internet (Tessa).

Just as many of the positive representations of blackness that the research subjects had encountered in film and television had come from the US, so too had the affirmative depictions of blackness on the Web. The Web has its equivalents of black film in that there were texts which had constructive portrayals of black people, which dealt with issues of race and ethnicity, which were produced from a black perspective and intended for black consumers (Ross 1996: p.154; Reid 1993: p.2); but apparently no British counterparts. In fact, any representations of ethnicity on the Web seemed, by and large, to be from the US. Likewise, Buruma's (1999) examination of Chinese Web sites shows that many were set up from North America. There is a sense from the research subjects that the US is more advanced in terms of its recognition of and catering for black media audiences as well as Internet users: as Tessa said in her interview, 'they have their own shows, they have a lot more than we have over in England but I think we are a little bit behind over here.' While the research subjects felt a solidarity with the 40 million strong African-American population (Mashengele 1997: pp.311-315; Morrissey 2003) through their blackness, they were also aware of their marginalisation because of their Britishness. This is understandable considering that Web users in all of western Europe combined numbered 23.7 million compared with 51.6 million in the US as at 1998 (Panos 1998). In 1999, 15% of the UK population was using the Internet compared with 25% of the US population (Pastore 1999). In 2000, this increased to 27% of the UK population (Pastore 2000a). From 2002 to 2004, the number of UK Internet users increased from 29 million to 34 million, while those in the US grew from 166 million to 182 million (Greenspan 2002; ClickZ 2004). The more specific the research subjects' ethnicities became, the more their minority status was exacerbated, as the difficulty of the task of representation increased:

> I could relate more to the sites that I found using the keywords Black British although this term does not reflect my history (Bella).

> I did not find anything that triggered a sense of belonging or ethnic bonding, but there was quite a lot of information on the Caribbean and Africa (Teti).

> I think it is a shame that we are not more catered for on the Internet. But obviously not enough British-born Jamaicans are involved in the Net and providing those kind of services (Askari).

> ...in England there was none and I couldn't believe that there was none and I wondered if it was the keywords I was using...The only thing [I found] on Yahoo is a few articles by black people but nothing to do with ethnicity, just that they are black and that is how the British web sites define ethnicity, if a black person wrote something...that is how they define Afro Caribbean Black British – a black man asking for a pen pal...a black man working for the *Guardian*...he is black but it had nothing to do with how we live in Britain as black people and what affects us as black people in Britain, I didn't get any of that information, I think it's disgusting, I really am disgusted with it (Roni – interview).

For Teti, there was no membership to any virtual community (Rheingold 1992), cyborg diaspora (Gajjala 1999) or electronic ethnic neighbourhood (Mitra 1997: p.62, 72). Instead, the connections appeared lax, loosely held together as they are in Chinese cyberspace by certain symbols and historical events (Buruma 1999).

Rather than experiencing significant changes in representations of black British ethnicities, the research subjects saw evidence of more of the same of what Nakamura (2002) identified as 'cybertypes', racial stereotypes in online environments. Her findings showed ethnic and gender stereotypes enacted in the characters of the LambdaMOO, particularly where the characters were Asian females. This eroticised representation of Asian women on the Web was both anticipated and confirmed by Noori:

> I guessed that there would be a lot of marriage bureaus and there was. When we went into it there was a whole lot, I think about 10 or 12 lists of mail-order brides and stuff like that...I was searching on HotBot and first I typed in "Asian Bangladeshi" and all I got was about the population and ethnic minority in Britain and the rest was just mail-order brides, marriage bureaus, something for single men and stuff like that (Noori – interview).

> None of these Web sites were aimed at women, they had men in mind and weren't bothered if women accessed them or not...apart from the one written by women, the rest are not going out of their way to cover issues important to women (Noori).

As in media representations of black women, the depiction of Asian women on the Web was intended for men. Noori felt alienated as a consumer of the Web because of her gender and ethnicity, showing an awareness of the imbalance in the Internet's gender ratio (Apple 1992: p.118; Spender 1996: p.118; ; Interrogate the Internet 1996: pp.125-127; Squires 1996: p.200; Panos 1998; ClickZ 2002; Pastore 2000a, 2001). As a woman, she was not the intended reader for these texts: that is, she is not the 'average' white, educated, affluent, employed Internet user (Terranova 1996: p.72; Hoffman and Novak 1998; Kendall 1999: p.63; Pastore 2000; ClickZ 2001; Greenspan 2003b). As an Asian woman, she experienced similar objectified representations seen in other media. As a Bangladeshi woman, her ethnicity is rendered invisible, subsumed under Asianness. Its specificity, like that of black Britishness, poses particular challenges to its representation:

> I couldn't find anything because I am Bangladeshi and I am a woman and there's nothing (Noori – interview).

Noori seems to consider herself simultaneously unrepresented and misrepresented, which in many respects, summarises the portrayal of ethnic minorities throughout history. Other research subjects had the same reactions to representations of their countries of birth:

> ...there wasn't much information on Nigeria apart from things like the role of politics, there wasn't much things of interest, killing and things like that so I wasn't really really prepared to go into and reflecting back to things that really irritate you or haunt you. It wasn't a good memory to really dig into...there wasn't much on the traditional things that we used to do back home. Women used to weave clothes you know this African material they used to do by hand and things like that...So I was expecting to see things on the Internet but I was disappointed that there wasn't much like that apart from politics and killing and killing so I wasn't too pleased (Oyen – interview).

Oyen detected a distinct masculinist orientation in Web representations of Nigeria in that the activities of Nigerian women were not apparent in either the production, representation or consumption of these images. But unlike in film and television, where the 'male gaze' has focused on the female as object (hooks 1992: p.62; Jones 1993: p.253), the gaze is, instead, white, and bears down on its male antithesis, dark Africa, which it constructs as barbaric and base (Hoch 1979: pp.44-46). So Oyen's point of contention is not only with the depiction of ethnicity itself, but who is the agent of representation and what is the basis of their authority to speak on behalf of her ethnicity? It seems to confirm Zurawski's (1996) claim that 'techno-elites' are controlling and shaping the representation of ethnicity on the Web. Indeed, Hall's (1998a) and Nakamura's (2002: p.xvi) critique of William Gibson's *Neuromancer* shows his futuristic representations of African ethnicity in cyberspace to be 'true to age-old racial stereotypes'. Historically, the West has claimed the right to name and 'speak for' the Orient and others it has defined as alien (Said 1995: p.3). However, in the interests of self-representation, this mandate has also been seized from within by leaders of ethnic groups, communities and nation states:

> I found there was lots of things about my country where I was born...Sudan. They had things on the money they use, like the geography of the country, the best place to go to for tourists, the food they eat. All that kind of stuff that I didn't think would be on the Internet...There was things on it that I didn't even know were in my country. They have places where you can go, like fun fair amusement places that they put on the Internet but when I was there I don't remember seeing those kind of things at all. I think they had just put that there for tourists so they'd see it and be impressed with it. When I was there things were never like that. On the Internet it says that there's plenty of food and everyone can eat...but it's not true because when I was there – even now when I get letters from my friends and stuff things are really hard. Things are really hard so I wish they wouldn't put stuff like that on the Internet...most of it is untrue. It's just to make the country look good enough for tourists to come and spend their money (Sasha – interview).

> When I did look up a Web site about where I was born, most of the information was not true so I did not feel that I would honestly write down all that information which was not true from what I remember and from what my friends who are back home tell me about what is going on there (Sasha).

Sasha challenges the official representations on the Web of Sudan using her own 'experiential authority' (Clifford 1988: p.35). She doubts the authenticity of the claims being made about Sudan, in part, because they are being directed at users and readers for whom the country might be considered exotic or 'otherworldly' (Hall 1998a), as well as because the legitimacy of such information on the Web, as discussed in Chapter 4, is difficult to verify. As the Web is a minority medium of 'demassified' consumers (Nguyen and Alexander 1996: p.110; Mitra 1997: p.73), a critical mass of outraged opponents to these statements is unlikely. The Web becomes a forum where information is presented (Zurawski 1996) or broadcast (Chandler and Roberts-Young 1998), rather than discussed. If that is the case, then the Web is a space where the struggle for representation occurs, between ethnicity's construction from without and within (Werbner 1997: p.18).

Fixing Ethnicity

While there was a consensus amongst the research subjects that media representations of their ethnicities were inadequate in terms of quality and quantity, there were differing responses to the Web's capacity to extend and/or transcend these depictions. Because the research tasks asked them to find Web sites which represented, as much as possible, how they located themselves ethnically, most chose texts which were consistent with the loose definitions given of their own ethnicities and produced by fellow members of their ethnic communities. This could be considered a rejection of the media's 'white gaze' and narrow portrayals of ethnicity.

However, this is not to say that there was a scarcity of representations of ethnicity on the Web which were constructed from without or seemingly produced from outside the realm of personal experience of that ethnicity, and which represented ethnicity as static and concrete. Indeed, my own and a few of the research subjects' journeys into cyberspace found a number of such Web texts, although our reasons for selecting them differed substantially. The Web sites are discussed here in the context of their appropriation of the media's representational strategies.

I was motivated by my personal interest in locating any contemporary Web-based examples of Orientalism, and identifying who was claiming to 'speak for' the Orient (Said 1995: p.20) and on behalf of myself as an 'Oriental'. Indeed, traditional media representations of Chinese ethnicity seemed to have been transferred to the Web, as if the Web were the logical successor of the historical constructions of race (Bobo 1993: p.273). This confirms Krysmanski's et al (1999) claim that digital technology merges with, rather than replaces, previous media.

Just as the Orient has been depicted as diametrically opposed to the West (Said 1995: pp.1-3), there were examples on the Web which articulated this, where Chineseness was represented as mutually exclusive, even fundamentally contradictory, to white or Western subjectivity. The first was a Web site publicising a video entitled 'Chinese Canadians' which purported to give a 'first-hand account' of business and community life in Vancouver's Chinatown.[1] The 'first-hand account' implies a kind of 'experiential authority' (Clifford 1988: p.35), but the authority, in this case, is not a person of Chinese ethnicity. Rather, the technology, the medium of video, is endowed with representational authority: it captures the 'reality' of Chineseness as if it were through the eyes of a Chinese person. Thus, it objectifies Chineseness by claiming it can be seized and portrayed in its entirety, just as notions of race have attempted to define blackness as static and unchanging.

'Western influence is apparent everywhere', the video's abstract proclaimed, as if this hybridisation is somehow surprising. There is a sense that this transcultural mixing whereby 'boundaries are crossed; cultures are mingled; identities become blurred' (Robins 1991: p.42) is unexpected. It suggests that as a result of this process, authenticity is eroded, something is lost. It is a regressive construction of ethnicity founded upon an idealised and imagined past (Ross 1996: p.xi), a sentimental notion of 'One China' (Buruma 1999) rather than an ethnicity comprised of numerous dialects and diverse inflections.

Chinese ethnicity's connotations of distinct and ancient cultural traditions, customs and religions is seen in other media, such as in *kung fu* movies, which Lee (1991: pp.52-72) argues represent Chinese values in their preoccupation with loyalty to and vengeance for family and friends. Perhaps it is because the Web site refers to the older medium of video that it almost necessarily borrows from these previous means of representing Chineseness.

The translation of representations of ethnicity from an older medium to the Web was also seen in another Web text called 'Ethics and Ethnic Newspapers', a feature article in the online edition of *The Age*, an Australian urban daily newspaper.[2] It examined a complaint made to the Australian Press Council against the *Daily Chinese*

Herald, a Chinese language newspaper published in Melbourne and Sydney, about the style in which a rape case was reported. It argued that ethnic media organisations are a law unto themselves because of the lack of regulation accorded to ethnic newspapers and magazines in Australia: 'As well as being almost impossible to monitor properly, the ethnic media, which in some cases is owned or part-owned by international interests, is exempt from the cross-media rules to which mainstream newspapers are subject' (Bone 1996) . This representation of Chinese ethnicity on the Web continues in the vein of depictions of ethnic minorities on film and television as 'problems' (Tulloch 1990: pp.143-144; Pines 1992: pp.9-10). The premise that the activities of ethnic media must be policed is reminiscent of the notion that ethnic minorities require control and surveillance. This is seen historically in colonial representations of black people as needing to be tamed by white imperialists (Hoch 1979: p.48; Silk and Silk 1990: p.viii; Pieterse 1992: p.78). In this case, the 'white gaze' is assumed by institutions such as *The Age* and the Australian Press Council, which ensure the activities of ethnic newspapers such as the *Daily Chinese Herald* continue to occupy a marginal position and ultimately do not threaten the status quo. In its portrayal of Chinese ethnicity, the Web article distinguishes between acceptable and unacceptable Chineseness, by including the views of the Chinese Inter-church Committee, a Christian association, to justify its condemnation of the *Daily Chinese Herald.* Thus, it is more than the behaviour of ethnic minorities which is regulated in this Web example, but their representation as well: the Christian articulation of Chinese ethnicity is encouraged while its politically incorrect expression is depicted negatively.

This kind of representation of ethnicity may be as much informed by the genre of news reportage as it is by the practices of the press or print media. That is, an article such as the one above is newsworthy, according to Hall et al (1978: pp.53-55) because the event it reports is extraordinary, has negative consequences and assumes a consensus against the actions of the *Daily Chinese Herald.* Credibility is given to the Australian Press Council as the arbitrator of the dispute and its 'objective' judgement, in part because it is one of the bureaucracies which media organisations rely upon for their news (Herman and Chomsky 1988: p.22). The depiction of Chineseness as a struggle between good and bad is given legitimacy because it has been sanctioned officially.

Similarly, the well-respected reputation of a media institution like the BBC lends weight to its news, despite criticisms of its portrayal of ethnic minorities and the biases of its white, male, Conservative, middle class management (Curran 1997; Tulloch 1990: pp.143-144). An article from BBC News Online on the Web selected by Gina[3] reports on the resignation of the Chilean Defence Minister, but associates him with Pinochet and human rights abuses. Therefore, like the Web text discussed previously, the depiction of Chile is one of 'problem', in which those in power cannot be controlled and cannot manage the country which they govern. As there are no direct quotes from representatives of the Chilean government, the BBC is the primary source of information and representation, so it speaks for both itself as well as the Chilean government.

In another of my Web examples, an article from an online edition of *Asiaweek*,[4] Loveard (1997) employs the tactics of Orientalism in speaking for both East and West

(Said 1995: p.3). But instead of emphasising difference, he stresses the commonality of Australianness:

> The young guy gamboling in the surf at Bondi with his girlfriend had 'Australia' printed large on the back of his swimming costume. The pair were a microcosm of the scene on Australia's best known beach, enjoying the arrival of warm weather like the thousands of others there. Both were unmistakably Chinese. Later they sat down amongst the others on the beach. Greeks, Lebanese, Arabs, South Americans and East Europeans by appearance and language, they were at this moment typical native Australians, who like nothing better than sun and surf (Loveard 1997).

Loveard speaks on behalf of ethnic minorities as an English-born migrant who empathises with the discrimination they face as he has been subject to being called 'Pommie bastard'. Yet he resorts to the same representational strategies as racism in his definition of ethnicities according to physiology (Hernton 1988: p.xii; Bottomley and de Lepervanche 1988: p.33): his 'unmistakable' assumption of Chineseness and other ethnicities 'by appearance'; and the treatment of such ethnic diversity as the same (Hall et al 1992: p.308) in terms of their 'typical native [Australianness], who like nothing better than sun and surf.'

The Web articles discussed so far in this chapter borrow from the traditions of the press and broadcasting, not only in terms of their direct connections with those media institutions, but also in the context of their news gathering techniques and representational practices. To see the Web as an extension of previous media not only highlights the background against which ethnic minorities have been represented over the course of time, but can also make it more visible than it otherwise might have been. The Web becomes another means of perpetuating the 'white gaze', often in ways that were not so obvious before: as detailed in Chapter 5, because texts on the Web are not at all coherently organised, and not all accessible at any one time (Kahle 1997; Fuller and Lovink 1999), it is possible to encounter Web texts that are not as accessible through other media. For example, while scholarly texts are traditionally confined to the peripheries of the print media, there were a number of academic contributions to the representation of Chinese ethnicity on the Web.

One was a Web-based abstract of a research study undertaken at Stockholm University.[5] Entitled 'Consuming the Other: Representations of Western Women in Chinese Women's Magazine Advertising', it argues that Chinese popular culture is subject to an imperialising Western aesthetic in its images of women. In accordance with the practices of Orientalism, it establishes a dichotomy between East and West (Said 1995: p.2) in terms of the relationship between Chinese and Western women. Furthermore, it refers to the West as a complete entity, powerful in its ability to pervade the Chinese media and dominate its images. The cultural imperialism thesis used here, whereby Chinese women consumers fall victim to the 'unrelenting, all-absorbing, linear process' (Ang 1996: p.152) of Westernisation, has extended from 'hypodermic needle' theories about the effects of television to fears that the Internet will compound the world's Americanisation (see Spender 1996: p.118).

This Web text claims to speak for both sides (East and West), yet simultaneously asserts that it attempts to develop 'still nascent understandings of Chinese consumer culture and of contemporary China in general' (Johansson 1997). That is, its representation of Chinese ethnicity is for the purpose of furthering the West's, admittedly rudimentary, knowledge of Chineseness. Therefore, it is clear that the ideal consumer of this Web page is not someone like myself, who identifies as Chinese. This became apparent in another academic Web text, 'Chinese in Australia: Challenging the Generalisations',[6] a report on research which found that the Chinese population of Western Australia were not a homogenous group but spoke different Chinese dialects. This information is hardly a revelation to me, so although knowledge about Chineseness is being broadcast across global networks for apparently educational purposes, it is to an audience which excludes the parties that are being discussed.

This exemplifies the Orientalist authority, of which Said (1995: pp.2, 20) was so critical, whereby the representation of Chineseness is completely out of the hands of Chinese people. Instead, knowledge of Chinese ethnicity is sought from those with academic authority, rather than 'experiential authority' (Clifford 1988: p.35). Chineseness is being depicted but is neither produced nor consumed from within the realm of personal experience of Chinese ethnicity. This is also evident in a Web-based message board on Chinese-Australian immigration history,[7] the original message being an appeal to academics for their expertise and assistance:

> I am a postgraduate student whose broad research topic is the nature of the relationship between Chinese in Australia and their places of origin from 1900 to 1950 with special reference to Zhongshan county. What I am seeking is contact with scholars who may be able to assist in locating relevant source material in Zhongshan and/or in directing me to further studies... (Williams 1997).

Here ethnicity is defined in terms of fixed geographical boundaries which tie Chineseness to a 'homeland'. There is no reference to how it is articulated locally in terms of an ethnic community in Australia (Gillespie 1995: p.6). This approach to examining ethnicity is quite averse to the one which my own research has employed: as discussed in Chapter 5, the personal experience of the research subjects, including myself, has been central to how ethnicity is conceptualised in this study. But even while autobiography has been used in this study as a rejection of 'objective' or 'certain' knowledge (Stanley 1997) so that ethnicity is not seen to be prescriptive or static, the Web examples I have shown demonstrate that scholars still construct it in such a way, that it continues to be represented and theorised from outside the subject and divorced from lived experience.

However, in many instances, as mentioned earlier in the chapter, the research subjects themselves resorted to representing their ethnicities as fixed, for example, through geography in order to give it a tangibility. This is seen in the Web texts selected by Gina, which featured maps of Latin America from the BGS Map Library[8] and KPMG.[9] This visual representation of 'where you are from' (Gilroy 1990/1: pp.3-16) helps Gina to articulate her ethnicity in a concrete way. Having found this difficult to do herself as 'most of the time people [think that] I am Spanish' (interview), she defers to scientific knowledge to do this for her. The dearth of readily available images of her ethnicity in popular culture is compensated somewhat by her appropriation of objectified scientific ones from the Web.

There also seems to be an element of identity tourism in the research subjects' interactions with Web representations of ethnicity produced from the 'white gaze', similar to that described by Nakamura (2002) in her study of characters in LambdaMOO. Just as young, white males adopt and play Asian characters in LambdaMOO so they can enact someone they cannot be in everyday life – one might call it a form of experiential learning – the research subjects reverse this process by looking to 'objective' forms of knowledge about their ethnicities through which they learn about things outside their own experiences. This type of tourism is a way of taking a hiatus from real life by travelling virtually to exotic places and living viacriously through the Internet (Nakamura 2002: p.40), yet it is also a means of strengthening diasporic connections to a conceptual 'home' (Mallapragada 2000: pp.179-185). This is illustrated in one of the Web texts selected by Sha, Caribbean-On-Line, which was sponsored by American Express:[10] 'There was a Web site that was looking at the different parts of Jamaica, the famous tourist parts like Ocho Rios is supposed to have good beaches...I didn't realise how close the Bahamas were to Jamaica...' (Sha – interview).

The site categorises Jamaica according to restaurants, shops and hotels. It claims an ethnic expertise which Sha admits she does not possess herself. The commercial orientation of the site and its representation of Jamaica does not faze Sha as it would many critics who argued that the corporatisation of the Web has inevitably reduced its content to the discourse of the market (see Schiller 1996: p.87; Johnson 1996: pp.94-96; Campaign for Press and Broadcasting Freedom 1996: p.10). Instead, Sha engages with the text and positions herself as its intended reader, as a foreigner to Jamaica, using the capacity of the Web to reconfigure time and space to partake in what Zurawski (1997) calls 'global tourism', to bring the unfamiliar to one's doorstep. But the outcome, according to Nakamura (2002: p.42), whether intentional or not, is often to 'fix the boundaries of cultural identity', to objectify it or to give it a static definition. To a certain extent, Sha does distance herself from her Jamaican ethnicity as we saw earlier in the chapter, but she clearly also has an insight into it that many tourists to Jamaica would not: that is, she would not be the targeted user of this site. Her choice of this site is indicative of her dissociation with her Jamaicanness but she also adapts it for her purposes, as an educational resource rather than as a travel guide, similar to the the strategies ethnic media audiences employ to derive pleasure from images created by white media industries for white viewers (Reid 1993: p.135; hooks 1992: pp.291-293; Diawara 1993: p.215).

Where there were commercial Web sites which attempted to appeal directly to ethnic minority users, these were not entirely successful. One example is the Australian Chinese Golden Pages, an interactive business directory for Chinese communities.[11] The option of viewing the site in Chinese characters after downloading special software demonstrates a cultural sensitivity. But the site does not provide any specialist advice or information. With hyperlinks such as 'shopping news', 'vehicle information' and 'adult sites and links', it mostly lists the names and addresses of businesses which could otherwise be found in a standard telephone directory. There are only a few instances where Chinese businesses are advertised. So the service provided to Chinese Web users is only cosmetic, akin to television's 'Cosby-isation' (its substitution of black characters in roles which could otherwise be played by white people) or what Hall (1995: p.22) calls the 'coconut' effect. Given that the site was produced by WebMedia Pty Ltd, one of the first and largest Web developers in the UK (Waldman 1998), the representation of Chinese ethnicity remains in the 'protective custody' (Guerrero 1993: p.239) of white, mainstream production in that it claims to 'speak for' the Chinese community by furnishing it with the information it deems it needs. This is not to say that the representation of ethnicity should only be left to ethnic minorities, or can only transcend simplification when it is self-constructed.

Rather, I am arguing for an awareness of the complexity of ethnicity in its representation, from whatever position this is taking place; that it should attempt to articulate ethnicity's dynamism, hybridity and constant reinvention (Ross 1996: p.xi). Moreover, there needs to be self-reflexivity on the part of the producer of such images, a consciousness of their relationship and responsibility to the ethnic communities they are depicting – in much the same way that as a researcher, I have had to be explicit about my role in representing the research subjects. This sensitivity was evident in a commercial Web site, 'Master Lu's Fortune Cookies' which had some sort of advertising function.[12] Its stylised fonts to mimic Chinese characters and the centrality of the fortune cookies demonstrates a knowledge of stereotypical signifiers of Chineseness, but its cartoon quality and the use of cariacatures suggest that they are being employed ironically. As it is well known that fortune cookies did not originate from China, but were an American invention, the producers of this site also seem to be declaring their Chineseness to be spurious, even non-existent. It is almost confirmed when the user is invited to crack open one of the three fortune cookies. Instead of a profound Confucian proverb, I was given the message: 'Small gifts will best maintain friendship'.

In place of the supposedly traditional Chinese values advocating loyalty and duty (Lee 1991: pp.52-72) conventionally found in fortune cookie messages was the promotion of Western materialism and consumer culture. The humour of the text exposes this representation of Chinese ethnicity (as well as its producers) as fraudulent and its primary motivation to be advertising and championing consumerism. The willingness of this Web text to declare its interests, to knowingly represent Chineseness but at the same time without making any claim to authenticity or to represent the Chinese community, makes it an enigma. In many respects, it is far more difficult to decipher whether it is a mocking self-construction of Chinese ethnicity, or a cheeky but astute attempt to represent it from outside the realm of personal experience (like the players in LambdaMOO) – than the other Web texts examined which automatically assert authority and validity in their depictions of ethnicity through association with other media and appropriation of their representational practices.

Conclusions

The findings presented in this chapter provide an insight into the ways the Web continues the traditions of the print and broadcast media in terms of its representations of ethnic minorities. This is most clearly illustrated where there is a direct connection with an older media form and/or a media organisation. Thus, news articles on the Web tended to reproduce their corresponding print-based versions and the processes of depicting ethnicity within the media institutions involved. Likewise, academic Web texts seemed to entrench the scholarly practice of speaking on behalf of minorities. This suggests that the Web is being deployed merely as another form of distribution for the same content and, as Nakamura (2002) found, 'cybertypes' – racist representations translated for new media.

These recurring patterns of ethnic representation in the media were more than evident to the research subjects. Their experiences of media consumption confirmed the gross simplification and dichotomisation in portrayals of ethnicity that have been shown in previous research studies. As a result, they were cautious in their expectations of the Web, but their increasing interactions with it spawned an awareness of its possibilities as a new technology to generate new representational practices and politics (Gillespie 1995: p.10), ones which are more reflective of how they construct their own diverse and complex ethnicities. This was also the case for those who sought Web representations of ethnicity which were fixed by geography or scientific 'facts' as these were a beacon by which to navigate the uncertainties of their ethnic identities.

While this seemingly wealth of representational potential resonates with the discourses of freedom that have pervaded the Internet, it is interesting to note that it was a commerical Web site which managed to humorously reappropriate and thereby critique traditional signifiers of (Chinese) ethnicity. The Web as a manifestation of the ultimate free market is played out in the aforementioned commercial site. In the appeal to a niche market of Web consumers, it sought a representation of ethnicity which went beyond the historical formulae. If the free marketeers are to be believed, then such solutions to the problem of lack of ethnic representation can be developed through technological enterprise. However, it seems to owe itself more to innovation, which can only be fully realised with an embracing of the specificities of the Web and a refusal to be bound by the representational practices of previous media forms. For example, the interactivity of the Web lends itself to a game-like engagement which can bring humour to representations of ethnicity. Likewise, its haphazard organisation juxtaposes depictions of ethnicity created from competing positions of academic/scientific and 'experiential authority' (Clifford 1988: p.35), setting it up as space of struggle for ethnic representation across global networks.

The next chapter discusses how ethnic minorities are appropriating the Web for these very purposes: to resist mainstream white constructions of ethnicity; to forge their own self-representations; and to participate in the production of images of ethnicity which, like independent black film, provides an alternative viewpoint and reading position to the 'white gaze'.

Notes

1 National Film Board of Canada (2002 online 19 May 2004) 'Chinese Canadians' at http:/ /cmm.onf.ca/E/titleinfo/index.epl?id=16275. The Web address has changed and the site has been redesigned, but the content for the page remains the same.
2 Bone, P. (7 October 1996 online 19 May 2004) 'Ethics and ethnic newspapers' at *The Age: News Store* http://www.theage.com.au/. The article was previously publicly available, but now requires a fee to access.
3 BBC World Service. (17 January 1998 online 19 May 2004) 'Chilean Defence Minister resigns in Pinochet row' at http://news.bbc.co.uk/1/hi/world/americas/48042.stm. The article remains the same despite a site redesign.
4 Loveard, K. (31 January 1997 online 19 May 2004) 'Australian reflections: most migrants have been the targets of prejudice' at http://www.pathfinder.com/Asiaweek/97/0131/ view.html. The Web address remains the same, although the article apart from the title and credit is no longer available.
5 Johansson, P. (1997 online 19 May 2004) 'Consuming the Other: Representations of Western Women in Chinese Women's Magazine Advertising' at http://www.aasianst.org/absts/1997/ abst/china/c85.htm. This abstract is no longer available from the author's homepage, but still resides on the Web site for the conference, along with those for other papers.
6 Edith Cowan University. (March 1996 no longer online) 'Chinese in Australia: Challenging the Generalisations' at http://ecuinfo.cowan.edu/ecuwis/docs/res/quest/mar96.html
7 Williams, M. (13 July 1997 no longer online) 'Chinese-Australian immigration history' at http://www.ercomer.org/wwwvl/merboard/messages/1350.html
8 British Geological Survey. (30 January 1998 no longer online) 'World Maps – South America' at http://www.bgs.ac.uk/bgs/w3/libr/s_america.html
9 KPMG Latin America. (1998 no longer online) 'KPMG Latin America Country Facts' at http://www.latinamerica.kpmg.com/country.html
10 Caribbean-On-Line. (1998 online 19 May 2004) 'Caribbean-On-Line Jamaica Maps & Guide 1998' at http://www.caribbean-on-line.com/jm/jmm.html. The site has migrated from its original Web address and has undergone a redesign, but retains some of the content.
11 WebMedia Pty Ltd. (1996 no longer online) 'Australian Golden Pages Chinese Version' at http://www.goldpages.com.au
12 'Master Lu Fortune Cookies' (no date, no longer online) at http://www.fortune-cookies.com/ uk/welcome.html

Chapter 8

Reconfiguring Ethnicity: The Web as Technology of Self-Representation

Representations of ethnicity in Web sites which are produced by ethnic minorities have a distinctly different orientation to those constructed from the 'white gaze' exemplified in the previous chapter. This is not to say that they are necessarily more progressive but like independent black cinema, they provide alternative positions of reading/consumption (Ross 1996: p.167). Their content is generally not commercially oriented (Reid 1993: p.5; Diawara 1993: p.6), but rather produced in the 'nooks and crannies' (Phillips 1995: p.72) of cyberspace. That is, there are black Web sites like there are black films which address black communities, are concerned with issues of race and ethnicity, and are created by black Web users.

But unlike the independent black film industry, the problem of distribution on the Web is not as apparent. Technically, the mechanism is the same for corporations as it is for ethnic minority groups. As a result, there seems to be black presence across a range of genres of Web texts, as opposed to its concentration in the realms of sport and music (Hall 1998b: p.43) in other media. Certainly, ethnic participation on the Web borrows from and extends upon print media genres in their provision of information services to ethnic minority communities, adapting magazine or newspaper formats in their Web sites. There is also evidence of a black education sector, which promotes 'Africentricity' (Mashengele 1997: pp.311-315) and personal experience as an alternative to the study of ethnicity from the 'white gaze'. Then there are home pages, the ultimate form of self-representation unique to the Web.

Without the same kind of structural impediments determining access to self-produced representations of ethnicity, as in the film industry, the Web is where objectified and subjective depictions of race and ethnicity contest each other within the same arena. The seemingly random, technical process of searching the Web (Kahle 1997; Fuller 1999a, 1999b; Fuller and Lovink 1999) juxtaposes images of ethnicity constructed from without with those from within. Given these intimate positionings, it is not surprising to find that they reappropriate strategies of representation from each other. Just as the commercial 'Master Lu's Fortune Cookies' Web site (discussed in the previous chapter) transformed traditional depictions of Chinese ethnicity from the 'white gaze', so too Web sites produced by ethnic minorities employ notions of 'ethnic absolutism' (Hall et al 1992: p.308) in the representation of their ethnicities.

The chapter begins by examining examples of ethnic expertise on the Web, whereby the 'white gaze' is mirrored by an ethnic one. That is, the claim to represent ethnicity is made from within rather than from without. But in doing so, it still employs the same tactic of depicting ethnicity as unified and homogenous. Self-produced ethnic Web sites which deploy ethnic expertise generally address a white audience and can be differentiated from those which are directed at an ethnic readership.

Where the audience is an ethnic community, the authority to speak is asssumed by its 'leaders', with appointments to this status mostly sanctioned by institutions. The chapter explores Web texts which illustrate various configurations of this ethnic author/ethnic reader relation: these range from the unofficial contributions of Web-literate individual members of that community affiliated to powerful institutions, to those which are formal representations made by ethnic community organisations. The chapter looks particularly at instances of ethnic self-representation in academic and news Web sites. The entrenched institutional practices that the academy and the media both have when it comes to representing ethnicity are contested on the Web by ethnic minorities participating in these industries as well as the Internet.

The difficulty in distinguishing between the genres of news and what might be termed 'community information' in self-produced ethnic Web sites points to their greater commonality with the black independent media sector than with mainstream media organisations in terms of their community-oriented consciousness and concern with issues of ethnicity. In particular, the distinctive female presence in the production of ethnic community-based Web sites align them with black womanist films (Reid 1993: p.111) in their negotiations of gender and ethnicity. Nonetheless, the masculinity of black cinema also has its parallels on the Web, given the predominance of male voices across the numerous genres of ethnic sites found. As such, there are many different manifestations of them: they speak on behalf of institutions, as 'leaders' or official representatives of communities and as individuals.

Given the array of genres in which representations of ethnicity produced by ethnic minorities themselves can be found on the Web, it could be said that the profile of Internet users is not as white as many commentators have believed, even in the latter part of the 1990s (see Apple 1992: p.118; Johnson 1996: p.98; Spender 1996: p.118; Interrogate the Internet 1996: pp.125-127; Lockard 1999). But while the barriers to ethnic participation on the Web may not be as fortified as for other media industries, it is important to remember that there are barriers nonetheless. The Web texts discussed in this chapter confirm the significant degree of black activity on the Web occurring as early as 1998 (see Hoffmann and Novak). However, it is also indicative of a particular ethnic class formation which, according to Terranova (1996: p.72), probably does not include 'the terminally unskilled and unemployed, single mothers on welfare, the old and poor, or the majority of residents in "underdeveloped" regions of the world'. Therefore, in spite of claims made by some to speak for entire ethnic communities, the representations of ethnicity examined below are representative only of specific identity positions, of particular intersections of ethnicity with class, nationality, age and other dimensions of subjectivity. The individualism of home pages are the extreme articulation of this. They highlight the quandary of representation: the ongoing struggle and yet the constant inadequacy of attempting to articulate ethnicity. This continuous process perhaps becomes more obvious in a medium like the Web which can accommodate a proliferation of images of ethnicity. The simple conclusion that the broadcast media portrayed ethnicity poorly was easily reached given its finite capacity for representation. But even with a technology such as the Web which offers vast opportunities in this area, the question of representation remains unresolved and ironically becomes more complex: can representation ever suffice?

Speaking to the 'White Gaze': The Claim of Ethnic Expertise from Within

The last chapter illustrated the ways in which Orientalist authority, the West's claim to represent the East (Said 1995: p.3), were being manifested on the Web. Almost as a response to this, there were instances where 'ethnic expertise' was reclaimed by ethnic minorities asserting their right to represent themselves. In doing so, they establish a dialectic between representations of ethnicity constructed from the 'white gaze' and those produced from positions of 'experiential authority' (Clifford 1988: p.35), in which the latter contests and provides an alternative perspective to the former. In much the same way, independent black media productions have effectively attacked racism in the mainstream media (Phillips 1995: p.72; Morris 1982: p.79).

For example, the Web site about Sudan[1] chosen by Sasha, gives a very different image of the country to those of starvation and famine seen in Western media. It suggests Sudan to be an ideal tourist destination: 'The capital, Khartoum, is connected by air to practically every part of the world and all the most important airlines operate there...The visitor [to] Sudan will find a wide variety of interests ranging from wildlife to archeology, from the Red Sea to folklore and handicraft.' As mentioned in the previous chapter, Sasha took exception to this portrayal of Sudan, partly because it is intended to attract tourists to the country. That is, this representation of the Sudan exists for the 'white gaze' and is so far removed from Sasha's personal experience of Sudan that she argues that the information is simply not true. Indeed, the site is also referred to by Zurawski (1996), who similarly questions its accuracy: 'Here the impression is created that this is the perfect country for a family vacation, as though there were no civil war – accompanied by massive ethnic cleansing – going on in the south of Sudan'. Zurawski uses the site as an example of the possible consequences of the struggle for representation on the Web. He argues that while the Web enables self-representation for ethnic minority groups, there is also the chance of exaggeration and misinformation because it is an environment where representation is forged almost without any regulation or control. This is reiteriated by Arnold and Plymire (2000: pp.186-193) who say that the potential for misrepresentation is inevitable if only a select few have access to the technology. However, as seen in Chapter 3, the representation of ethnicities from the perspective of the 'white gaze' has likewise been subject to much distortion, relegated to invisibility (Silk and Silk 1990: p.128), the antithesis to white identity (Hoch 1979: pp.44-46), or the areas of sport and music (Hall 1998b: p.43). The Web site seems to be an attempt by a person of Sudanese ethnicity to present a positive image of Sudan, at the expense of some omissions – just as in the 1980s *The Cosby Show* sought to depict a black American family but did not reflect the growing poverty amongst the black US population at that time (Jhally and Lewis 1992: pp.1-33).

A criticism that was levelled at *The Cosby Show* at the time and indeed, could also apply to the Web site is that despite them being examples of self-produced representations of ethnicity, the intended audience is white. That is, they are created in order to be consumed by the 'white gaze'. For Fanon (1967: p.11), this demonstrates the internalisation of colonial ideology, whereby black people are determined to prove as much as possible that they share more similarities than differences with their white colonisers. Thus, instead of the usual Western portrayal of Sudan as yet another anarchic and base African society (Pieterse 1992: p.78), the Web site represents it as a destination that would appeal to the tastes of white tourists.

The Web site's claim to knowledge of widely unknown aspects of Sudan assumes the foreignness of the country to the reader. This sets up the mutual exclusivity of the native expert and the ignorant tourist like the East/West dichotomy of Orientalism (Said 1995: pp.1-3). As illustrated in the previous chapter, this is often prevalent in sites pertaining to travel, which represent ethnicity in terms of exoticism. But instead of the West speaking on behalf of the East, representation is reclaimed by ethnic minorities in an act of self-determination. In the case of this Web site's portrayal of Sudan, the representation is not being made on behalf of its government or an organisation. Rather, the ~ symbol in its Web address indicates that it is a home page (Rubio 1996) and therefore, the work of an individual, Tarig Monawar, who also claims copyright of the content on the site. The home page's location in Columbia University (www.columbia.edu) is suggested by the Web address and particularly the 'edu' suffix which shows it to be an educational institution (ibid); and provides a tentative profile of the author as a person of Sudanese ethnicity or nationality living and studying or working in the US. In short, Tarig Monawar is a member of that general class formation of Internet users identified as highly educated and affluent (Terranova 1996: p.72; Hoffman and Novak 1998; Kendall 1999: p.63; Pastore 2000; ClickZ 2001; Greenspan 2003b). However, the justification of this single-handed construction of ethnicity lies in the allusion to an 'experiential authority' (Clifford 1988: p.35) which suggests that the author has lived in Sudan.

Ethnic expertise emanating from within an ethnic minority community or individual seems to be predicated on the importance of personal experience, which often alleges an authenticity. This is evident in another site, called 'De Web Site on Jamaica' chosen by Sha, subtitled 'a taste of de real Jamaica'[2] It suggests to the user that the information on the site is legitimate because it is produced by 'real' Jamaicans. Sha also clearly engaged with its representation of Jamaica because it was not produced from the perspective of the 'white gaze', nor was she excluded from its ideal readership:

> ...it relates to me because of the home [cooked] recipes...that's what I cook at home now and my parents had taught me. The patois [is] what we speak to each other when the family get together. The reggae music which is illstrated on the Web site I listen to. Even the culture, [the] ways which my parents have taught me, some of the ways which I was [accustomed] to I still used today to help bring up my daughter. I feel that this particular site has got quite a few things which it relates to me as a person (Sha).

De Web Site on Jamaica seemed to serve as a resource for excavating Sha's 'lost' ethnicity, reminding her of the Jamaican language and cuisine on which she was brought up, but from which she also feels somewhat estranged. But while the site was a point of rediscovery for Sha, it is also clearly a source of discovery for potential tourists to Jamaica seeking background information: it coaxes the reader to 'be a Jamaican tourist' with 'tips for tourists visiting Jamaica'. Its representation of Jamaicanness as being constituted by food (as seen in the section 'cook Jamaican'), people (in its sample of 'the characters who make up the Jamaican society') and language ('learn to speak Jamaican using conversational sentences and realtime audio'), implies a reader with a 'white gaze' who has never travelled to Jamaica, who is unfamiliar but interested in Jamaican culture. This construction of Jamaicanness in terms of food, language and people employs a kind of 'ethnic absolutism' (Hall et al 1992: p.308) but gives its claim of expertise credibility by speaking as a person/s of Jamaican ethnicity. It is perhaps this identification which led Sha to favour this site over Caribbean-On-Line (discussed in the previous chapter): that is, she felt that the 'insider' position from which this site spoke was more closely aligned with her own experience. Indeed, the phone details given at the bottom of the Web pages show that the producers are based in the US and like Sha, part of the Jamaican diaspora rather than resident Jamaicans.

Addresses to the 'white gaze' are not only differentiated by the position from which an address is made, but also the subsequent mode of address. That is, there are qualitative differences between self-produced and objectified representations of ethnicity. This has been argued extensively in the study of black independent film and music which are seen as overt declarations of black authorship and political rejections of the mainstream media industries (Reid 1993: p.5; Diawara 1993: p.6; Gilroy 1987: p.168). Certainly, in relation to the Web, Sha's chosen Web sites on Jamaica illustrate how representational practices vary according to where producers are ethnically located. Self-produced ethnic Web sites strongly indicate the author's membership to that ethnicity, especially where ethnicity is the primary subject of the site. Web sites which objectify ethnicity do not make explicit the author's relationship to that ethnicity while making similar claims of expertise and presumptions about the fixed and unchanging nature of ethnicity. However, as discussed in Chapter 4, the Web also makes producers' identities elusive and thus problematises the task of distinguishing between self-produced and objectified representations of ethnicity.

For example, during my own forays into the Web, I encountered the 'New Age Network China' site[3] which aimed to introduce 'the western new age movement to China and Chinese thoughts, religion, philosophy and *qigong* to the world' as stated in the description given by the search engine. Here an image of Chineseness is constructed which is complete, pure and wholly independent of the West. In a typically Orientalist outlook, East and West are regarded as cultural opponents (Said 1995: pp.2-3) which need to be reconciled by bringing a 'white gaze' to the former and the mystique of Chineseness to the latter. Nonetheless, the textual information given on the 'New Age Network China' site was entirely in Chinese and the 'cn' suffix of the e-mail address provided indicates it emerges from mainland China. Effectively, this was a self-produced representation of Chineseness, but one which, to some extent, appeals to the 'white gaze' in its promise to reveal some of the mysteries of Chineseness to the Western reader, although any such expectations are difficult to fulfil given that it is a Chinese language site and hence intended for Chinese readers.

Is the Web being used as a technology of resistance here? In the same way that urban, black youth have adopted and transformed principles of free market enterprise (Hall 1996a, 1996b, 1998b) in music production, the 'New Age Network China' site, although clearly created by Chinese people, appropriates the tactics of racism and Orientalism in its binary delineation of East and West, as well as by claiming to represent Chineseness in its entirety. Yet in doing so, it wrests the right of representation away from the West or the 'white gaze', where it has traditionally resided. Also, by assuming the speaking position, it constructs a very different ideal reader: it directs its address away from the 'white gaze' by excluding English language and instead nominating Chinese to mediate the representation. It elects an ethnic minority as the intended audience.

Cultural Commentary from the Inside: Addressing the Ethnic Reader

The representational opportunities the Web provides to ethnic minorities also enable debate amongst those communities. There is arguably as much contention when ethnicity is defined internally as it is externally (Werbner 1997: p.18). While the notion of a virtual ethnic community falsely implies unanimity, perhaps the term 'cyborg diaspora' (Gajjala 1999) more appropriately articulates the differences embodied in the experience of ethnicity (Gillespie 1995: p.6). However, the diversity implied in the concept of a diaspora does not represent the relationships of power within it. As Walkerdine and Lucey (1989: p.4) argue, contradicitions of power and powerlessness are invoked through intersections of class, gender and ethnicity.

As seen earlier in the chapter, the authority to represent the Republic of Sudan was assumed by a student or academic, Tarig Monawar, presumably of Sudanese ethnicity, living in the US and studying or working at Columbia University. Similarly, 'The Bangladeshi Home Pages'[4] appear to be the work of one person, Zunaid Kazi, who claims copyright on the content and the right to nominate as well as choose the Bangladeshi of the year 1997, 'who, for better or for worse, has had the most impact on Bangladesh and Bangladeshis'. Like Tarig Monawar, Zunaid Kazi also seems to be a student or academic, but presumably of Bangladeshi ethnicity, at a US university, as indicated by the 'edu' suffix in the site's Web address (Rubio 1996). The same applies to Heng Yuan, whose 'Chinese Web Directory' is hosted by another US university, of which he is apparently a student or member of staff.[5] What does this indicate about relationships of power within ethnic minorities when it comes to Web production, representation and possibly consumption?

It suggests that Web production by ethnic minorities, at least in the late 1990s, was located largely in the US, despite that Internet growth was faster in developing countries than anywhere else (Panos 1998). This corresponds with Mitra's (1997: p.63) study of the soc.culture.indian newsgroup, which found that most participants were from the US with only a minority in India itself. In 1999, the number of Web users in the US outnumbered those from developing regions of the world by nearly 7:1 (Panos 1998). By 2002, Internet users in the US still outnumbered those in China, which had the second largest online population in the world, by threefold (Greenspan 2002). This ratio has remained up until 2004, except that Japan has replaced China in second position (ClickZ 2004). With 80% of Web content being in the English language (Warschauer 2000: p.156; Lockard 2000: p.178; Hill 2001: p.25) and 44% of US Internet users (approximately 53 million Internet users) having contributed online content in some form (Greenspan 2004; Pew Research Center 2003), it would appear that much Web production still resides in the US, although this needs to be studied more accurately, particularly as it relates to ethnic minority content creators (Nakamura 2002: p.108). According to Zurawski (1999), it seems that the representation of ethnicities from developing nations on the Web, is being led and possibly manipulated by 'techno-elites' from outside those homelands. This demonstrates Hall's (1998a) argument that new digital technologies allow new forms of individual power which, in the above cases, are being applied in the name of self-determination as well as to forge a kind of ethnic expertise.

The expertise is claimed from a position of assumed authority on the part of the producers of these Web texts. At times, they speak as representatives of the ethnic communities concerned, or they defer to the opinions of community leaders. An example would be a site, 'Our Story',[6] selected by Oyen, which yet again, seems to be the homepage of a student or member of staff at a US university. The site is an ethnic portal site linking to Web-based resources on cultures of the African diaspora, but the author's presence is more pronounced: '...we have played a HUGE role in the formation, culture and life of most societies currently on the planet. I am going to attempt to weave a story for you of the history of a people.' The author, Cardell Orrin, expresses himself in the first person ('we', 'I') and addresses the reader as a fellow member of the African diaspora, thus establishing himself as part of a community. However, he also distinguishes himself from it through his professed knowledge of African history and subsequently, the implication that other people of African ethnicities do not possess this because it has been 'stolen from Africans'. His credibility is perhaps enhanced through his affiliation to an educational institution, combining his 'experiential authority' (Clifford 1988: p.35) with academic authority. Other ethnic minority sites have invoked other types of institutions to legitimise their right to represent their ethnicities as a whole.

A Web article, 'Zimbabwean Culture on the Death Bed?',[7] selected by Bella as part of the Panafrican News Agency site, not only has the reputation of the media organisation to support its argument; it also draws on the opinions of cultural leaders. The article contends that young people in Zimbabwe are rejecting traditional customs because of Western influences:

> ...Vice-President Simon Muzenda attacked disgraceful youths for shunning their culture. It is a terrible shame that some of our young people seem to be bent on throwing away anything that is African, including our language, preferring to imitate Western values which can never be ours even in a million years, he said...Godfrey Mahachi, National Museums and Monuments deputy executive director, says many aspects of traditional life [were] discouraged by colonialism, the education system and christianity which labelled it as primitive and barbaric.

This essentialist construction of Zimbabwean culture as polluted by Western imperialism demonstrates what Hall et al (1992: p.308) call 'ethnic absolutism'. The desire for a return to origins, also evident in the abovementioned 'Our Story' Web site, is made more persuasive by the status of those imploring for cultural purity. Just as 'authenticity' can be an effective form of political mobilisation (Yuval-Davis 1998: pp.138-139), it can also be central to the formation of political and, indeed, representational power. Nevertheless, to some extent, Bella does not contest this portrayal of Zimbabwe by 'experts' as requiring cultural cleansing:

> This site was particularly appropriate because of the topic of discussion...and my feelings on culture and the need to embrace and recapture what once was ours especially in order to [pass] this onto our children. Otherwise inevitably it will be lost as we become more and more assimilated into Western ways (Bella).

Rather, Bella is almost grateful that the leaders of Zimbabwe can highlight this kind of 'hypodermic needle' effect by which African ethnicities fall victim to the 'unrelenting, all-absorbing, linear process' (Ang 1996: p.152) of Westernisation, so that people like herself become aware and can take action. On the other hand, she also feels that she is not being represented: 'The article focuses on Zimbabwean youth and ignores the hundreds of us who have grown [up] elsewhere – such Britain or the States...' (Bella).

Bella realises that she is partly the 'problem' as a person of Zimbabwean origins who has been raised in a Western country. Therefore, the subject of the criticism is not as simplistic as it might seem. Although she seeks an image of Zimbabwe which is untainted, she challenges the accusations of those who speak on behalf of Zimbabwe. The Web is not only a space where representations constructed by ethnic minorities contest those made from the 'white gaze', but it is also where power relations within ethnic minorities are manifest.

A Web article that I found, titled 'Chinese to enter politics to stop anti-Asian sentiment',[8] is a direct address from Chinese ethnic leaders to their communities. The article, part of the 'Taiwan Headline News' Web site, exploits the credibility of the news organisation as well as the spokesperson it quotes, to make its singular message more compelling.

> Australian citizens of Chinese ancestry are urged to become more integrated into Australian society, particularly in the field of politics, so that they can help prevent the rise of anti-Asian sentiments...An Son Hong, managing director of the Melbourne Chinese News...said it was now time for Chinese Australians "to join more activities in mainstream society. We

> need all Australian Chinese migrants to understand the duty of ours in Australia. We are Chinese Australian, not Chinese...If every Chinese Australian can do their duty in Australia, I think that any damage from racist statements will come to a standstill."

Because the appeal is for integration, not separatism, this could not be considered an example of 'ethnic absolutism' (Hall et al 1992: p.308). However, it does construct a one-dimensional representation of Australian Chineseness in its appeal for the community to act as a whole. Where ethnic leaders assume responsibility for representation, there is little room for dissent or diversity. The depiction of ethnicity, while out of the 'protective custody' (Guerrero 1993: p.259) of the 'white gaze', becomes influenced by those members of ethnic minorities who perceive themselves as leaders of the communities of which they are part. In addition, it is likely that these self-proclaimed ethnic leaders are also those at the centre of the Internet, who, as discussed in Chapter 4, are socially and economically privileged in real life (Johnson 1996: p.90; Kendall 1999: p.63; Pastore 2000; ClickZ 2001; Greenspan 2003b). Furthermore, those participating in cyberspace and who have the power to represent the ethnic communities of which they are part appear to reside in the West and are closely linked to prestigious institutions such as universities or the media.

Countering the 'White Gaze' of the Academy

As we have seen, many of those speaking on behalf of ethnic communities are at least affiliated with, if not representatives of, educational institutions. Academic discourse on the Web seems to open up a space where subjective and objectified representations of ethnicity can be juxtaposed and debated; and ethnic minorities can make their experiential voices heard with legitimate institutional support.

In the previous chapter, examples were discussed of how the 'white gaze' prevails in scholarly texts on the Web and in the representational practices of academic culture. In some alternative examples of educational Web sites found by Lorraine and Teti, the 'white gaze' of the academy is negated in that 'experiential authority' (Clifford 1988: p.35) is treated as an integral part of academic authority, so that the subjective is privileged over the objective. The sites function to present other approaches to the academic study of ethnicity apart from that of the 'white gaze' to scholars operating within and outside the ethnic communities under their scrutiny.

Lorraine's chosen Web site was that for 'New Beacon Books',[9] which specialises in 'multi-ethnic books'. The site is premised on providing an alternative to Eurocentrism in the publishing industry and the failure to address ethnic minority readers through books that are not intended to be consumed from the 'white gaze'. This mainstream exclusion of the ethnic minority writer/reader at the level of both production and consumption has become translated at the level of representation. As Lorraine noted: '...black people are not normally depicted as intellectuals...although education is an important part of our culture' (Lorraine).

For Lorraine, the rare association of blackness with scholarly activity made the 'New Beacon Books' site a representation of ethnicity in which the 'white gaze' was contested: 'The New Beacon bookshop was the best site I visited because it gave a positive image of African Caribbean by consisting of lots [of] literature on a wide range of topics, of which to read and learn' (Lorraine).

The site not only challenged traditional depictions of blackness as the antithesis of white intellectual and moral superiority (Hoch 1979: pp.44-46), but also engendered a sense of inclusion for Lorraine as the intended reader/consumer: '...they do books on Black British and African, African-American, European, Asian but it really appealed to me because it deals with so many books. A lot of the book titles that I clicked on, well all of them that I clicked on just seemed to talk to me...' (Lorraine – interview).

The books 'spoke' to Lorraine in a way which suggests that the production/ consumption equation was different to what she has experienced before. Given that the site offered 'Third World' books and autobiographies from Africa and America, perhaps Lorraine believed the ethnic identities of the authors to be similar to her own. Like myself, Lorraine suggests that 'experiential authority' (Clifford 1988: p.35) is key to any examination of ethnicity, particularly in an educational context. This also seems to be borne out in Teti's choice of Web sites below.

Unlike the site for 'New Beacon Books' which commercially promotes multicultural educational resources, the 'African Centred Research Group'[10] and 'Religious Traditions of the African Diaspora'[11] sites are based in higher education institutions in the UK (as indicated by the 'ac.uk' suffix in the Web address) and the US respectively. While the 'African Centred Research Group' site refers to people engaged in a particular kind of academic project, 'The Religious Traditions of the African Diaspora' site appears to be a component of a university course. However, both seem to have corresponding approaches to the study of ethnicity.

They both demonstrate what Mashengele (1997: pp.311-315) calls 'Africentricity': concern with issues affecting people of the African diaspora beyond the geographical boundaries of Africa itself. More importantly, they propose that the analysis of such issues should be done from an African-centred perspective or what might perhaps be termed a 'black gaze'. For example, the 'Religious Traditions of the African Diaspora' site refers to an 'Afrocentric worldview', as opposed to a 'Eurocentric worldview'. In other words, in the study and representation of ethnicity, alternative positions to the 'white gaze' need to be considered. The African Centred Research Group argues that this is only realised through the production of subjective, not objective, knowledge:

> The African Centred Research Group (ACRG) was established in June 1994, initially as an informal support for researchers of African descent engaged in African-centred research...[and] to promote African centred scholarship and research that is grounded in the lived and historical experiences of people of African descent on the African Continent and the Diaspora.

In other words, in the examination of African identities and communities, the ethnicity of the researcher matters. In the academic representation of ethnic minorities, how and where the researcher is ethnically located in relation to the research subject is relevant – just as in media depictions of ethnic minorities, who does and doesn't participate in the production of such images requires reflection (Diawara 1993: p.11). The approach recommended by the African Centred Research Group seems to be one which combines 'experiential fieldwork' (Williams 1990: p.254), in which the attempt to understand ethnicity is done through one's own experience; and where knowledge of ethnicity emanates from and is constructed by people from ethnic minorities.

There is a sense that the abovementioned education sites are contesting a dominant paradigm – the Eurocentrism of curricula, the notion of 'objective' knowledge of ethnicity – yet there is little sense of their marginalisation on the Web. These sites were found as easily as the contentious ones I found on academic studies of Chinese ethnicity: in the process of searching the Web using a keyword search with a search engine, they were mainly in the first thirty results given. This implies the Web to be effective in flattening the hierarchies of large institutions: marginalised viewpoints on the peripheries of universities become juxtaposed with those at the centre and pinnacle of those organisations. Self-produced representations of ethnicity become the neighbours of those depicted from the 'white gaze'. This can also be seen in competing depictions of ethnicity from media organisations on the Web.

Headlines vs Hard Lines: Alternatives to Institutionalised Representations of Ethnicity in the Media

Where the academy fosters a space for conceptualisations of ethnicity on the Web to be contested internally, the representational practices of news and journalism and their associated institutions are challenged externally by ethnic minorities. That is, ethnic minorities active in the production of news on the Web seem to be outside of the large news organisations, located in their own independent sector. While the criteria for newsworthiness – negative consequences, human tragedy and drama (Hall et al 1978: p.54) – are generally the same, the approach to representing ethnic minorities is distinguishable between when it is self-produced compared with when it is from the 'white gaze'. The portrayal of black people as 'problems' by the mainstream media (as discussed in Chapter 3) is, instead, given a more charitable and introspective viewpoint by ethnic news producers.

A site selected by Chwime, 'Repression of Nigerian Students and Academics'[12] reports on student demonstrations against Nigeria's military government. While this has had coverage in the wider media, it does not attempt to claim objectivity in its reportage, as seen in the online news items by the BBC and *The Age* discussed in the previous chapter (see notes 3 and 2 in Chapter 7). Rather, it invites action from the reader: 'In addition to targeting the Nigerian Embassy and supporting the sanctions bill...we urge members to develop local work on their campuses and communities'.

It utilises the us/them dualisms of racism (Hoch 1979: pp.44-46) and Orientalism (Said 1995: p.2), which were also evident in the online news items by the BBC (Britain vs Chile) and *The Age* (ethnic media vs mainstream media). In this case, it is the Association of Concerned African Scholars vs the Nigerian government. However, it makes its position explicit: in providing information about events in Nigeria, it is also opposing the actions of Nigeria's military government.

Like the research subjects' responses to other sites produced by ethnic minorities, Chwime felt that she was being addressed directly as the ideal reader, especially as someone who is both a student, identifies herself as 'British-born Nigerian' and can therefore be described as a 'concerned African scholar':

> ...I found this site interesting and moving because the country itself is beautiful, it is the leadership that is wrong and there are people suffering for these sinful killings. There is no freedom of speech or press coverage (Chwime).

Indeed, the appeal for action seems intended for those who are located closely to the situation through personal experience and therefore want to do something about it. Thus, the production of Web-based news items by ethnic minorities seems to employ feminist principles of making the personal the political, the emotional overt and struggling against oppression (Stanley 1990: pp.12-15), but specifically with the ethnic minority subject in mind. This approach is also illustrated in the site chosen by Tessa, which is particularly concerned with ethnic minority women.

The Web article 'Women Struggle as Heads of Dominican Households'[13] was syndicated from the New York Times News Service by LatinoLink, presumably a site aimed at Latin American ethnic communities. It reports on the high proportion of single motherhood and social disadvantage amongst immigrants from the Dominican Republic living in New York City.

Like the 'Repression of Nigerian Students/Academics' site, the subject matter is pessimistic and therefore the sites could be regarded as negative representations of ethnicity: the former could be said to perpetuate the image of Africa as anarchic and in need of law and order (Pieterse 1992: p.78); while the latter could be considered a depiction of Latino men as promiscuous and irresponsible (Hoch 1979: pp.44-46), and of Latino women as suffering the consequences of their ill-considered dalliances with Latino men (Jones 1993: p.253; hooks 1992: p.62).

However, both sites are sympathetic to who they identify as the 'victims' in the respective situations. The 'Women Struggle as Heads of Dominican Households' article represents immigrant Dominican women living in the US as bearing all the financial and emotional responsibilities for their families. But it does not attempt the simplistic good/bad dualisms of racism (Hoch 1979: pp.44-46) and Orientalism (Said 1995: p.2). It acknowledges that the reasons for the vulnerability of Dominican immigrant women are complex: the circumstances of emigration; gender relations in Dominican culture; language barriers; immigrant women's employment prospects.

Again, there is a spur to action, with the article inviting comments from readers: 'To share your thoughts about this article or any other in LatinoLink, send e-mail...'. Tessa seems to have been inspired by this call to act, given the parallels with her own identity and life situation:

> This site summarises the struggle that black women face bringing up a family on their own...Although [this site was] based in the States, women in the Caribbean and in England

> face the same problems ie bringing up a family on their own, absent fathers. (I could relate to this, because I am a single parent.) (Tessa).

Like Chwime, Tessa felt that the site 'spoke' to her as an ethnic minority woman, mother and immigrant. In this sense, such news items on the Web which represent as well as target ethnic minorities (that is, where the 'white gaze' is absent), not only deal with issues in a way which is sensitive and pertinent to their readers, but simultaneously engender a feeling of community amongst them. Through the 'Dominican Women...' Web article, Tessa positions herself as part of a community of diasporic ethnic minority single mothers. In the 'Repression of Nigerian Students and Academics' Web article, Chwime identifies herself as part of a community of Nigerian students opposing the military government. These texts provide an insight into how the Web creates a 'we' feeling (Miller 1993: p.185) by defining a population. They exemplify what Rheingold (1992) might term a 'virtual community' or even, as Gajjala (1999) describes, a 'cyborg diaspora', a virtual online *ethnic* community.

This sense of community seems to be intensified when such Web-based news stories are encompassed in larger dedicated Web sites. For example, the report on the repression of Nigerian students and academics was part of the site and work of the Association of Concerned African Scholars; and the article on Dominican women was incorporated into the LatinoLink site. It is the community that is defined and constructed by the Web site that seems to inspire and mobilise readers to action when help is sought.

A sort of virtual ethnic neighbourhood (Mitra 1997: p.62, 72) is seen in the Web site of 'The Chronicle',[14] which came to the attention of Roni. Its slogan 'Changing Black Britain' declares the ethnic community it seeks to represent. This confirms Miller and Mather's (1998) argument that the Web is utilised by people to emphasise who they are rather than to play out an alternative existence. Like the sites discussed above, 'The Chronicle' is a news service for ethnic minority communities: 'The Chronicle is Britain's first Internet magazine monitoring Britain's Black urban communities...[it is an] international digital magazine on changing black urban communities in Britain and abroad'.

Although it does provide news for black British Internet users, its magazine format with date and number of issue, suggests that it is more than a news service. Certainly, the headings on its front page ('Evolving Black Urban Experience', 'Regeneration Time', 'Share the Dream', 'Expand Your Universe', 'Speak Out on the Black Millenium') are not hard news headlines of the kind in the previous Web news articles. Rather, it seems to offer a wider range of ethnic community information. This is confirmed by Roni:

> The site looked at Britain from a 'real' perspective, was honest in its coverage and it covered a lot, hardly leaving a stone unturned. It not only examined the ghettos and the social conditions black people experience, it also considered the policies that engineer the fate of black communities and the weaknesses of those policies, placing the blame on the black communities, which is common practice, but questions the inadequacies of policies past and present...It merely addressed what black people address everyday, misrepresentations,

> inequality and social deprivation which the government purport to be self-inflicted saying we are the cause of our own devastation, because we choose to rob, pillage, and have babies at the expense of welfare, rather than work and improve our lot... (Roni).

Roni's use of 'we' indicates that she identifies with the community to which this site is targeted and which the site claims to represent. The site seems to have the equivalent aims of independent black film in its focus on black communities and issues of race and ethnicity (Ross 1996: p.154; Reid 1993: p.2). It acknowledges the complex and dynamic state of black Britishness in its slogan 'Changing Black Britain', and in its critical analysis of policy issues. Although Roni says its approach is abstract and theoretical, the site's community orientation associates it with those which might be called ethnic community self-help sites.

Community Information and Services in the 'Cyborg Diaspora'

If the 'The Chronicle' Web site can be regarded as a virtual ethnic neighbourhood (Mitra 1997: pp.62, 72), then ethnic community self-help sites are more like the epicentres from which the Web user travels to those neighbourhoods. They are the launch pads, the points of departure to places on the Web which have a connection with the ethnicity concerned, with links to a range of information and services in addition to news. They can be described as portal sites in that they direct the user to resources (Patelis 1999).

For example, Askari chose the 'Blacknet UK' site,[15] which she noted as linking to a plethora of other Web-based information and services for black Britons, so many that it would require a significant amount of time to even visit only the ones that were just of interest to her:

> This site led to sites I felt that I could relate to (eg http://www.blink.org.uk) black bookshops...news about pro-black issues, black chat rooms aimed at students...sisterhood groups offering ways of getting spiritual guidance (educational) and much more I have not yet gone in to surf! (Askari).

As such sites are not self-contained, but are rather the hub of a network of community-based information and services, they seem to encourage the user to wander. Askari suggests that it is almost impossible to stay within the 'Blacknet UK' site, and in any of the other sites to which it links. This is also evident when other research subjects chose similar portal sites. Rosie selected one representing and targeting Pakistani ethnic communities:[16]

> I found Indian film stars, the film industry. It gave information about the film stars. Especially the ones you are interested in you can find out about their profiles. They give you their height, what their favourite food is, everything. I think I am more into music and that's why I went to this site and then I tried to learn if I can learn Arabic because although I am Pakistani but we are connected with being Muslims...They gave lots of things and they actually have lessons and things that you can download and I visited that site about learning

another different language. You can learn any language...So actually it's something I could not have found from one book, there is no way I could have found one book with all those answers on it (Rosie – interview).

Rosie displays a sense of being lost amongst the sites she visited because of the array of material available relating to Pakistani ethnicities. Some of the sites she mentioned were not apparent links from the Pakistani portal site, but were probably secondary links. Her disorientation is illustrated in the difficulty of deciphering the trail of sites visited beginning from the portal. Similarly, Noori's visit to a portal site called 'The Bangladesh Home Pages' perhaps led her to comment that it was impossible to nominate one as most representative of her ethnicity: 'There was not one site that summarised my ethnicity...I couldn't pick just one and say that represents me!' (Noori).

Noori points to the diversity and complexity of self-produced representations of ethnicity that is facilitated by the Web, as well as to the inherent difficulties of capturing the nuances of ethnicity in spite of such multiplicity. The overwhelming display of Web texts produced by ethnic minorities not only depict ethnicities, but construct specific audiences for them through intersections with other aspects of ethnic identity. This can be seen in links to sites for black business enterprises; Bangladeshi cricket stars; Pakistani poets; and the Internet Chinese Librarians Club. Ethnic portal sites depict a range of positions within diasporas: they are a Web representation of the global dispersal of local ethnic communities who have a shared culture or history (Gillespie 1995: p.6) consolidated into a single text.

Sites such as 'Blacknet UK', 'The Bangladesh Home Pages' and 'Heng Yuan's Chinese Web Directory' mobilise the Web as a technology of resistance for ethnic minorities. Whereas portals have been criticised as a means of limiting access to the Web and directing users to commercial content (Franck 1998; Patelis 1999; Cisler 1998a; Eisenberg 1998; Stalder 1998; Fuller 1999b), here they provide access to representations of ethnicities which are difficult to locate in other media:

You are not going to see or hear these kind of images on television or film, especially if they are written from a person of another race's point of view (Askari).

...it's something I could not have found from one book, there is no way I could have found one book with all those answers on it (Rosie – interview).

In the previous chapter, Tessa remarked that she was excluded from cosmetics advertisements on television because she is not the intended consumer for those products. In contrast, 'Blacknet UK' links to beauty salons for black women, thus positioning her as the ideal reader. Therefore, there seems to be a common element of self-help and community service in the sites to which these portals link.

The dispersed but networked relations between sites work against the tendency in the broadcast media to construct audiences in the image of the 'white gaze' and concentrate the portrayal of ethnic minorities in particular areas, such as sport (Hall 1998b: p.143). Instead, production, representation and consumption is undertaken by and for ethnic minorities. Communities speak to and on behalf of themselves. Diverse representations are made behind a united front that is the site, akin to 'black' being a term of political solidarity, signifying active coalition rather than physiological similarity (Hall et al 1992: p.308). Ethnic self-help sites subsume diverse groups and services wanting to be associated with each other under a common umbrella, such as in the 'Black Information Link' site,[17] visited by Askari, which states its mission as follows: 'This site aims to [provide] the much needed self-help information especially to the Asian, African and Caribbean people living in the United Kingdom'.

The notion of self-help suggests an absence of the 'white gaze' and simultaneously its presence; that communities are utilising something which has previously been unavailable to them by establishing an alternative system to the mainstream. The 'Black Information Link' site illustrates black communities' helping themselves to Web information, representation and technology, as their access to them, it suggests, has been hampered by imperialising forces:

> The inventions of humankind are not the property of any one race to be used to gain artifical superiority. Technology can be as much an instrument of liberation as it is of domination. Liberators must gain control of these new technologies and employ them for the proper advancement of all humanity.

The premise of the Web being a technology of liberation, while explicitly proclaimed in the 'Black Information Link' site, also seems to be the subtle basis of other ethnic self-help sites, such as the 'South Asian Women Together' site,[18] visited by Noori. It is constructed by a collective of women of south Asian ethnicities who are 'committed to challenging the stereotypes we encounter in Canada by emphasising our diverse experiences'. Although it encourages women from ethnic minorities to take responsibility for their own representation, the function of technology in doing this is only insinuated in their appeal for e-mail submissions for a print anthology of stories by young ethnic minority women. Nonetheless, the role of women in this discourse of self-help was significant. Despite the general mantra that they are under-represented in cyberspace (Apple 1992: p.118; Spender 1996: p.118; Interrogate the Internet 1996: pp.125-127; Squires 1996: p.200; Panos 1998; ClickZ 2002; Pastore 2000a, 2001), the evidence indicates that they are particularly noticeable in this area of the Web, which may imply a very strategic use of the technology.

Communal Female Spaces

The prominence of women was evident in my own visits to Chinese self-help Web sites (without even having to actively search for sites produced by women), particularly those pertaining to dating and introductions, in which women initiated the process of finding a mate:

> ...we are a group of some 20 mainland Chinese ladies, who have joined together to share facilities and make contact with Western and overseas Chinese gentlemen.[19]

> Asian girls/women from Singapore, Indonesia, and the Philippines, including Japanese,

> Vietnamese, and Chinese, want to know American/Western men. See our photo biographies![20]

One of these sites, called 'Meow-Meow's Club', with all its connotations of Asian tiger/Siamese cat-like Oriental mystique, could be interpreted as yet another example of the sexual objectification of the non-white female body (hooks 1992: p.62; Jones 1993: p.253), and particularly the exoticisation of Asian women (Nakamura 2002). However, these representations of Asian femininity are not ones of passivity and demureness, but the overt statement of the personal, as seen in the use of the autobiographical 'we' and 'us', is consistent with feminist praxis (Stanley 1997; 1990: pp.12-15). Also, it resists one-dimensionality through its fusion of images of heterosexuality with those expressing a desire to build diasporic and cross-cultural connections.

These syncretic intersections and interactions were similarly apparent in a site addressed www.ibride.com,[21] suggesting that it may be for either Internet or international brides, and therefore aimed at a specific female readership. The site had an 'Etiquette Meeting Room' in which advice was sought on conducting cross-cultural weddings:

> [Message from Terry] I am Korean and my fiance is Chinese. We are having a big western wedding, but I would also like to incorporate both Chinese and Korean traditions into our ceremony and reception. Anybody run into similar situations and/or may have ideas on how to do this?

> [Follow-up message from Shirley] I too am in the same type of situation. I'm Chinese and husband to be is Irish. We're going to have the invitation both in English and Chinese. We're going to have an American buffet, but all the announcement[s] [will] be in both language[s].

Such sites are illustrative of the ways in which ethnic minority women are applying the Web to the building of communities and how the Web's interconnectivity facilitates the participation of women (Plant 1997), especially those from ethnic minorities, who, as Luttrell (1998: pp.249-254) argues due to their marginalisation, have a community-oriented consciousness. It is perhaps through this technical and social networking that ethnic minority women can affirm their status as the knowledge bearers within their families and communities (ibid). It constructs a kind of ethnic expertise but one that is not for the 'white gaze'.

All the abovementioned ethnic community self-help Web sites where women are discernible in their production have their own idiosyncratic forms of ethnic expertise. But their common characteristic seems to be that the distinction between those who are the experts and those who aren't is not marked; and the relationship between the former and latter is more horizontal than hierarchical. 'Experiential authority' (Clifford 1988: p.35) and self-representation, is privileged over institutional authority or the right to speak on behalf of others. However, it would be incorrect to designate this as a female quality in Web texts: it merely implies ethnic minority women's preference for communal kinds of self-representation, perhaps ones that do not reveal highly personal information. Ethnic minority women's marginalisation may steer them towards Web texts which have a more community-oriented consciousness (Luttrell 1988: pp.249-254).

In contrast, any discussion of the personal by men is highly individualised rather than in affiliation with other men. For example, Miller and Mather (1998) found there were five times more home pages by men than women. In addition to home pages, the empirical research shows that the lone male voice surfaces in other types of Web texts and contexts.

The Lone Male Voice

The lone male voice in representations of ethnicity can be seen in a Web article 'Commentary: US gives black Briton a new kind of racism',[22] chosen by Champagne. The article is part of the online edition of *The Detroit News*, so it has the backing of the media organisation. The writer, Gary Younge, refers to the politics of identity and identification that takes place within ethnic minorities through his personal experience of being a black British journalist in the US:

> Often people just think I am showing off. This is especially the case with African Americans. All I have to do is open my mouth and they prime themselves to ask 'Who are you trying to impress with that accent?'...Here in America, I look local and sound foreign...At home, I look foreign and sound local – and everybody tries hard not to notice. To say one is better or worse than the other would be too simplistic. The bottom line is that I will soon return to a racism I understand.

This individual representation of ethnicity by Gary Younge, made on his own behalf, resists attempts by ethnic 'leaders' to speak for him as clearly, he encountered obstacles in being embraced as a member of the black community in the US. His blackness was judged on the basis of his national affiliation, as marked by his accent, and became the grounds for his exclusion rather than inclusion. This conflict is akin to the one that took place in Britain in regard to the representation of Asians as black (Brah 1992: pp.127-128). Younge refers to his ostracism as a kind of racism from within, one that he does not comprehend, presumably because the Black Power movement, which originated in the US reconstructed blackness as a sign of political solidarity amongst diverse black ethnicities (ibid). Younge's experience exemplifies the construction of ethnicity as a site of struggle, one, in this case, he has overcome with his participation in media which gives him the authority to speak and access to the representational tools of the Web.

This individualised form of cultural commentary on the Web raises more anomalies and contradictions in the representation of ethnicity than generalised forms, whether they be from the 'white gaze' or ethnic community representatives. The Web allows these juxtapositions to be made, so that each contests the other in the same arena where there can be adjacent confrontations as well as fluky finds. The lone voice in a cultural critique on the Web is a reminder that there is diversity, hybridity and even disagreement within every ethnic community or diaspora; that the representation of ethnicity cannot be simply executed or easily resolved. A series of short stories, 'What Confucius Didn't Say',[23] published on the Web by writer Marty Chan as part of an Asian Canadian community site, exemplify the ambiguous relationships between constructions of Chineseness I found on the Web.

Chan examines, through Chinese food, the impossibility of cultural authenticity: 'Kung Pao Chicken. Eggrolls. Mu Shu Pork. Egg Foo Yung. Which China did this food come from?' Chan's point illustrates the constant process of adaptation, integration, incorporation and mutation in Chinese cuisine, changing according to the supplies and demands of a particular locality. This dynamism not only applies to culinary matters: food is only a metaphor for the continuous translation and reconfiguration of ethnicities. But this sort of depiction of Chineseness as inevitably hybridised, could be considered a thorn in the side of ethnic 'experts' or community leaders and the images of Chinese ethnicity they have constructed: it presents a direct contradiction to the notion of purely Chinese philosophy and customs like *qigong*, or of a singular history which connects all Chinese people as 'descendents of the dragon' (Buruma 1999, pp.9-12). It is an erosion of the authenticity of Chineseness on which they trade and mobilise people of Chinese ethnicity to act as one.

Nevertheless, Chan's description of his parents' efforts to give their children a 'White' Christmas experience would please those Chinese ethnic community leaders calling for more assimilation from their members into their host society:

> Back in the Seventies, my parents hadn't a clue about the holiday season. They were fresh off the sleigh, but they tried to get into the spirit of the season. While our neighbours trimmed their trees, dad screwed together a Zeller's Everlast Tree Facsimile. Instead of tinsel and Christmas ornaments, he hung shredded Chinese newspapers and Oriental pin cushions...Christmas dinner hit a little nearer to the mark. It wasn't turkey, but it was close: Peking Duck...Every year, I got money from "Santa" in a Chinese red packet...Dear old deluded mom and pop thought they were celebrating a 'White' Christmas.

Chan's use of humour undermines the sobriety and didacticism of the previously mentioned 'Taiwan Headline News' Web site imploring people of Chinese ethnicity to enter politics. Chan demonstrates that integration can be articulated locally, at the micro-level of everyday life, not just through representation in political structures. He also illustrates the pathos of when such cultural hybridisation is contrived. In this sense, Chan's Web texts have many parallels with the 'Master Lu's Fortune Cookies' site discussed in the last chapter (see note 12 in Chapter 7) in that both deconstruct traditional representations of Chineseness and reveal the fragility of notions of cultural authenticity.

It is evident from Chan's short stories and Younge's article, that the Web enables individual representations of ethnicity to be made and seen. Nevertheless, these examples are the work of professional writers: Chan is described as a playwright and Younge a reporter for *The Guardian*. Both are individual cultural commentaries which have institutional approval to represent membership to respective ethnic communities.

Earlier in the chapter, Web texts by individuals with institutional affiliations were also examined, although the lone voices in these disguised themselves as collective ones. There were other instances of sole-authored texts on the Web which foregrounded personal experience, as Chan and Younge do, but were more introspective, and by people from ethnic minorities preoccupied only with representing themselves.

Home pages are representations by (largely male) individuals on the Web (Miller and Mather 1998). They have different manifestations, but generally, do not claim to speak for anyone else except the author. More specifically, Chandler and Roberts-Young (1998), call these *personal* home pages because they have been created by the individual to whom it refers. As a result, they are concerned with personal experience and, indeed, rely upon it to give credence to their content. That is, they exude 'experiential authority' (Clifford 1988: p.35) as they are premised upon the self.

The egocentrism of home pages is implied ironically in 'Eon's Opinionated Page',[24] which was chosen by Champagne. It is simply a page of text with no links to other Web sites or pages, so it is completely self-contained and firmly in the category of home pages Miller (1995) defines as 'Hi, this is me (as an individual)': '...I'm not African-American. I'm Black... Very few of the Black people you're likely to meet on the street in the US are actually African-Americans. What they are is Black Americans. Anyway, you can just call me Black'. Eon emphasises his individuality by dissociating himself from African-American ethnicity and locating himself within the black diaspora. Therefore, his home page is not only a statement of his personal identity, it is also a declaration of his membership to a particular community (Miller and Mather 1998). More often, home pages represent the intersection of various, even numerous communities, of which the author is part.

At the top of Lawrence Lam's home page[25] is a picture of a knight in shining armour on horseback, followed by: 'Hello World out there! I am an Australian Chinese, just arrived [in] this part of the planet for good. I am also a new comer to this network and would like to make friends. Please do not hesitate to drop me a note or whatever attachment you like. GOODDAY MATE'. Lam has appropriated Australianness as part of his identity by calling himself 'Australian Chinese'. He therefore locates himself within a particular area of the Chinese diaspora. This is consistent with the intended audience of the Web site, whose address www.hkabc.net, suggests that it may be for Hong Kong (and) Australian-born Chinese (HKABCs). But by virtue of its presence on the Web, this particular 'cyborg diaspora' (Gajjala 1999) is assumed to be global and is confirmed by Lam's exclamation 'Hello World out there!'

However, Lam is not only part of an ethnic community and its online manifestation. His inclusion of an image of a knight in shining armour on his Web page, complete with its connotations of romance and bravery, also emphasises his masculinity and heterosexuality. The emphasis on the words 'GOODDAY MATE' through the use of upper case suggests a couple of possible readings: as an Australian expression and one which has masculine connotations, it is an assertion of his identity as an Australian male. The ambiguity of the term 'mate' may imply that he is not only looking for a friend (just a mate), but possibly a partner (a sexual mate) as well. Like a knight in shining armour, Lam deploys his Australian Chineseness with honour: to a potential audience of women of Chinese ethnicity, he says he would like to make 'friends', but incorporates signifiers of Australian heterosexual masculinity to modestly imply that he is seeking a 'mate'. It is the intersection of ethnicity, gender and sexuality (Brah 1992: p.131) which illustrates the multi-dimensionality of Lam's identity.

Like 'Eon's Opinionated Page', Lam's page is almost entirely link-free except for the provision of his e-mail address. That is, there are no electronic connections to the communities of which he claims to be part. The Web is not used to faciliate community development, it is merely used for self-representation, or as Miller (1995) describes it, self-advertisement. In contrast is the home page of Errol Welch,[26] which consists primarily of links to other sites. The site, which Welch calls 'Meth's UK Crib', does not explicitly state much about the author at all: 'This is my home page. It's about what I'm into! I'm Errol G, aka The Meth, aka The Godfather, aka Magnum!' Apart from this brief introduction in the first person, most of what the user learns about Welch is implicit in the sites to which his home pages link. It is through such connections that the user develops a sense of Welch's identity and his position as a node within various extended communities (Miller and Mather 1998). The range of names he is known by indicate his multi-dimensionality, and this is confirmed in the links from his Web page, which show that he has various interests including rap and R&B music and writing poetry. The link to 'Jamaica Online' and the use of the colours of Rastafaria (red, green and yellow) suggest he is probably of Jamaican ethnicity, but also takes an interest in other 'black voices', partly because, as the Web address shows, he is located in the UK and so may be a black Briton. He demonstrates the business enterprise that Hall (1996a, 1996b, 1998b) considers to be characteristic of black, British youth in that one of the headings on the home page is 'virtual resume', implying that the content of the Web page could be regarded as an electronic CV. Indeed, the intention of the page is also to promote Welch's skills as a Web designer: 'Do you like this Web site? Want your own Web page?' Thus 'Meth's UK Crib' straddles several categories in Miller's (1995) classification of Web home pages, including 'Hi this is me', 'This is what I think is cool', 'This is an advertisement for myself and the service I can provide', as well as 'the electronic curriculum vitae'. It exemplifies the process of 'bricolage' in the production of home pages (Chandler 1998) and in the construction of ethnic identities. The Web enables information to be constantly adapted, arranged and changed; facilitating the work of the ethnic 'bricoleur' as they 'duck and dive' from objectified representations of their ethnicities in the generation of their own.

This dynamism is evident in 'David Yuan's Home on the Internet' which, as a multifarious Web page, also acts as a metaphor for the author's identity. 'Bricolage' is demonstrated in its temporality: the pages are scattered with signifiers of Christmas like holly wreaths, trees and the heading 'Happy Holidays'; also there are specific items which are marked as 'new': 'The first Internet Chinese version of the Holy Bible is now available'. The practice of adding and subtracting aspects from his home page also highlights particular facets of Yuan's identity at different times. The recent link to a site in which the bible can be read in Chinese, depicts his ethnicity and (possibly new) religious affiliation. The prominent logo for La Trobe university indicates his proud membership to an Australian educational institution, which he verifies more specifically later on: 'I am now a postgraduate student in the Department of Computer Science and Engineering, La Trobe University in Melbourne, Australia...Of course, I can never stop learning about the fantastic world of computing and writing my C codes'.[27] This can be defined as the type of home page Miller (1995) describes as 'This is me as a member of an organisation', but it also has more informal qualities in its incorporation of quite personal information and its connotations of the communities with which Yuan is associated. It is through this inclusion of small detailed pieces of data that the process of 'bricolage' in his identity construction becomes apparent: thus far, he has represented himself as a Christian computing student of Chinese ethnicity living in Australia. His reference to his favourite kinds of software and hardware perhaps define him as a 'nerd', although as Squires (1996: p.200) argues, this image has been largely assigned to young, white, North American males. However, Asians males are demographically more experienced and active computer users than their white counterparts (ClickZ 2001).

The German subheading 'Herzlich willkommen auf meiner Homepage', combined with Yuan's claim that he is currently learning Spanish and his apparent Chinese literacy, show that he is mutli-lingual. His exhaustive list of places where he has lived and institutions where he has studied; his favourite cinema, airline, colours, sports, supermarket, and telephone company, amongst many other things; further expands exponentially his identity as a Christian computing student of Chinese ethnicity living in Australia. Therefore, the home page seems to be an idiosyncratic form of representation with which Web authors stake their unique place in the world. As Miller and Mather (1998) propose, the Web is where people emphasise who they are, not where 'people go to be someone else'. The Web becomes an extension of offline identities, where authors can be public and proud of who they are (Berry and Martin 2000: pp.74-81).

For ethnic minority home page authors, the Web seems to be the ultimate medium of self-representation, where the individual and personal is prioritised over the communal. Nevertheless, the communities to which the Web author belongs are always a constituent part of the self-representation (Wakeford 2000: p.35), whether this is subtle (with no direct references or links) or unequivocal (in the form of links from the Web page), albeit their membership to ethnic minorities is not necessarily privileged. For Nakamura (20002: p.111), the links from a Web site are as much representations of ethnicity and social networks, as the content within. This sort of relationship between the individual and community parallels autobiographical and feminist praxis (Stanley 1997; 1990: pp.12-15). However, the overwhelming majority (allowing for those that were gender-ambiguous) home pages found were created by men. This is affirmed by Nakamura's (2002: p.115) research showing women of colour to be under-represented in Web production.

It may have been due partly to the masculinity of home pages, as well as their recent introduction to searching on the Web, that the texts the research subjects found were not wholly representative of their ethnicities and identities:

> This site is better than the others I thought were appropriate...[and it] does summarise my ethnicity to some extent, otherwise I would love to see things like the traditional woven

> cloth that women [used] to do (Oyen referring to the 'Our Story' site).

> ...it does not summarise my ethnic identity because it does not have much information on how black British people live...most of the information was on famous Black people... (Sasha referring to 'Meth's UK Crib' site)

This points to the difficulties inherent in the representation of ethnicity, even if it is defined from within (Werbner 1997: p.18). While the Web has the capacity to depict the diversity and dynamism of ethnicities (Hall 1998b: p.39; Ross 1996: p.xi), the experiential differences emerging from its inflection by gender, class, sexuality and other aspects of identity (Brah 1992: p.310), make the task of speaking on behalf of anyone but oneself ever more problematic. Home pages take self-representation to its logical conclusion, but as Rubio asks, who is listening as everyone is exercising their right to express themselves? 'It's a denial of community, an orgy of solipsism...' (Rubio 1996).

Home pages make the Web appear to be a cacophony of heterogenous voices. For those who participate in their production, the Web enables the portrayal of complex ethnicities and identities, as well as resistance to traditional modes of ethnic representation. Paradoxically, for those consuming home pages, they are problematic tools of representation because of their particularity: they become simply another means of looking at others, never quite able to nor wanting to articulate the broader themes connecting communities. In short, they embody the tensions between the individual and the communal in the construction of ethnicity and identity.

Conclusions

This chapter has attempted to examine the multifarious configurations in the relationship between Web production, consumption, representation, the 'white gaze' and ethnic minority Web authors/users; in addition to the ways in which these different assemblages are expressed in particular Web genres. While those ethnic minorities participating on the Web could be considered the 'techno-elites' of the ethnic communities of which they are part, they nevertheless deployed the Web as a technology of resistance, inverting the traditional dynamics of power which tend to endow the 'white gaze' with the right to speak on behalf of ethnic minorities who are then the object of representation.

The white producer/white consumer equation was interrupted by ethnic minority claims of 'ethnic expertise'. Mostly directed at the 'white gaze', and asserted from within institutions, such as in Web sites for media and education, as well as individually in home pages; the equation was transformed into one of ethnic producer/white consumer. Employing both experiential and institutional authority, this kind of contestation of the 'white gaze' could be considered to be at the 'frontline' of the politics of representation on the Web, given that it is challenging a history of images of ethnicity which have not been self-produced.

Nevertheless, resistance to the 'white gaze' is also apparent on the peripheries of these representational activities in more localised forms on the Web where the equation has been that of ethnic producer/ethnic consumer. That is, sites in which ethnic Web producers appeal to their ethnic communities bypass the 'white gaze' altogether in that the white reader is excluded from the interaction. In addition, the hierarchies usually associated with the producer/consumer relationship are flattened to some extent through the very necessity of providing self-help services, and alternative ways of seeing and mobilising ethnicities that may not otherwise be available in other media.

But there is a gap between Web production and consumption nonetheless. By appealing to their communities through the technology, ethnic minority voices on the Web assume unhindered access to it. This is because for 'techno-elites' – those ethnic minorities who are members of educational, media, cultural and political institutions and networks in the West – there are few obstacles to Web access. They are the ones who travel and migrate virtually as well as geographically. They are also the ones who claim the right to speak on behalf of their ethnic communities.

There is not only a social, economic, occupational and geographical bias to ethnic participation on the Web, but a related gendered one too. While the presence of ethnic minority women was apparent in cyberspace, Web production could still be largely defined as 'men's work' (Nakamura 2002: p.115), given the prominence of representations by ethnic males and their particular tendency to assume an advocacy or leadership role on behalf of their communities. The claim that, like many other technologies, women are relegated to the realm of consumption on the Web is not borne out in the empirical research, as seen especially in community-based ethnic self-help sites. But statistically speaking, it has been shown that men dominate consumption too, with Internet users in all countries except the US and Canada being 52-63% male (Pastore 2001), which is also reflected in visitor data from the top domains (ClickZ 2002). The unique situation in which this research was conducted tends to suggest Web consumption to be a predominantly female activity, as the research subjects had only basic IT skills which excluded them from Web production. However, even in their Web consumption, through their selection of Web texts, they mirror the activities and images of Web producers by ducking and weaving themselves into and through the Web at the same time as they dodge and resist attempts for their identities to be defined simplistically. That is, ethnic minority Web producers and consumers are able to deploy the Web to reconfigure ethnicity in their own image.

Notes

1 Monawar, T. (1994-1996 no longer online) 'Republic of Sudan' at http://www.columbia.edu/~tm146/sudan.html. While this page no longer exists, there is a link to it from http://www.eng.fsu.edu/~abdelraz/links2.htm

2 XK. (1995-1998) 'De Web Site on Jamaica' at http://www.jamaicans.com/jam.htm. This site has since been redesigned, but retains some of the previous content.

3 'New Age Network China' at http://newage.net.cn/. This site has since been redesigned for Chinese language users, where previously, the Yahoo search results appeared in English.
4 Kazi, Z. (1998) 'The Bangladeshi Home Pages' at http://www.virtualbangladesh.com/polls/BOTY97.html. This site has since been redesigned with a new Web address, but the content remains the same.
5 Yuan, H. (26 December 1997 online 4 June 2004) 'Chinese Web Directory' at http://www.ag.arizona.edu/~heng/chinese.chinese.html. The Web address remains the same and Heng Yuan's personal homepage still exists, but the directory is now defunct.
6 Orrin, C. (no date, no longer online) 'Our Story' at http://homepages.seas.upenn.edu/~cardell/africa.html. While this page no longer exists, there is a link to it from http://www.abyssiniacybergateway.net/exodus.html
7 Panafrican News Agency. (26 January 1998 no longer online) 'Zimbabwean Culture on the Death Bed?' at http://www.africanews.org/PANA/news/19980126/feat3.html
8 Taiwan Headline News. (1996 no longer online) 'Chinese to enter politics to stop anti-Asian sentiment' at http://apec.gaspa.washington.edu/apec/media/tainews/october/961021anti_tn.html
9 New Beacon Bookshop. (no date, no longer online) 'New Beacon Books' at http://www.newbeacon-books.com. The domain name seems to have changed ownership, but the bookshop is referred to in sites such as http://www.wguides.com/city/1/233_3537.cfm
10 African Centred Research Group (no date, no longer online) 'African Centred Research Group' at http://www.shef.ac.uk/uni/projects/jitol/africa.html
11 The College of New Jersey. (1997 no longer online) 'Religious Traditions of the African Diaspora' at http://www.tcnj.edu/~afamstud/diaspora/. Whilst the page doesn't exist in its previous form, most of its content is still available as an updated course description at http://dickinsg.intrasun.tcnj.edu/diaspora/intro.html
12 Association of Concerned African Scholars. (2 July 1996 no longer online) 'Background: Repression of Nigerian Students and Academics'at http://www.prairienet.org/acas/nalert2.html. Whilst the page doesn't exist in its previous form, its content is still available as part of a new Web site at http://www.africaaction.org/docs96/nig9607.htm
13 New York Times News Service. (16 December 1997 no longer online) 'Women Struggle as Heads of Dominican Households'at http://www.latinolink.com/news/news97/1216ndom.htm
14 The Chronicle (1997-2003 online 4 June 2004) *The Chronicle: Changing Black Britain* at http://www.chronicleworld.org. The publication still exists although the Web address has changed and the site has been redesigned.
15 Blacknet UK. (1996-2004) 'Blacknet UK' at http://www.blacknet.co.uk. The Web address remains the same although the site has been redesigned.
16 The Official Pakistan Page. (1995-1997 no longer online) 'TOPP Site Awards' at http://www.pak.org/ncgibin/topps/list/others. Whilst the page doesn't exist in its previous form, the main Web address is still a Pakistani portal site.
17 The 1990 Trust. (no date, online 4 June 2004) 'Black Information Link'at http://www.blink.org.uk. The site has since been redesigned.
18 Mallal,N. (no date, no longer online) 'South Asian Women Together' at http://www.uoguelph.ca/~nmallal
19 Extreme-FX Personals. (1997 no longer online) 'Re: Chinese ladies' at http://www.extreme-fx.com/personals/wmessages/79.html
20 Asian Meow-Meow's Club (no date) at http://www.meow-meow.com. The domain name appears to have changed ownership although the original site is still linked from many dating and matchmaking sites.

21 Etiquette Meeting Room. (1997 no longer online) 'Re: Cross Cultural Marriages' at http://www.ibride.com/ibride/meetings/etiqroom/276.html
22 Younge, G. (13 October 1996 no longer online) 'Commentary: US gives Briton a new kind of racism' in *The Detroit News* at http://www.detnews.com/1996/menu/stories/69327.htm
23 Chan, M. (1997 online 4 June 2004) 'What Confucius Didn't Say' at *China City: Bringing an Asian Canadian community to you* at http://www.asian.ca/media/chinacity/confu.htm
24 Eon. (no date, no longer online) 'Eon's Opinionated Page' at http://www.camilleon.com/~eon/rant.html
25 Lam, L. (no date, no longer online) 'Welcome to Lawrence Lam's Home Page' at http://www.hkabc.net/~fwlam. While this page no longer exists, the main domain name is still in operation.
26 Welch, E. (no date, no longer online) 'Meth's UK Crib' at http://www.bogo.co.uk/magnum/
27 Yuan, D. (January 1997) 'David Yuan's Home on the Internet' at http://www.cs.latrobe.edu.au/~yuand/. While this page no longer exists, it is linked from several Christian Web sites.

Chapter 9

Conclusions

In this chapter, I reiterate and reflect upon the achievements of the research, that is, what I intended to do, what I did, how I felt about it, what I learnt from it and what I might have done differently in hindsight.

What Did I Do? What Did I Intend?

In summary, the research could be described as an enquiry into ethnic minority production, representation and consumption on the World Wide Web. But despite the apparent breadth of the research topic, the contribution made by this book is only small. Limiting the research to a study of the Web, as opposed to the entire Internet, within a well-defined population of ethnic minority women research subjects was a deliberate strategy, in part to allow a focus on the UK at a time when it was leading Internet use in Europe in terms of the proportion of the overall population which was online (Pastore 2000a). The empirical specificity was a response to the weight of US-centric work about the Internet. As an in-depth body of work (in contrast to a collection of essays), it adds to the much needed qualitiative, grounded studies (Nakamura 2002: p.xviii; Wakeford 2000: p.34; Sterne 1999: p.270 that have focused on particular aspects of the Internet, such as chat rooms and newsgroups. Its purpose was to focus on the areas of cyberspace which do not fulfil the widely accepted mantra that it is white and male.

The originality of the research lies in its tackling of issues of ethnic minority production, representation and consumption on the Web, as well as the environment in which the research was conducted. The study of Web consumption by the research subjects was a by-product of our involvement in the larger research framework of Project @THENE and its concern with enhancing access to higher education to women from ethnic minorities through computer-mediated distance learning. This context provided unique opportunities for examining the technology's use both within educational and domestic environments. These concrete settings were important in highlighting the relationships of power in the everyday lives of the research subjects which, in turn, informed their interactions with the Web and searches for online representations of their ethnicities.

Indeed, it is the question of Web representation that has been at the core of the research and upon which the study of both production and consumption have hinged. That is, it has been through the analysis of Web texts, the points of representation, that the practices of Web production and consumption have been examined. It is through the analysis of representations of ethnicity that particular patterns and practices of representation on the Web and in other media could be closely scrutinised and contrasted. For example, self-produced Web representations of ethnicity could be compared with objectified ones; and those constructed by institutions could be juxtaposed with those of individuals.

The intention of the research tasks was to treat representation as a realm of engagement – between producer and consumer; author and reader; who is speaking on behalf of whom and who is being spoken to; the micro level of the text and the macro level of the world it seeks to depict. But they also tried to do so without surrendering too much power to the text: the Web illustrates the redundancy of investing too much responsibility in texts for portraying 'the truth' given the difficulties of verifying the legitimacy of claims made. Rather, I wanted representation to be considered a point of departure for the research subjects to critically analyse ethnic minority activity on the Web, the extent to which it spoke to their personal experiences and the strategies used in the constant struggle to speak and be adequately represented.

Representation was also an an anchor by which a comparison between the Web and other cultural forms could be made. Applying theories of race and representation in media studies to the Web, for example, allowed for a broader interrogration of the relationship between ethnicity and technology. The connections between structural representation at the level of production, and representation in the text or image could be explored on the Web as they had been in the broadcast media. The extent to which the latter differed and paralleled the former distinguished the unique qualities of the Web's mode of production and representation. Media and cultural studies also provided models of consumption against which ethnic Web participation could be gauged.

The interdisciplinary nature of the research not only contributed the desired multiple perspectives on technology but was absolutely necessary. In addition to the ethnicity/technology equation explored in media and cultural studies, the women and technology relation as examined in feminist studies was also pertinent, and so too studies of the use of technology in education. While each discipline has its own 'take' on technology and how it should be studied, it was always clear from the beginning that using the ideas and frameworks from other academic disciplines to study the Web would be limited. This is, in part, due to the idiosyncracies of the Web, especially the intimacy of its processes of production, distribution and consumption which does not seem to be a characteristic of any previous technology. Also, there are so few prior studies of technology which consider the various dimensions covered in this research simultaneously.

As such, the research has implications not only for how the Web might be studied in future, but also how ethnicity can be conceptualised, how educational research might be done, how feminist studies could be expanded and how disciplines might intersect in the course of doing research.

What Did I Learn?

Despite the dynamic nature of technological change, the necessity for currency and contemporaneity in Web research is not absolute. As I write this in 2004, the snapshot of cyberspace in the last years of the 20th century that this book provides remains relevant. While the US no longer dominates Internet use as much as it once did, it still has the highest number of Internet users in the world. Similarly, the gender ratios are not as skewed as they were, but the majority of Internet users in all countries (bar the US and Canada) are male nonetheless. Irrespective of the continued uptake of the Internet, home computer ownership generally remains the preserve of the educated and affluent. Although the media landscape has been dramatically transformed, the relations of production, consumption and representation seem to be undergoing a slower metamorphosis.

The preoccupation in the research with representation on the Web has highlighted ongoing areas of debate. It has shown the issue of representation to be complex. Looking at it in relation to the Web has necessitated a rethinking of the representation of ethnicity, especially how this has been scrutinised in other media such as film and television. Previous media studies of the representation of race and ethnicity which have conclusively found ethnic minorities to have been depicted negatively or inadequately seem far too simplistic for the Web in light of the findings of the research. The multitude of depictions of ethnicity found on the Web demonstrated the eternal difficulties of representation. Being only a microcosm of the possibilities which were not explored, they reinforced the conceptual mobility of ethnicity, its constant redefinition and reconstruction from both inside and outside ethnic communities.

Such multifarious articulations of ethnicity in Web texts were evident in: claims of cultural purity and authenticity founded upon notions of originality and homogeneity; reinventions of racial dichotomies and binary oppositions, both unconscious and strategic; as well as tributes to diversity under diasporic commonality. These portrayals of ethnicity on the Web were further exponentially differentiated by their intersections with gender, age, sexuality, nationality and other aspects of identity. While these representations were made from within as well as outside ethnic communities, they were distinguished by how they located its producers and consumers in terms of modes of address and the degree of visibility given to the author's ethnicity. Thus, questions of representation on the Web cannot be isolated from questions of production, distribution and consumption, just as ethnicity cannot be understood separately from other elements of subjectivity. That is, neither representation nor ethnicity are self-contained in ways which make them easy to theorise. The Web exacerbates this to the extent of warranting new approaches to studying ethnicity and representation which avoid redundant positive/negative dualisms or wholesale dismissal of texts. However, this focus on representations of ethnicity on the Web was resisted by the research subjects in their regular use of the Web for other purposes. That is, the research compelled them to seek representations of ethnicity on the Web when the technology was clearly applied very differently outside the scope of the course. The research subjects' extra-curricular participation on the Web showed that it was not primarily used to access representations of ethnicity.

But perhaps it was the various perceptions and high expectations of the nature of representation itself that were problematic. As discussed in Chapter 3, media studies research on representation has been based on certain assumptions. One is that representation should be a true and accurate reflection of reality. The second, based on the first, is that past representations form a trajectory by which present and future representations are produced. Indeed, the research subjects anticipated experiencing the same either non-existent or racist representations of ethnicity on the Web that they had encountered previously in other media, premised upon the ideas that racism in the media is symptomatic of racism in society, and further that new media reproduces the racist representational practices of its predecessors. Their resignation to the impossibility of locating Web representations of their ethnicity seemed to be founded upon a notion that no text could ever articulate their ethnicity completely and/or precisely.

Categorisations as to which representations of ethnicity could be said to be objectified or self-produced were found to be fragile where the Web is concerned, as its heterogeneity works against any form of organisation or generalisation. While the objectifying 'white gaze' was found in academic Web sites, these were countered by those produced from positions of 'experiential authority' (Clifford 1988: p.35) and subjective knowledge. Similarly, mainstream media organisations seemed to repeat and extend the representational practices of older media on the Web, yet equivalent sites developed by ethnic groups rejected aspirations to 'objective' reportage in their news gathering techniques, preferring instead to appeal directly to their ethnic audience/ readership and provide community information services. It could not be said that 'ethnic absolutism' (Hall et al 1992: p.308) and claims of authenticity, in which ethnicity is depicted as pure and whole, were only made from the 'white gaze' because they were equally employed by representatives of ethnic minorities as a form of 'strategic essentialism' (Spivak 1993: pp.2-5). Whether this right to represent was asserted from within or without, it was subject to contestation, making redundant any portrayal of ethnicity as static and complete. The Web allows individual representations of ethnicity to challenge and intersect with those of communities and institutions and vice versa, so that innovative texts can emerge from the commercial realm just as regressive ones can come from ethnic minorities. This crossing of traditional boundaries is facilitated by the Web's interconnectivity, its capabilities for networking, which enables dynamic and multiple forms of mobilisation and tribalisation. Transient communities can be established, which then borrow and apply representational practices from previous temporary solidarities before disbanding and moving on. This makes the issue of representation all the more thorny and fraught with dangers, and the sensitivity of the research subjects to this demonstrates it to be the case.

The Web is a medium that is complicated and complicates. Not only is this apparent in relation to the representation of ethnicity, but also in the production of these representations for the Web. Ethnic minority Web production seems to capitalise on its technological capacity for declassification. That is, there is no conspicuous separation of dominant and resistant forces: the 'white gaze' resides next to and is engaged in representational struggle with ethnic communities and spokespeople, as much as ethnic individuals and groups do so with each other. Despite the biases of search engines, no party has a stranglehold on representational power which can only be contested independently or externally, as seen in the minority media sector's relationship to mainstream media organisations. Instead, the Web is a hybridised version of these industries, in one sense a minority medium in its appeal to niche audiences, and yet in another, a mass medium in terms of its global accessibility. This means that freedom of expression is not necessarily sacrificed to the freedom of the market: because the latter is demassified, the commercial imperatives are perhaps more lax. The dissolution of these sorts of dichotomies makes the Web a derivative of previous technologies while simultaneouly totally unlike them. For ethnic minorities, the possibilities for participation in Web production are potentially as great as that of its consumption, unlike in older media where they have been relegated to readership, spectatorship or audience. In light of research showing more users are also becoming producers (Pew Research Center 2003; Greenspan 2004), it is this blending of what was once distinct which encourages ethnic minority Web activity, as it allows for easy movement between the realms of production and consumption; the private and the public; the individual, institutional and community. These manoeuvres are analagous to the ones relating to the construction of ethnicity and to the notion of the postmodern 'virtual self' (Nakamura 2002: p.xv), which are characterised by a similar sense of dynamism. As witnessed in the research subjects, people from ethnic minority backgrounds 'duck and dive' amongst representations of ethnicity, in permanent states of transition between 'where you are from' and 'where you are at' (Gilroy 1990/1: pp.3-16), in response to the difficulties of defining their difference. While the Web has this flexibility which lends itself to ethnic community mobilisation, it is not to say it is devoid of certain hierarchies and biases.

The loose structure of the Web I have described merely enhances accessibility to ethnic minorities, but is not universally accessible. Although the incalculable number of texts on the Web and the mysterious idiosyncracies of search engines render it problematic to make any broad generalisations, the findings from this study suggest that the responsibility, whether this be sanctioned or self-proclaimed, for representing ethnic communities on the Web rests with only a few members of those communities who typically reside in the West and are affiliated with institutions which give them the authority to speak on behalf of others. By and large, they are also male across most genres of Web text, indicating that it is men that are at the helm of production or at least in positions as community or institutional representatives, thereby giving them representational power. This profile is supported by statistical surveys of global Internet use. On the other hand, this research found ethnic minority women to have a central involvement in developing communities in cyberspace. But again, I would refrain from resorting to the familiar dualisms of mainstream media versus independent media, which equate institutional representations with conservatism, the 'white gaze' and masculinity; and community-based ones with more progressive and innovative imagery (as argued in studies of black film). At the same time as women from ethnic minorities seemed to be marginalised to community development Web sites, ethnic minority men also seemed to be adopting a feminist praxis in the highly personalised and experiential nature of individual home pages.

This criss-crossing of genres obviously contains new possibilities, such as men experimenting in areas traditionally demarcated as feminine. However, there are also drawbacks to this representational mobility. Access to the means of production is important for ethnic minorities in enabling this but enterprising representations of ethnicity are not always the result. Where there is crossover, there is also borrowing of the best and worst kind. Thus, as men reveal subjective experiences in the production of their home pages, where are the women? That is, the exchanges are not necessarily even.

Furthermore, as the Web increases opportunities for the representation of ethnicity, those undertaking Web production have their representational power magnified exponentially. Not only can they take up various positions of representation (as individuals and/or on behalf of groups, communities or institutions), but the positions from which they speak are easily transformed or disguised. That is, who is speaking and their legitimacy in doing so is not always transparent. The sheer mass of texts on the Web, coupled with their transience, undermines the authority of representation whilst it makes it easier to claim. In an educational context, this particular feature of the Web may be frustrating to students, as it was to the research subjects, but it assists in developing their abilities to question the authenticity of texts.

As the research tasks were built into the curriculum, the research subjects' critical analytical skills that were being honed as part of their studies were also applied to the research. However, it was difficult to distinguish the motivations and the position (of student or research subject) from which a response was made. It was also unclear whether it was directed at my capacity as a tutor or a researcher. Therefore, the intersection of the researcher/researched relationship with that of a tutor/student one invariably added a level of complexity. Where research is conducted in an educational setting, there is an inevitable crossover between what students learn as part of the curriculum and what they learn as research subjects participating in a study.

Nevertheless, I recognised that mine was an opportune research situation. The students were readymade research subjects. Their access to computers and the Web was supplied as part of the course. The research tasks were built into the curriculum, giving me the chance to learn from my teaching as much as from the research itself. That is, the educational context was a foundation from which various research initiatives, including my own, could easily grow. The immediacy of this empirical setup was both a gift and a constraint in that it lent a predetermined dynamic of power to the study. The inherently unequal power relations of a formal learning environment have to be acknowledged irrespective of the extent to which they were minimised. Certainly, in spite of my own identification as an ethnic minority woman and participation as a research subject, this power discrepancy served to illuminate the important differences between the other research subjects and myself, differences which overshadowed our commonalities.

Doing it Differently: Implications for Future Research

Given the multi-faceted nature of the study, there are many things which, in hindsight, could be altered and improved about the research. As mentioned previously, it was apparent that the research tasks were negotiated with reluctance by some of the research subjects, who felt that the representation of ethnicity had been tackled unsuccessfully in other media and been consistently insufficient in one sense or another, setting a precedence for the Web. With such apprehensions surrounding the issue of representation, it may have been justifiable to lessen its emphasis and concentrate, instead, on ethnic minority Web production and consumption.

The research tasks may have unknowingly fostered the belief, in requiring the research subjects to find Web sites that summarised their ethnicities, that there would be something to find! Without any extended debate or discussion surrounding the research tasks or the concept of representation, they may have implied a search for Web texts which necessarily portrayed the complexities and subtleties of ethnicity with stark realism. In addition, I did not envisage the lasting effects of the disappointment and dissatisfaction with representations of ethnicity on film and television which would compound the research subjects' negativity about issues of representation. But the alternatives of simple resignation that representation will never suffice, or a celebration of 'erase-ism', the capacity for the Web to render ethnicity invisible, are otherwise eternally unsatisfactory in their avoidance of the difficult debates surrounding representation, which have to be confronted. The complexities of representation and ethnicity are not an argument for their dismissal.

In terms of research, there is much scope for the further study of ethnic minority Web producers and production. In this particular study, it is approached in a limited way only through analysis of representations of ethnicity made in Web texts. As mentioned previously, the study avoided getting into truth/falsity debates because the focus was on what sort of representations of ethnicity were being made by whom and how they might be interpreted, rather than their accuracy. As the research subjects were primarily consumers of the Web, it oriented the research towards scrutinising the ways in which a group of ethnic minority women might engage with representations of ethnicity on the Web. But there is future potential in conducting a similar investigation of a group of ethnic minority Web producers' creations of representations of ethnicity, which likewise employs methodologies from cultural studies, feminist praxis, action research and ethnography. After all, Web texts also offer insights into modes of production, as has been demonstrated in this study. Furthermore, the transience of Web texts is driven by authors not readers (Mitra and Cohen 1999: pp.181,191). Perhaps even the same group of research subjects could be studied as they gain skills and experience in Web production.

Just as the research subjects were identified as atypical Web consumers in terms of their socio-economic, ethnic minority and gender status; a study of ethnic minority Web producers could also be assessed accordingly and in terms of their relationship to the dominant forces operating in cyberspace. Nonetheless, this study demonstrated that questions of Web consumption cannot be considered in isolation from issues of

Web production and representation. Given their intimacy, the transition between Web production and consumption for Web producers is only one of the kinds of border crossings that could be scrutinised in prospective research.

The sort of ethnography of ethnic minority Web consumption in the domestic sphere undertaken in this research may be applied to Web production as well, particularly as the research illustrated the close connection between the personal and the public in Web texts such as individual home pages. By examining the specificities of Web consumption, the research subjects' activities in the virtual world were set against their day-to-day existence as homemakers, mothers and students. There is certainly as much that could be explored about how ethnic minority Web producers weave their virtual work into their everyday lives, although it would not have to be limited to domestic contexts, but could be examined in professional environments as well.

Is Web production characterised by time-shifting, as seen in the research subjects' consumption of the Web at unsociable hours? If so, is this a result of domestic or childcare responsibilities, or the financial necessity of making the most of the Web during off-peak times? Is there the same oscillation between technical euphoria and dismay for Web producers as was seen in the research subjects? Indeed, there is scope, even within this study, to gain more insight into ethnic minority Web consumption, let alone production. But because the research relied on interviews and transcripts derived from Project @THENE, another study with different purposes, and written responses to a lesser degree, it is difficult to attribute accurately the extent to which the findings were culturally, gender or socio-economically specific. A more detailed, possibly observational study, concentrating mainly on the research subjects' Web consumption may be able to disentangle this, and an equivalent investigation into the intricacies of Web production would also be worthwhile.

Observation of the research subjects' interactions with the Web, whilst inappropriate for this study, might be a potentially fruitful methodology for later inquiry into ethnic minority Web consumption and production. It would provide the researcher with a direct view of the ways in which the research subject integrates information technology into their domestic (or other) situation, and participates in the Web according to the demands of the latter. It would also give an indication of the research subjects' computer usage in relation to their engagement with other media in those surroundings. For example, for the group of ethnic minority women in this study who were jaded television viewers, the Web was used as a replacement for television as it was a new and unknown technology for them which offered the hope of alternative kinds of texts that acknowledged and addressed their marginalisation instead of making them feel powerless and invisible because of it. The opportunity of observing the processes of Web consumption and/or production would allow for the research to be less directed, as it was in this study. That is, because the findings were garnered from set research tasks, the Web texts which the research subjects were looking at outside of these were largely ignored. Yet these are important as they arguably provide a different perspective of the representations and affiliations which appeal to ethnic minority women Web consumers, and they may or may not make reference to ethnicity at all.

The directed nature of the research was influenced by the educational context in which it took place and it is for this reason that observation of the research subjects in their home settings was unsuitable. The researcher/researched relationship was intersected by an additional tutor/student one, making the dynamics of power a difficult negotiation even within a straightforward interview situation. The intention of the @THENE Year Zero, the computer-mediated distance learning course on which the research subjects were enrolled, was for them to develop as independent learners: having the tutor in their home observing them for research purposes would seemingly defeat that objective. Furthermore, unlike in ethnographies of television viewing, where families are observed in their living rooms watching their favourite television programmes, the practices of Web production and consumption are more individualistic pursuits, where the researcher might find it either difficult to participate or to minimise his/her presence given the lack of communal interaction.

However, the context of the research did present an opportunity to look closely at the fuzzy boundaries between the private sphere of the home and the formal sphere of education. Not only does this have implications for how the Web might be studied in similar environments in the future, but also how educational delivery and research may be conducted. With the Internet becoming central to teaching, the Web is not only a technology of representation but also a learning resource. Therefore, it ought to be considered as a multi-purpose tool, with education as one of its primary applications. Irrespective of the formal educational context of Project @THENE, the Web was still used for extra-curricular learning by the research subjects and their children. Further inquiry could potentially investigate the diverse ways in which the Web is appropriated in students' learning, both informally as well as officially. Questions of representation may figure in this, but perhaps more inadvertently than was the case in this study. Integrating the research tasks into the curriculum meant there was minimal negotiation between the student research subjects and myself as both tutor and researcher about the inclusion of issues of representation in their learning contract.

A less structured approach could be constructive in exploring the Web's possibilities as a facilitator of experiential learning, where students' journeys into cyberspace are self-directed and attuned to their personal needs and interests. In this way, what is learnt in the virtual realm is relevant to their everyday lives, so the Web cannot be easily regarded as a neutral arena where questions of (in)equality don't matter. Indeed, this empirical sudy of a group of ethnic minority women's consumption of the Web has highlighted the need to promote equality of access in order to achieve equality in representation. An educational environment which gives primacy to personal experience and ensures that its students are not technologically disadvantaged in either their Internet skills or access can successfully make the connection between the real and the virtual, and subsequently encourage deep learning.

Finally...

The particularity of this study's examination of ethnic minority production, representation and consumption on the World Wide Web is a small contribution to research into ethnicity and technology; and a response to the dominance of US-based research about the Internet. Despite its specificity, it offers numerous points of departure for future examination of the Web, whether or not it is related to ethnic minorities. There is potential to focus primarily on Web production, representation or consumption, although these are inevitably linked. The practices of Web production amongst ethnic minorities or other marginalised communities could be examined, as there are too many representations of ethnicity on the Web for any researcher to exhaust. Alternatively, representations of other aspects of identity on the Web, such as gender, age, sexuality or nationality, are possible areas of investigation. Study of Web consumption amongst ethnic minorities or other marginalised communities in alternative environments to the home is also feasible. The research has also demonstrated the possibilities for adapting methodologies from a range of disciplines to study the Web, and the need to be innovative in their application in accordance with the participating group or community and the idiosyncracies of that technology. In addition, it has illustrated how theoretical models pertaining to a particular technology (such as television) might be translated to another (such as the Web) and in the process of doing so, offer new perspectives and critiques of both. In this way, this book has critically analysed as well as experimented with the ways in which the Web is studied and conceptualised. This balance between pioneering knowledge and understanding it through existing frameworks applies to any exploration of new technology.

Bibliography

Abbate, J. (1994). 'The Internet Challenge: Conflict and Compromise in Computer Networking' in Summaton, J. (ed) *Changing Large Technical Systems*. Boulder: Westview.

Ackers, H. (1993) 'Racism, Sexuality and the Process of Ethnographic Research' in Hobbs, D. and May, T. (eds) *Interpreting the Field: Accounts of Ethnography*. Oxford: Clarendon Press.

Akeroyd, A. (1991) 'Personal Information and Qualitative Research Data: Some Practical and Ethical Problems Arising from Data Protection Legislation' in Fielding, N. and Lee, R. *Using Computers in Qualitative Research*. London: Sage Publications.

Alkalimat, A. (1996) 'Technological Revolution and Prospects for Black Liberation in the 21st Century' *in cyRev: A Journal of Cybernetic Revolution, Sustainable Socialism and Radical Democracy.* Issue 4 Summer/Fall at http://www.net4dem.org/cyrev/archive/issue4/articles/liberation/Liberation1.htm

Ang, I. (1996) *Living Room Wars: Rethinking Media Audiences for a Postmodern World*. London: Routledge.

Ang, I. (1994) 'On Not Speaking Chnese: Postmodern Ethnicity and the Politics of Diaspora' in *New Formations: On Not Speaking Chinese*. London: Lawrence and Wishart. 24. Winter.

Apple, M. (1992) 'Is the New Technology Part of the Solution or Part of the Problem in Education' in Beynon, J. and Mackay, H. (eds) *Technological History and the Curriculum*. London: The Falmer Press.

Argyle, K. and Shields, R. (1996) 'Is There a Body on the Net?' in Shields, R. (ed) *Cultures of Internet*. London: Sage Publications.

Arnold, E. and Plymire, D. (2000) 'The Cherokee Indians and the Internet' in Gauntlett, D. (ed) *Web Studies*. London: Arnold.

Baginski, N. (15 October 1997 online 4 June 2004) 'The Human and the Machine: Interview with Nick Baginski' at http://www.nettime.org/Lists-Archives/nettime-l-9710/msg00025.html

Baker Jr, H. (1991) 'Hybridity, The Rap Race and Pedagogy for the 1990s' in Penley, C. and Ross, A. (eds) *Technoculture*. Minneapolis: University of Minnesota Press.

Bandyopadhyay, N.; Leung, L. and Stepulevage, L. (2001) 'Otherness Negotiated through Technology: Stories by Three Women Technologists'. Unpublished.

Barker, J. and Tucker, R. (eds) (1990) *The Interactive Learning Revolution: Multimedia in Education and Training*. London: Kogan Page.

Barry, A. (1996) 'Who Gets to Play? Art, Access and the Margin' in Dovey, J. (ed) *Fractal Dreams: New Media in Social Context*. London: Lawrence and Wishart.

Beaty, L. (1997) *Developing Your Teaching Through Reflective Practice*. Birmingham: Staff and Educational Development Association.

Becker, H. (1992) 'The Methodology of a Writing Observed' in Clough, P. *The End(s) of Ethnography*. Newbury Park: Sage Publications.

Benjamin, W. (1992) 'The Work of Art in the Age of Mechanical Reproduction' in Frascina, F. and Harris, J. (eds) *Art in Modern Culture*. London: Phaidon Press.

Berelson, B. and Salter, P. (1973) 'Majority and Minority Americans: an analysis of magazine fiction' in Cohen, S. and Young, J. (eds) *The Manufacture of News: Social Problems, Deviance and the Mass Media*. London: Constable.

Bernstein, B. (1975) *Class, Codes and Control: Towards a Theory of Educational Transmissions.* London: Routledge and Kegan Paul.

Berry, C. and Martin, F. (2000) '"Queer" and Asian On and Off the Net: The Role of Cyberspace in Queer Taiwan and Korea' in Gauntlett, D. (ed) *Web Studies*. London: Arnold.

Blumer, H. (1992) 'A Methodology for Writing Observation' in Clough, P. *The End(s) of Ethnography.* Newbury Park: Sage Publications.

Bobo, J. (1993) 'Reading Through the Text: The Black Woman as Audience' in Diawara, M. (ed) *Black American Cinema.* New York: Routledge.

Bottomley, G. and de Lepervanche, M. (eds) (1988) *The Cultural Construction of Race*. Sydney: Sydney Association for Studies in Society and Culture.

Boud, D. (1988) *Developing Student Autonomy in Learning*. London: Kogan Page.

Boud, D. and Miller, N. (1996) *Working with Experience: Animating Learning*. London: Routledge.

Brah, A. (1992) 'Differences, Diversity and Differentiation' in Donald, J. and Rattansi, A. (eds) *'Race', Culture and Difference*. London: Sage.

British Broadcasting Corporation. (1997) *The Net.* Monday 13 January. 11:15pm to 12am. BBC2.

British Broadcasting Corporation. (1996) *The Hollow State*. Saturday 28 September. 8:10pm to 9:00pm. BBC2.

Brown, A. (1997) 'Making the invisible visible by challenging the myth of the universal teacher' in *SCUTREA 25th Anniversary CD-ROM Conference Proceedings 1970-1997.* London: Standing Conference on University Teaching and Research in the Education of Adults.

Buckingham, D. (1993) *Reading Audiences*. Manchester: Manchester University Press.

Buruma, I. (4 November1999 online 5 June 2004) 'China in Cyberspace' in *New York Review of Books*. Volume 46, number 17 at http://www.nybooks.com/articles/article-preview?article_id=316

Butler, T. (2000) *Easterm Promise: Education and Social Renewal in London's Docklands.* London: Lawrence and Wishart.

Campaign for Press and Broadcasting Freedom. (1996) *Media Manifesto.* London: Campaign for Press and Broadcasting Freedom.

Carstephen, M. and Lambiase, J. (1998) 'Domination and Democracy in Cyberspace: Reports from the Majority Media and Ethnic/Gender Margins' in Ebo, B. (ed) *Cyberghetto or Cybertopia? Race, Class and Gender on the Internet.*

Chan, A. (1997) 'Diversity and Institutional Change: Current and Proposed Research' in *Crossing Boundaries, Breaking Borders: Research in the Education of Adults 27th Annual SCUTREA Conference Proceedings.* London: Universityof London Birkbeck College. 1-3 July.

Chandler, D. (1998 online 4 June 2004) 'Personal Home Pages and the Construction of Identities on the Web' at http://www.aber.ac.uk/media/Documents/short/webident.html

Chandler, D. and Roberts-Young, D. (1998 online 4 June 2004) 'The Construction of Identity in the Personal Homepages of Adolescents' at http://www.aber.ac.uk/media/Documents/short/strasbourg.html

Chung, Y. (1990) 'At the Palace: researching gender and ethnicity in a Chinese restaurant' in Stanley, L. (ed) *Feminist Praxis: Research, Theory and Epistemology in Feminist Sociology.* London: Routledge.

Cisler, S. (31 January 1998 online 5 June 2004) 'The Internet and Indigenous Groups' in *Cultural Survival Quarterly.* Issue 24.1 at http://www.culturalsurvival.org/publications/csq/

Cisler, S. (18 September 1998a online 4 June 2004) 'Electronic Public Space in 1998' at http://www.nettime.org/Lists-Archives/nettime-l-9809/msg00062.html

ClickZ Stats staff. (12 February 2004 online 22 March 2004) 'Population Explosion!' at *http://www.clickz.com/stats/big_picture/geographics/article.php/5911_151151*

ClickZ Stats staff. (29 January 2004a online 22 March 2004) 'Active Internet Users by Country, December 2003' at *http://www.clickz.com/stats/big_picture/geographics/article.php/3305941*

ClickZ Stats staff. (22 January 2002 online 22 March 2004) 'Men Still Dominate Worldwide Internet Use' at *http://www.clickz.com/stats/big_picture/demographics/article.php/5901_959421*

ClickZ Stats staff. (18 December 2001 online 22 March 2004) 'Asians Among Most Wired Americans' at *http://www.clickz.com/stats/big_picture/demographics/article.php/5901_942621*

Clifford, J. (1988) *Predicament of Culture*. Cambridge: Harvard University Press.

Clough, P. (1992) *The End(s) of Ethnography*. Newbury Park: Sage Publications.

Cohen, P. (1997. *Rethinking the Youth Question: Education, Labour and Cultural Studies*. Basingstoke: Macmillan.

Costigan, J. (1999) 'Forest, Trees and Internet Research' in Jones, S. (ed) *Doing Internet Research*. London: Sage.

Cox, J. (1994) *London's East End: Life and Traditions*. London: Weidenfeld and Nicholson.

Crane, D. (2000) 'In Medias Race: Filmic Representation, Networked Communication, and Racial Intermediation' in Kolko, B; Nakamura, L. and Rodman, G (eds) *Race in Cyberspace*. New York: Routledge.

Cubitt, S. (1996) 'It's Life Jim, But Not As We Know It: Rolling Backwards into the Future' in Dovey, J. (ed) *Fractal Dreams: New Media in Social Context*. London: Lawrence and Wishart.

Curran, J. (1997) 'Rupert the Bear'. *Great Expectations: Six Seminars of the New Governance*. Monday 17 February. London: Signs of the Times.

Dawson, K. (2 February 1999 online 4 June 2004) 'TBTF for 1999-02-01: Squammers' at http://www.nettime.org/Lists-Archives/nettime-l-9902/msg00007.html

Delgado-P, G and Becker, M. (31 January 1998 online 5 June 2004) 'Latin America: The Internet and Indigenous Texts' in *Cultural Survival Quarterly*. Issue 21.4 at http://www.culturalsurvival.org/publications/csq/

Denzin, N. (1999) 'Cybertalk and the Method of Instances' in Jones,S. (ed) *Doing Internet Research*. London: Sage.

Dery, M. (1994) *Flame Wars: The Discourse of Cyberculture*. Durham: Duke University Press.

Diawara, M. (1993) *Black American Cinema*. New York: Routledge.

Donath, J. (1998) 'Identity and Deception in the Virtual Community' in Smith, M. and Kollock, P. (eds) *Communities in Cyberspace*. London: Routledge.

Dovey, J. (ed) (1996) *Fractal Dreams: New Media in Social Context*. London: Lawrence and Wishart.

DP Connect. (1997) *Women in IT Campaign Brief*. Bromley: DP Connect.

Eisenberg, R. (2 December 1998 online 4 June 2004) 'Re: netscape' at http://www.nettime.org/Lists-Archives/nettime-l-9812/msg00003.html

Fanon, F. (1967) *Black Skin, White Masks*. New York. Grove Weldenfeld.

Faulkner, W. (1997) 'The Power and the Pleasure? or "making gender stick" to engineers' in *NECSTS Workshop on Gender, Science and Technology*. Trondheim, Norway. 27-31 May.

Faulkner, W. (1996) 'Feminism and Technology: Tools of a Masculine Trade or Female Empowerment' in *VII Jornada Internacionales de Coeducacion en Ciencia, Technologia y Sociedad*. Valencia, Spain. 17-19 October.

Feldman, T. (1997) *An Introduction to Digital Media*. London: Routledge.

Fernback, J. (1999) 'There is a There There: Notes Towards a Definition of Cybercommunity' in Jones, S. (ed) *Doing Internet Research*. London: Sage.

Franck, P. (22 August 1998 online 4 June 2004) 'Technological Revolution: Repression, Fascism and the Potential for the Release of Desire' at http://www.nettime.org/Lists-Archives/nettime-l-9808/msg00067.html

Freeth, T. (1982) 'Racism on TV: Bringing the Colonies Back Home' in Cohen, P. and Gardener, C. (eds) *It Ain't Half Racist, Mum: Fighting Racism in the Media*. London: Comedia Publishing Group.

Fuller, M. (27 September 1999a online 4 June 2004) 'Linker' at http://www.nettime.org/Lists-Archives/nettime-l-9909/msg00154.html

Fuller, M. (21 September 1999b online 4 June 2004) 'Break the Law of Information' at http://www.nettime.org/Lists-Archives/nettime-l-9909/msg00126.html

Fuller, M. and Lovink, G. (10 August 1999 online 4 June 2004) 'trash txt' at http://www.nettime.org/Lists-Archives/nettime-l-9908/msg00029.html

Gajjala, R. (6 August 1999 online 4 June 2004) 'Cyborg Diaspora and Virtual Imagined Community: Studying SAWNET' in *Cybersociology Issue 6: Research Methodology Online* at http://www.cybersociology.com

Gauntlett, D. (2000) *Web Studies*. London: Arnold.

Giddens, A. (1991) *Modernity and Self-Identity: Self and Society in the Late Modern Age*. Cambridge: Polity Press.

Gilbert, J. (1997) *New Labour's Blurred Vision: A Signs of the Times Discussion Paper*. London: Signs of the Times. May.

Gillespie, M. (1995) *Television, Ethnicity and Cultural Change*. London: Routledge.

Gilroy, P. (1995) 'Intervention for what? Black TV and the Impossibility of Politics' in Givanni, J. (ed) *Remote Control*. London: BFI African and Caribbean Unit.

Gilroy, P. (1993) *The Black Atlantic: Modernity and Double Consciousness*. London: Verso.

Gilroy, P. (1990/1991) 'It Ain't Where You're From, Its Where You're At...The Dialetics of Diasporic Identification' in *Third Text*. Volume 13. Winter.

Gilroy, P. (1987) *There ain't no Black in the Union Jack*. London: Hutchison.

Givanni, J. (ed) (1995) *Remote Control*. London: British Film Institute African and Caribbean Unit.

Godell, L. (2000) 'Europe's free Internet lunch fades away' in *Fletcher Research Internet Analysis Newsletter*. Volume 3, Number 5. 26 April.

Gonzales, J. (2000) 'The Appended Subject: Race and Identity as Digital Assemblage' in Kolko, B; Nakamura, L. and Rodman, G. (eds) *Race in Cyberspace*. New York: Routledge.

Graham, B. (1996) 'Play with Yourself: Pleasure and Interactive Art' in Dovey, J. (ed) *Fractal Dreams: New Media in Social Context*. London: Lawrence and Wishart.

Greed, C. (1990) 'The Professional and the Personal: A Study of Women Quantity Surveyors' in Stanley, L. (ed) *Feminist Praxis: Research, Theory and Epistemology in Feminist Sociology*. London: Routledge.

Greenspan, R. (1 March 2004 online 22 March 2004) 'Creating, Contributing Content Catching on' at http://www.clickz.com/stats/big_picture/applications/article.php/3319651

Greenspan, R. (2 January 2004a online 22 March (2004) 'Ethnic Personalities Apparent Online' at http://www.clickz.com/stats/big_picture/demographics/article.php/3294691

Greenspan, R. (21 October 2003 online 22 March 2004) 'Europe on Different Sides of the Gender Divide' at http://www.clickz.com/stats/big_picture/demographics/article.php/5901_3095681

Greenspan, R. (26 September 2003a online 22 March 2004) 'African-Americans Create Online Identity' at http://www.clickz.com/stats/big_picture/demographics/article.php/3084241

Greenspan, R. (16 April 2003b online 22 March 2004) 'Internet Not For Everyone' at http://www.clickz.com/stats/big_picture/demographics/article.php/2192251

Greenspan, R. (22 April 2002 online 22 March 2004) 'China Pulls Ahead of Japan' at http://www.clickz.com/stats/big_picture/geographics/article.php/5911_1013841

Guerrero, E. (1993) 'The Black Image in Protective Custody' in Diawara, M. (ed) *Black American Cinema*. New York: Routledge.

Hall, M. (1998a online 4 June 2004) 'Africa Connected' in *First Monday.* Issue 3 at http://www.firstmonday.org/issue3_11/hall

Hall, S. (1998b) 'Aspirations and Attitude...Reflection on Black Britain in the '90s' in *New Formations: Frontlines, Backyards*. London: Lawrence and Wishart. Number 33. Spring.

Hall, S. (1996a) 'Frontlines, Backyards: Changing Geographies of "Race", Nation and Ethnicity' Open Plenary Session of *Frontlines, Backyards: A Conference with Differences*. London: University of East London Centre for New Ethnicities Research. 6-7 December.

Hall, S. (1996b) 'New Ethnicities' in Morley, D. and Chen, K. (eds) *Stuart Hall: Critical Dialogues in Cultural Studies*. London: New York.

Hall, S. (1995) 'Black and White TV' in Givanni, J. (ed) *Remote Control*. London: British Film Institute African and Caribbean Unit.

Hall, S. (1993) 'Ethnicity, Race and Nation' in the *Empire, Nation and Language Conference*. London: University of London Institutes of Advanced Studies. December 3.

Hall, S. (1992) *Rethinking New Ethnicities: Three Blind Mice (One Black, One White, One Hybrid)*. London: New Ethnicities Unit, University of East London.

Hall, S. (1981) 'The White of their Eyes' in Bridges, G. and Brunt, R. (eds). *Silver Linings: Some Strategies for the Eighties*. London: Lawrence and Wilhart.

Hall, S.; Critcher, C.; Jefferson, T; Clarke, J. and Roberts, D. (eds) (1978) *Policing the Crisis: Mugging, the State, and Law and Order.* Oxford: Polity Press.

Hall, S.; Held, D. and McGrew, T. (eds) (1992. *Modernity and its Futures*. Oxford: Polity Press in association with the Open University.

Hall, T. (1996c) *Utilising Multimedia Toolbook 3.0*. Danvers: Boyd and Fraser Publishing Company.

Halleck, D. (1991) 'Watch Out Dick Tracy! Popular Video in the Wake of *Exxon Valdez*' in Penley, C. and Ross, A. (eds) *Technoculture*. Minneapolis: University of Minnesota Press.

Hamman, R. (7 August 1998 online 4 June 2004) 'Introduction to Digital Third Worlds: overcoming the economic and educational barriers to Internet access and online publishing' in *Cybersociology Issue 3: Digital Third Worlds and Questions of Net Access* at http://www.socio.demon.co.uk/magazine/3/is3intro.html

Hammersley, M. and Atkinson, P. (1995) *Ethnography: Principles in Practice*. London: Routledge. 2nd edition.

Haraway, D. (1985) 'A Manifesto for Cyborgs: Science, Technology and Socialist Feminism in the 1980s' in *Socialist Review*. Volume 80.

Hartmann, P. and Husband, C. (1973) 'The Mass Media and Racial Conflict' in Cohen, S. and Young, J. (eds) *The Manufacture of News: Social Problems, Deviance and the Mass Media*. London: Constable.

Herman, E. and Chomsky, N. (1988) *Manufacturing Consent: The Political Economy of the Mass Media*. New York: Pantheon Books.

Hernton, C. (1988) *Sex and Racism in America*. New York: Grove Weidenfeld.

Hesse, B. (1996) 'The Futures of Racism and Representation' Workshop Session of *Frontlines, Backyards: A Conference with Differences*. London: University of East London Centre for New Ethnicities Research. 6-7 December.

Hill, L. (2001) 'Beyond Access: Race, Technology, Community' in Nelson, A. and Tu, T. (eds) *Technicolor: Race, Technology and Everyday Life*. New York: NYU Press.

HMSO. (1995) *London: Facts and Figures*. London: HMSO.

HMSO. (1991) *The 1991 Census on CD-ROM*. Cambridge: Chadwyck-Healey.

Hobbs, D. (1989) *Doing the Business: Entrepreneurship, the Working Class and Detectives in the East End of London*. Oxford: Oxford University Press.

Hoch, P. (1979) *White Hero, Black Beast: Racism, Sexism and the Mask of Masculinity*. London: Pluto Press.

Hoffman, D. and Novak, T. (2 February 1998 online 4 June 2004) 'Bridging the Digital Divide: The Impact of Race on Computer Access and Internet Use' at http://elab.vanderbilt.edu/research/papers/html/manuscripts/race/science.html

Holme, A. (1985) *Housing and Young Families in East London*. London: Routledge and Kegan Paul.

hooks, b. (1993) 'The Oppositional Gaze: Black Female Spectators' in Diawara, M. (ed) *Black American Cinema*. New York: Routledge.

hooks, b. (1992) *Black Looks*. London: Turnaround.

Horsman, M. (1996) 'Manifesto for a new media age' in *New Statesman*. London: Statesman and Nation Publishing Co. 15 November.

Hossfeld, K. (2001) '"Their Logic Against Them": Contradictions in Sex, Race and Class in Silicon Valley' in Nelson,A. and Tu, T. (eds) *Technicolor: Race, Technology and Everyday Life*. New York: NYU Press.

Hutnyk, J. (1997) 'Adorno at Womad: South Asian Crossovers and the Limits of Hybridity-talk' in Werbner, P. and Modood, T. (eds) *Debating Cultural Hybridity: Multicultural Identities and the Politics of Anti-Racism*. London: Zed Books.

Ifekwunigwe, J. (1998) 'Multiple Occupancies: Locating Home Base' in *New Formations: Frontlines Backyards*. London: Lawrence and Wishart. 33. Spring.

Interrogate the Internet. (1996) 'Contradictions in Cyberspace: Collective Response' in Shields, R. (ed) *Cultures of Internet*. London: Sage Publications.

Jain,S. (1997) 'Cultural Mapping' in *Wired Women: Virtual Worlds, Real Lives – A Conference for International Women's Day*. Portsmouth: University of Portsmouth School of Art Design and Media. March 8.

Jhally, S. and Lewis, J. (1992) *Enlightened Racism*. Oxford: Westview Press.

Johnson, F. (1996) 'Cyberpunks in the White House' in Dovey, J. (ed) *Fractal Dreams: New Media in Social Context*. London: Lawrence and Wishart.

Jones, J. (1993) 'The Construction of Black Sexuality: Towards Normalizing the Black Cinematic Experience' in Diawara, M. (ed) *Black American Cinema*. New York: Routledge.

Jones, S. (ed) (1999) *Doing Internet Research*. London: Sage.

Kahle, B. (7 October 1997 online 4 June 2004) 'Brewster Kahle: Archiving the Internet' at http://www.nettime.org/Lists-Archivea/nettime-l-9710/msg00014.html

Karpf, A. (1987) 'Recent feminist approaches to women and technology' in McNeil, M. (ed) *Gender and Expertise*. London: Free Association Press.

Keats, D. (1993) *Skilled Interviewing*. Hawthorn, Victoria: Australian Council for Educational Research.

Kelly, K. and Wolf, G. (1997) 'Push! Kiss your browser goodbye: the radical future of media beyond the Web' in *Wired*. March.

Kendall, L. (1999) 'Recontextualising "Cyberspace": Methodological Considerations for Online Research' in Jones,S. (ed) *Doing Internet Research*. London: Sage.

Kennett, P (1994) 'Exclusion, post-Fordism and the "New Europe"' in Brown, P. and Crompton, R. (eds) *A New Europe? Economic Restructuring and Social Exclusion*. London: UCL Press.

Khan, F. (1988) 'The Inner City Context and the Generation of Curricula in Adult Education' n *SCUTREA 25th Anniversary CD-ROM Conference Proceedings (1970-1997)*. London: Standing Conference on University Teaching and Research in the Education of Adults.

Kleiner, K. (1997) 'Surfing Prohibited' in *New Scientist*. London: IPC Magazines. 25 January.

Kolko, B; Nakamura, L. and Rodman, G. (2000) *Race in Cyberspace*. New York: Routledge.

Krysmanski, H.; Teubener, K. and Zurawski, N. (1999 online 4 June 2004) 'Broadcasting the Web: Interfaces for Sciences and the Mass Media (TV and Internet)' at http://www.uni-muenster.de/EuropeanPopularScience/nonpublic/99063.html

Kumar, A. (2001) 'Temporary Access: The Indian H-1B Worker in the US' in Nelson, A. and Tu, T. (eds) *Technicolor: Race, Technology and Everyday Life*. New York: NYU Press.

Landow, G. (1994) 'Bootstrapping Hypertext: Student-created Documents, Intermedia, and the Social Construction of Knowledge' in Barrett, E. (ed) *Sociomedia: Multimedia, Hypermedia, and the Social Construction of Knowledge*. London: The MIT Press.

Lee, P. (1991) 'The Absorption of Foreign Media Culture' in *Asian Journal of Communication*. Volume 1. Number 2.

Leicester, M. (1999) *Disability Voice*. London: Jessica Kingsley Publishers.

Leicester, M. (1993) *Race for a Change in Continuing and Higher Education*. Buckingham: Open University Press and Society for Research into Higher Education.

Leung, L. (2001) 'From Set Menu to All-You-Can-Eat: comparing representations of my ethnicity in broadcast and new media technologies ' in Henwood, F.; Kennedy, H. and Miller, N. (eds) *Cyborg Lives? Women's Technobiographies*. York: Raw Nerve Books.

Leung, L. (1996-1997) *Project @THENE Diary*. Unpublished and confidential.

Lévi-Strauss, C. (1977) *Structural Anthropology: Volume II*. London: Allen Lane.

Lichtman, J. (December 1998 online 5 June 2004) 'The Cyber Sisters Club: Using the Internet to Bridge the Technology Gap with Inner City Girls' in *T.H.E. Journal* at http://www.thejournal.com/magazine/vault/A2004.cfm

Lillie, J. (1997 online 5 June 2004) 'Possible roles for electronic community networks and participatory development strategies in access programmes for poor neighborhoods' at http://www.ibiblio.org/jlillie/310.html

Lillie, J. (1998 online 5 June 2004) 'Cultural uses of new, networked Internet information and communication technologies: implications for US Latino identities' at http://www.ibiblio.org/jlillie/thesis.html

Linn, P. (1987) 'Gender Stereotypes, Technology Stereotypes' in McNeil, M. (ed) *Gender and Expertise*. London: Free Association Press.

Lippard, L. (1992) 'Mapping' in Frascina, F. and Harris, J. (eds) *Art in Modern Culture*. London: Phaidon Press.

Lockard, J. (no date, no longer online) 'Virtual Whiteness and Narrative Diversity' at http://darkwing.uoregon.edu/~ucurrent/uc4/4-lockard.html

Lockard, J. (2000) 'Babel Machines and Electronic Universalism' in Kolko, B; Nakamura, L. and Rodman, G. (eds) *Race in Cyberspace*. New York: Routledge.

Lull, J. (1990) *Inside Family Viewing*. London: Routledge.

Luttrell, W. (1988) 'Different Ways of Knowing: A Feminist Perspective on the Intersection of Gender, Race and Class in the Social Construction of Knowledge' in *SCUTREA 25th*

Anniversary CD-ROM Conference Proceedings (1970-1997). London: Standing Conference on University Teaching and Research in the Education of Adults.

Mallapragada, M. (2000) 'The Indian Diaspora in the USA and Around the Web' in Gauntlett, D. (ed) *Web Studies*. London: Arnold.

Marriott, M. (1998) ' Frank Racial Dialogue Thrives on the Web' *in New York Times*. Sunday 8 March. Page 1.

Mashengele, D. (1997) 'Africentricity: New Context, New Challenges, New Futures' in *SCUTREA 25th Anniversary CD-ROM Conference Proceedings (1970-1997)*. London: Standing Conference on University Teaching and Research in the Education of Adults.

Mashengele, D. (1995) 'The Creative Management of Biography: A Strategy of Survival and Resistance for One Black Researcher' in *SCUTREA 25th Anniversary CD-ROM Conference Proceedings (1970-1997)*. London: Standing Conference on University Teaching and Research in the Education of Adults.

Mason, E. (no date, online 5 June 2004) 'Resisting Erase-ism on the Net' in *Brillo Magazine* No. 3 at http://www.brillomag.net/No3/erasism.htm

McDonald, J. (1995) 'Te(k)nowledge: Technology, Education, and the New Student/Subject' in *Science As Culture*. London: Process Press. Volume 4. Part 4. Number 21.

McPherson, T. (2000) 'I'll Take My Stand in Dixie-Net: White Guys, the South, and Cyberspace' in Kolko, B; Nakamura, L. and Rodman, G (eds) *Race in Cyberspace*. New York: Routledge.

Melkote, S. and Liu, D. (1999) 'The Role of the Internet in Forging a Pluralistic Integration: A Study of Chinese Intellectuals in the United States'. Unpublished article.

Meridian. (1996) *Cyberspace*. Sunday 8 December. 10:45pm to 11:45pm. Antelope Productions.

Miller, H. (June 1995 online 4 June 2004) 'The Presentation of Self in Electronic Life: Goffman on the Internet' at http://ess.ntu.ac.uk/miller/cyberpsych/goffman.htm

Miller, H. and Mather, R. (1998 online 4 June 2004) 'The Presentation of Self in WWW Home Pages' in *IRSS '98 Conference Proceedings* at http://www.sosig.ac.uk/iriss/papers/paper21.htm

Miller, N. (1993) *Personal Experience, Adult Learning and Social Research: developing a sociological imagination in and beyond the T-group*. University of South Australia: Centre for Research in Adult Education for Human Development.

Mitra, A. (1997) 'Virtual Commonality: Looking for India on the Internet' in Jones, S. (ed) *Virtual Culture: Identity and Communication in Cybersociety*. London: Sage.

Mitra, A. and Cohen, E. (1999) 'Analysing the Web: Directions and Challenges' in Jones, S. (ed) *Doing Internet Research*. London: Sage.

Modood, T. (1997) '"Difference", Cultural Racism and Anti-Racism' in Werbner, P. and Modood, T. (eds) *Debating Cultural Hybridity: Multicultural Identities and the Politics of Anti-Racism*. London: Zed Books.

Morley, D. (1993) *Television, Audiences and Cultural Studies*. London: Routledge.

Morris, G (1982) 'Employment, Training and the Work of the Black Media Workers' Association' in Cohen, P. and Gardener, C. (eds) *It Ain't Half Racist, Mum: Fighting Racism in the Media*. London: Comedia Publishing Group.

Morrissey, B. (28 February 2003 online 22 March 2004) 'Black Online Population Narrows Adoption Gap' at http://www.clickz.com/stats/big_picture/demographics/article.php/1855931

Mosco, V. (1982) *Pushbutton Fantasies: Critical Perspectives in Videotex and Information Technology*. Norwood: Ablex Publishing Corporation.

Mulgan, G (1996) 'High Tech and High Angst' in Dunant, S. and Porter, R. (eds) *The Age of Anxiety*. London: Virago.

Murdoch, R. (1989) 'The technology of freedom' in *The Weekend Australian*. November 11-12. pp.25-27.

Nakamura, L. (2002). *Cybertypes: Race, Ethnicity and Identity on the Internet*. New York: Routledge.

Negroponte, N. (1995) *Being Digital*. London: Hodder and Stoughton.

NCET. (1996a) *Gender and IT Information Sheet*. Coventry: National Council on Educational Technology.

NCET. (1996b) *Attracting Girls to IT Project Sheet*. Coventry: National Council on Educational Technology.

Nelson, A. and Tu, T. (2001) *Technicolor: Race, Technology and Everyday Life*. New York: NYU Press.

Nguyen, D. and Alexander, J. (1996) 'The Coming of Cyberspace Time and the End of the Polity' in Shields, R. (ed) *Cultures of Internet*. London: Sage Publications.

Nguyen, M. (2001) 'Tales Of An Asian Geek Girl' in Nelson, A. and Tu, T. (eds) *Technicolor: Race, Technology and Everyday Life*. New York: NYU Press.

Ow, J. (2000) 'The Revenge of the Yellowfaced Cyborg Terminator' in Kolko, B; Nakamura, L. and Rodman, G. (eds) *Race in Cyberspace*. New York: Routledge.

Panos. (1998 online 4 June 2004) 'The Internet and Poverty: Real Help or Real Hype?' at http://www.panos.org.uk/resources/reportdetails.asp?id=1049

Pascall, A. (1982) 'Black Autonomy and the BBC' in Cohen, P. and Gardener, C. (eds) *It Ain't Half Racist, Mum: Fighting Racism in the* Media. London: Comedia Publishing Group.

Pastore, M. (26 July 2001 online 22 March 2004) 'Internet Remains a Man's Domain' at *http://www.clickz.com/stats/big_picture/demographics/article.php/5901_809341*

Pastore, M. (18 June 2001a online 22 March 2004) 'Woman Maintain Lead in Internet Use' at *http://www.clickz.com/stats/big_picture/demographics/article.php/5901_786791*

Pastore, M. (20 March 2001b online 22 March 2004) 'British Internet Market Continues to Grow, Mature' at *http://www.clickz.com/stats/big_picture/geographics/article.php/5911_718651*

Pastore, M. (15 June 2000 online 22 March 2004) 'Digital Divide More Economic than Ethnic' at *http://www.clickz.com/stats/big_picture/demographics/article.php/5901_395581*

Pastore, M. (1 May 2000a online 22 March 2004) 'European Internet Use Still Behind the US' at *http://www.clickz.com/stats/big_picture/geographics/article.php/5911_351591*

Pastore, M. (25 October 1999 online 22 March 2004) 'Netwatch Demographic Stats' at *http://www.clickz.com/stats/big_picture/demographics/article.php/5901_225371*

Patelis, K. (22 March 1999 online 4 June 2004) 'Political Economy of the Internet' at http://www.nettime.org/Lists-Archives/nettime-l-9903/msg00068.html

Pew Research Center (19 March 2004 online 22 March 2004) 'Daily Internet Activities' in *Pew Internet & American Life Project* at http://www.pewinternet.org/reports/chart.asp?img=Daily_Activities_3.19.04.htm

Pew Research Center (19 March 2004 online 22 March 2004) 'Internet Activities' in *Pew Internet & American Life Project* at http://www.pewinternet.org/reports/chart.asp?img=Internet_Activities_3.19.04.htm

Pew Research Center (2003 online 22 March 2004) 'Summary of findings' in *Pew Internet & American Life Project* at http://www.pewinternet.org

Phillips, M. (1995) 'Black and White in Colour' in in Givanni, J. (ed) *Remote Control*. London: British Film Institute African and Caribbean Unit.

Pieterse, J. (1992) *White on Black: Images of Africa and Blacks in Western Popular Culture*. London: Yale University Press.

Pillinger, J. (1988) 'Methodological Problems of Small-Scale Community-Based Action Research' in *SCUTREA 25th Anniversary CD-ROM Conference Proceedings (1970-1997)*.

London: Standing Conference on University Teaching and Research in the Education of Adults.

Pines, J. (1992) *Black and White in Colour: Black People in British Television Since 1936*. London: British Film Institute.

Plant, S. (1997) Keynote speech at *Wired Women: Virtual Worlds, Real Lives – A Conference for International Women's Day*. Portsmouth: University of Portsmouth School of Art Design and Media. March 8.

Preece, J. (1996) 'Positions of Race and gender in Adult Continuing Education: Excluded Discourses' in *SCUTREA 25th Anniversary CD-ROM Conference Proceedings (1970-1997)*. London: Standing Conference on University Teaching and Research in the Education of Adults.

Reid, E. (1989) 'Television Viewing Habits of Young Black Women in London' in *Screen*. Volume 30. Numbers 1 and 2. Winter/Spring.

Reid, M. (1993) *Redefining Black Film*. Oxford: University of California Press.

Rheingold, H. (1992 online 5 June 2004) 'A Slice of Life in my Virtual Community' in *Media Literacy Review* at http://interact.uoregon.edu/MediaLit/mlr/readings/articles/aslice.html

Rix, V. (1997) 'Industrial Decline, Economic Restructuring and Social Exclusion in London East (1980s and 1990s)' in *Rising East: The Journal of East London Studies*. London: University of East London. Volume 1. Number 1.

Robins, D. and Cohen, P. (1978) *Knuckle Sandwich: Growing Up in the Working Class City*. Harmondsworth: Penguin.

Robins, K. (1991) 'Tradition and translation: national culture in its global context' in Corner, J. and Harvey, S. (eds) *Enterprise and Heritage: Crosscurrents of National Culture*. London: Routledge.

Robinson, P. (1998) 'Equity and Acess to Computer Technology for Grades K-12' in Ebo, B. (ed) *Cyberghetto or Cybertopia? Race, Class and Gender on the Internet*.

Rose, T. and Coleman, B. (2001) 'Sound Effects' in Nelson, A. and Tu, T. (eds) *Technicolor: Race, Technology and Everyday Life*. New York: NYU Press.

Roseneil, S. (1993) 'Greenham Revisited: Researching Myself and My Sisters' in Hobbs, D. and May, T. (eds) *Interpreting the Field: Accounts of Ethnography*. Oxford: Clarendon Press.

Ross, A. and Greaves, M. (2001) 'Net-working: The Online Cultural Entrepreneur' in Nelson, A. and Tu, T. (eds) *Technicolor: Race, Technology and Everyday Life*. New York: NYU Press.

Ross, K. (1996) *Black and White Media: Black Images in Popular Film and Television*. Cambridge: Polity Press.

Rubio, S. (February 1996 online 4 June 2004) 'Home Page' in *Bad Subjects: Political Education for Everyday Life*. Issue 24 at http://eserver.org/bs/24/rubio.html

Ruhmann, I. (18 August 1997 online 4 June 2004) 'Langer/Ruhmann: Germany's Multimedia Law' at http://www.nettime.org/Lists-Archives/nettime-l-9708/msg00082.html

Said, E. (1995) *Orientalism*. London: Penguin.

Said, E. (1993) 'Cultural War: Insiders and Outsiders' in the *Empire, Nation and Language Conference*. London: University of London Institutes of Advanced Studies. December 2.

Sceats, C. (2000) 'Dot com TV ads pay off, but for how long?' in *Forrester Research Internet Analysis Newsletter*. Volume 1, Number 1. 24 July.

Schiller, H. (1996) *Information Inequality: the Deepening Social Crisis in America*. London: Routledge.

Shields, R. (ed) (1996) *Cultures of Internet*. London: Sage Publications.

Silk, C. and Silk, J. (1990) *Racism and Anti-Racism in American Popular Culture*. Manchester: Manchester University Press.

Silver, D. 'Margins in the Wires: Looking for Race, Gender and Sexuality in Blacksburg Electronic Village' in Kolko, B; Nakamura, L. and Rodman, G. (eds) *Race in Cyberspace*. New York: Routledge.

Silverstone, R. (1997) 'Technologies, Texts and Discursive Spaces: Notes Towards the Interactive' at *University of East London Department of Cultural Studies Seminar*. London: University of East London. 6 March.

Solomos, J. and Back, L. (1996) *Racism and Society*. London: Macmillan Press.

Sosnoski, J. (1999) 'Configuring as a Mode of Rhetorical Analysis' in Jones, S. (ed) *Doing Internet Research*. London: Sage.

Spender, D. (1996) *Nattering on the Net: Women, Power and Cyberspace*. North Melbourne: Spinifex Publishing.

Spivak, G. (1993) *Outside in the Teaching Machine*. New York: Routledge.

Squires, J. (1996) 'Fabulous Feminist Futures and the Lure of Cyberculture' in Dovey, J. (ed) *Fractal Dreams: New Media in Social Context*. London: Lawrence and Wishart.

Stalder, F. (1999 online 4 June 2004) 'Beyond Portals and Gifts: Towards a Bottom-Up Net-Economy' in *First Monday*. Issue 4 at http://firstmonday.org/issues/issue4_1/stalder

Stanley, L. (1997) *Auto/Biography: it may be fun but is it science? Department of Innovation Studies Research and Development Seminar*. London: University of East London. March 12.

Stanley, L. (ed) (1990) *Feminist Praxis: Research, Theory and Epistemology in Feminist Sociology*. London: Routledge.

Sterne, J. (1999) 'Thinking the Internet: Cultural Studies versus the Millennium' in Jones, S. (ed) *Doing Internet Research*. London: Sage.

Sudan, R. (2000) 'Sexy SIMS, Racy SIMMS' in Kolko, B; Nakamura, L. and Rodman, G. (eds) *Race in Cyberspace*. New York: Routledge.

Terranova, T. (1996) 'Digital Darwin: Nature, Evolution and Control in the Rhetoric of Electronic Communication' in *New Formations: TechnoScience*. London: Lawrence and Wishart. Number 29. Autumn.

Thomas, R. (1998) *Conducting Educational Research*. London: Bergin and Garvey.

Tulloch, J. (1990) 'Television and Black Britons' in Goodwin, A. and Whannel, G. (eds) *Understanding Television*. London: Routledge.

Tunstall, J. (1993) *Television Producers*. London: Routledge.

Tunstall, J. (1977) *The Media are American: Anglo-American Media in the World*. London: Constable.

Turkle, S. (1996) *Life on the Screen: Identity in the Age of the Internet*. London: Weidenfeld and Nicholson.

Turner, G. (1990) *British Cultural Studies: an introduction*. London: Unwin Hyman.

UEL. (1997a) *@THENE: Year Zero to New Technology Degrees Validation Document*. London: University of East London. May.

UEL. (1997b) *@THENE: Year Zero to New Technology Degrees Student Handbook (1997-8)*. London: University of East London. May.

Usher, R. (1996) 'Textuality and reflexivity in educational research' in Scott, D. and Usher, R. (eds) *Understanding Educational Research*. London: Routledge.

Usher, R. (1995) 'Telling the story of the self/deconstructing the self of the story' in *SCUTREA 25th Anniversary CD-ROM Conference Proceedings (1970-1997)*. London: Standing Conference on University Teaching and Research in the Education of Adults.

Verges, F. (1996) 'Esperanto Continued: The Dream of Universal Language' in *Frequencies: Investigations into Culture, History and Technology Seminar 1 Translating Technologies*. London: International Institute of Visual Arts. November 21.

Wajcman, J. (1991) *Feminism Confronts Technology*. Cambridge: Polity Press.

Wakeford, N. (2000) 'New Media, New Methodologies: Studying the Web' in Gauntlett, D. (ed) *Web Studies*. London: Arnold.

Waldman, S. (1998) 'Web pioneer admits defeat over agency' in *The Guardian*. January 12.

Walkerdine, V. and Lucey, H. (1989) *Democracy in the Kitchen: Regulating Mothers and Socialising Daughters*. London: Virago Press.

Warschauer, M. (2000) 'Language, Identity and the Internet' in Kolko, B; Nakamura, L. and Rodman, G. (eds) *Race in Cyberspace*. New York: Routledge.

Werbner, P. (1997) 'Introduction: The Dialectics of Cultural Hybridity' in Werbner, P. and Modood, T. (eds) *Debating Cultural Hybridity: Multicultural Identities and the Politics of Anti-Racism*. London: Zed Books.

Williams, A. (1990) 'Reading feminism in fieldnotes' in Stanley, L. (ed) *Feminist Praxis: Research, Theory and Epistemology in Feminist Sociology*. London: Routledge.

Williams, B. (2001) 'Black Secret Technology: Detroit Techno in the Information Age' in Nelson, A. and Tu, T. (eds) *Technicolor: Race, Technology and Everyday Life*. New York: NYU Press.

Witmer, D.; Colman, R. and Katzman, S. (1999) 'From Paper and Pencil to Screen and Keyboard' in Jones, S. (ed) *Doing Internet Research*. London: Sage.

Young, L. (1995) 'Questions of Colour' in Givanni, J. (ed) *Remote Control*. London: British Film Institute African and Caribbean Unit.

Yuval-Davis, N. (1998) '[Racial] Equality and the Politics of Difference' in *New Formations: Frontlines Backyards*. London: Lawrence and Wishart. 33 Spring.

Yuval-Davis, N. (1997) 'Ethnicity, Gender Relations and Multiculturalism' in Werbner, P. and Modood, T. (eds) *Debating Cultural Hybridity: Multicultural Identities and the Politics of Anti-Racism*. London: Zed Books.

Zellen, B. (31 January 1998 online 5 June 2004) 'Surf's Up!: NWT's Indigenous Communities Await a Tidal Wave of Electronic Information' in *Cultural Survival Quarterly*. Issue 22.1 at http://www.culturalsurvival.org/publications/csq/

Zipp, S. (19 March 1997 online 5 June 2004) 'What Color Is the Net?' in *Hotwired* at http://www.hotwired.com/netizen/97/11/index2a.html

Zuber-Skerritt, O. (1996) *New Directions for Action Research*. London: Falmer Press.

Zurawski, N. (1996 online 4 June 2004) 'Ethnicity and the Internet in a Global Society' at http://www.uni-muenster.de/PeaCon/zurawski/inet96.html

Zurawski, N. (1998 online 4 June 2004) 'Culture, Identity and the Internet' at http://www.uni-muenster.de/PeaCon/zurawski/Identity.html

Zurawski, N. (1997 online 4 June 2004) 'Beyond the global information frontiers: what global concepts ('Weltbilder') are there on the Internet and why?' at http://www.uni-muenster.de/PeaCon/zurawski/global.html

Zurawski, N. (1996a online 4 June 2004) 'What can the Internet do? Possiblities and limits of negotiating ethnicity and resolving ethnic conflicts on the Internet' at http://www.uni-muenster.de/PeaCon/zurawski/incore96.html

Index